Nov 2015 Gift from Ivan E.

‖‖‖‖‖‖‖‖‖‖‖‖‖‖‖‖‖

Directory of Visual Anthropology

edited by
Thomas D. Blakely
Pamela A. R. Blakely

FROM THE
LIBRARY OF

ANDREW
CAUSEY

A publication of the Society for Visual Anthropology,
a Unit of the American Anthropological Association

OFFICERS OF THE
SOCIETY FOR VISUAL ANTHROPOLOGY
1989

President   Karl G. Heider

President-elect   Richard M. Chalfen
                               (*Anthropology Newsletter* column editor)

Secretary/Treasurer   Joanna Cohan Scherer

Executive Board   Timothy Asch
                               (*SVA Newsletter* editor)
                             Joan S. Williams
                               (Film/Video Festival
                                   and AAA Film Screenings)

General Board   Ira R. Abrams
                             Peter S. Allen
                               (*American Anthropologist* Film Reviews editor)
                             Margaret B. Blackman
                             Thomas D. Blakely
                               (Visual Research Conference
                                   and SVA program chair for AAA meetings)
                             Jack R. Rollwagen
                             Nancy J. Schmidt
                             Anne C. Zeller

CONTENTS

INTRODUCTION

The *Directory of Visual Anthropology* provides fresh ammunition for countering the annoyingly persistent misconception among anthropologists and some others that "visual anthropology" mostly entails expertise in threading projectors, changing bulbs, and providing films as substitutes for out-of-town or unprepared teachers. For many contributors to this directory, visual ethnographic materials are a substantive part of their curriculum, are actively examined and discussed, and are even interwoven synergistically with written ethnographic materials. Another widespread misunderstanding is that the field of visual anthropology is concerned mainly with the production of presentation films and videos about Bangobangoland. This sterotype—while focusing on a very visible, vigorous, and vital part of visual anthropology—fails to take account of a lot of excellent anthropological photography, video, and film done in a rich variety of situations worldwide, and further ignores a great many kinds of <u>visual research</u> (and the visual aspects of professional practice) currently undertaken in anthropology and related fields.

It is not as if the exciting recent years of work on visual signification and communication, visual means of description and analysis, and visually oriented theory have emerged full-blown without antecedents. Cine film and photography, for example, have been used both in anthropological research and presentation since the nineteenth century and have enjoyed a robust if varied development well up through the middle decades of the twentieth century, as Luc de Heusch (1962), John Collier (1967), and Emilie de Brigard (1975) have so expertly chronicled and discussed. De Brigard further notes that

> In anthropology, the middle of the 1930's was the watershed between film's unimportance and its acceptability. [To earlier anthropological researchers] film was an illustration, not an integral part of research to be used in understanding and cited in publication.... By contrast, Gregory Bateson and Margaret Mead's decision to use cameras in Bali and New Guinea, 1936–38, was dictated by the needs of their research. They innovated both in the scale of their filming and photography (22,000 feet of 16-mm film, 25,000 stills) and in its aim, the description of an "ethos" of a people. [p. 26]

Bateson and Mead elaborated visual methodologies to examine aspects of behavior and interaction that could not be studied as well, or perhaps not much at all, with just language-based ways of doing ethnography. In their innovative monograph Balinese Character (1942), they also made advances in systematic scholarly presentation through the ways they closely interrelated written and visual description and analysis. This work remains a major milestone in the history of visual anthropology.

Most anthropologists did not immediately—or in some cases ever—understand or effectively utilize Bateson's and Mead's new methods, their expansion of what could now be more thoroughtly studied and presented, and their explorations in devising new concepts for dealing with the new topics, preferring instead to continue to limit the anthropological purview to that which proves most easily studied with the more logocentric, glottocentric, or numerocentric kinds of inquiry.

In the following decades, however, there were important exceptions to the general anthropological antipathy to thoroughgoing kinds of visual research. For example, Ray L. Birdwhistell's studies of body motion communication (kinesics), and his work with research filming and frame-by-frame microanalysis of film records of face-to-face interaction, drew inspiration from Bateson and Mead and from communication theory, cybernetics, and general systems theory (Birdwhistell 1970). Alan Lomax' cross-cultural research in choreometrics (Lomax 1969) involved painstaking analysis and comparison of film footage of dance and movement from a wide variety of cultures. Edward T. Hall's pioneering work on out-of-awareness culture, intercultural communication, and proxemics (Hall 1959, 1966, 1974) has demonstrated the potential of systematically investigating communication in various sensory modalities and working toward better understanding of the differing perceptual worlds in which people live. Partly as a result of the interesting possibilities emerging from these and other investigations, plus a number of other considerations, Hymes importantly modified his "ethnography of speaking" into a broader emphasis on "ethnography of communication" (Hymes 1964). Sol Worth and John Adair (1972), Jay Ruby (1976), and Richard Chalfen (1987), among others, have further developed and modified such formulations and have delved into collateral topics in productively energetic ways.

John Marshall's "The Hunters" and Robert Gardner's "Dead Birds" ushered in a new era of ethnographic filmmaking in North America that has increasingly expanded ever since: the difference in size between Karl Heider's first edition of Films for Anthropological Teaching (1966) and the seventh edition in 1983 is astounding, and the preparation of an eighth edition will be a truly daunting task. Similarly, the Directory of Visual Anthropology listings and bibiography show an energetic expansion and elaboration of the quality and number of published works, categories of research, terminologies, interests, and ways of doing time-honored as well as new kinds of visual anthropology in the last 30 years, and particularly during the last decade or so. These works have built upon well-known antecedents and a refreshing variety of other theoretical and methodological precursors from within anthropology and from other disciplinary and conceptual wellsprings.

The Directory is intended to serve as an aid to networking among persons interested in visually oriented anthropological research, teaching, production, or practice, and as an introduction to the panorama of topics in visual anthropology (noone is expert in all the visual anthropology specialities existing today). It gives key places to start inquiring further: each contributor represents a node in networks of other scholars and practitioners. Teachers should also find the Directory to be a useful resource for helping students explore the full variety of visual anthropology, and as an encouragement to continued creativity in the next half-generation of scholarly and professional contributions.

Editors' notes on format

Initially we had planned to include a filmography/videography as well as the bibliography following the directory listings. Citations submitted for many films and videos were incomplete, however, especially concerning distributors and other means of access. So, films, videos, slide-tapes, photo exhibitions, museum displays, slide shows, and television programs are noted under "visual productions" at the contributor's directory listing, near their address, phone number, and information on their interests and expertise.

The bibliographic citations were more detailed on the whole, though we still devoted substantial time to completing and checking them. Following searches in libraries and with computerized reference concordances, plus attempts to telephone authors, the eight written works that remain insufficiently documented for the bibliography are included under "other information" in the individual directory listings, again near to information about the author and the ways he or she can be contacted.

In designing the information form and in editing the Directory, we have tried to facilitate contributors' self-characterization of interests and specialties. Our goal here was to enhance our collective understanding of the breadth and multifaceted nature of the field of visual anthropology by encouraging formulations in contributors' own words rather than reifying procrustean-bed categories. Where practicable, we retain the original phrasings, in the hopes of making the Directory a more interesting and informative read. Though attention to indigenous categories and phrasings is hardly new to anthropology, this practice does depart significantly from directory questionnaires (some even done by anthropologists) that ask contributors to check their interests from a preestablished list. This emphasis has been especially appropriate for a field that is diversifying as rapidly as is visual anthropology.

The Directory includes those who submitted an information form [p. 178] to the Society for Visual Anthropology, regardless of whether they are or ever have been an SVA member. Contributions were actively sought through several strategies. Everyone on SVA mailing lists (including some past lists) were written letters and sent as many as three follow-up letters. Announcements were repeatedly placed in the *SVA Newsletter*, the SVA column in the *Anthropology Newsletter*, and also the *CVA Newletter*. Forms were made available at the various visual anthropology activities at the American Anthropological Association annual meetings for three consecutive years. In addition, forms were given to potential contributors at other national meetings we attended and other fortuitious occasions. Thus, this first edition of the Directory especially emphasizes visual anthropology by people based in North America, with some notable exceptions.

One frustration of doing a directory is keeping the more-ephemeral information current. People move, finish projects listed in "work in progress" (or abandon those projects for some exciting new pursuit), change phone numbers, and even change their names. This point was made particularly clear through a couple of rather dramatic instances where the individuals were in the process of moving on the day they were called to verify their address and phone information. For each individual included in this directory, we have checked that at least one of the listed addresses and phone numbers is current for him or her in April 1989 or is an institution that maintains this person's updated address and phone information.

This project was done with the institutional support of the Anthropology Department of Brigham Young University which we gratefully acknowledge. We want to express our appreciation to former students at Brigham Young University—Barbara McKillop, David Shuler, Terry Shuler, Lisa Romney, Mark Staker, and Kim Staker—who contributed to this endeavor by corresponding with directory contributors, organizing data, doing bibliographic research, and helping to prepare a preliminary manuscript. We also wish to thank Dick Chalfen, Karl Heider, and Joan Williams for their advice and support in bringing the Directory to completion, and Van Pelt College House and the Linguistics Lab (Bill Labov, Gillian Sankoff, Mary Beth Lemoine) at the University of Pennsylvania for providing computer facilities for printing it. Finally, we would like especially to thank Allison Jablonko for her crucial guidance in the initial conceptualization of this directory and her generous, thoughtful, and collegial midwifery throughout the process of producing it.

The directory is organized in two main parts: "Directory Listings" and "Bibliography." The Directory Listings are short biographical entries that include addresses, phone numbers, affiliations, training, interests, work in progress, geographic focus, languages, expertise, additional information, and visual productions (limited to eight), written from information furnished by the contributors. The Bibliography lists up to eight published or forthcoming works by directory contributors. The Directory Listings are proceeded by a short overview history of institutional arrangements in visual anthropology in North America, 1966–1989. Following the Bibliography is an Index of Contributors' World Area Expertise (including scholarly and fieldwork languages), a reduced facsimile of the blank directory form used by contributors, a

SVA/AAA membership and subscriber's form, and on the back cover a working statement entitled "What is the Society of Visual Anthropology (SVA)?"

A directory of visual anthropology could never be complete. There are always more people who could enhance the directory with their interests, concepts, projects, productions, and publications. We hope that the publication of this first edition of the Directory will stimulate others to contribute to an updated and expanded second edition. We welcome letters from those wishing to be in this proposed next edition, including contributors based outside North America. We would also like to urge visual anthropology organizations based in other regions of the world to publish directories.

Thomas D. Blakely
Pamela A. R. Blakely
University of Pennsylvania
April 20, 1989

Works cited:

Bateson, Gregory and Margaret Mead (1942). Balinese Character: Photographic Analysis. New York: New York Academy of Sciences.

Birdwhistell, Ray L. (1970a). Kinesics and Context: Essays on Body Motion Communication. Philadelphia: University of Pennsylvania Press.

Chalfen, Richard (1987). Snapshot Versions of Life. Bowling Green, Ohio: Bowling Green University Popular Press.

Collier, John R. (1967). Visual Anthropology: Photography as a Research Method. New York: Holt, Rinehart, and Winston. [2nd edition, 1988, with Malcolm Collier. Albuquerque: University of New Mexico Press.]

de Brigard, Emilie (1975). The History of Ethnographic Film. *In* Principles of Visual Anthropology. Paul Hockings, ed. Pp. 13–43. The Hague: Mouton.

de Heusch, Luc (1962). Le Cinéma et Sciences Sociales. Paris: UNESCO.

Hall, Edward T. (1959). The Silent Language. New York: Doubleday.

Hall, Edward T. (1966). The Hidden Dimension. New York: Doubleday.

Hall, Edward T. (1974). Handbook for Proxemic Research. Washington, D.C.: SAVICOM [now SVA]/American Anthropological Association.

Heider, Karl G., ed. (1966–1983). Films for Anthropological Teaching. 7 editions. Washington, D.C.: American Anthropological Association.

Hymes, Dell H. (1964b). Introduction: Toward Ethnographies of Communication. *In* The Ethnography of Communication. John Gumperz and Dell H. Hymes, eds. American Anthropologist 66(6, pt. 2):1–34.

Lomax, Alan (1969). Choreometrics: A Method for the Study of Cross-cultural Pattern in Film. Research Film 6(6):505–517.

Ruby, Jay (1976). Anthropology and Film: The Social Science Implications of Regarding Film as Communication. Quarterly Review of Film Studies 1(4): 426–445.

Worth, Sol and John Adair (1972). Through Navaho Eyes. An Exploration in Film Communication and Anthropology. Bloomington: Indiana University Press.

PIEF, SAVICOM, SVA:
North American Visual Anthropology Organizations
1966–1989+

The Directory of Visual Anthropology surveys a wide range of visual anthropology topics, and it chronicles the diversity of interests of scholars and practitioners actively working in one or more domains of this multifaceted field. Amid this wealth of activities and opportunities, however, there remains a dearth of bibliographic and review essays on particular topics, perspectives, and approaches in visual anthropology, with several fortunate exceptions such as the "extended notes" by Paolo Chiozzi (1984; reviewed in Jablonko and Jablonko 1987; English translation Chiozzi 1989).

Even more rare is systematic study of the institutional forms, professional networks, conferences, institutes, festivals, and other formal and informal means that have been used to facilitate productive discussion and interchange among those interested in visual anthropology. Summaries and overviews of such activities would be useful in helping record and illuminate the history of visual anthropology in various areas of the world. The following sketch focuses on some formal institutional activities in North America, particularly in the United States, since 1966.

In 1966 the Program in Ethnographic Film (PIEF)—dedicated to facilitating "teaching, production, and training" in visual anthropology—was organized by Robert Gardner and Asen Balikci, who were soon joined on the Executive Committee by Karl Heider and Irven Devore, and later in an "advisory capacity" by Margaret Mead, Walter Goldschmidt, Colin Young, and Sol Tax (Gardner 1970). PIEF initially received support from the Wenner-Gren Foundation, and functioned as a subcommittee of the American Anthropological Association. Among other activities, an active program at the AAA annual meetings was initiated and maintained.

In the fall of 1969, the PIEF office moved from Harvard University to Temple University, Jay Ruby became PIEF Executive Secretary, and in March 1970 the first issue of the *PIEF Newsletter* was published, with Jay Ruby and Carroll Williams as editors. Ruby and his students organized several conferences on visual anthropology in the early and mid–1970's, a tradition that has continued at Temple University in various forms under other conference organizers. Also, a master's degree program in visual anthropology (in collaboration with the Anthropology Film Center, Santa Fe, New Mexico, co-directed by Joan Williams and Carroll Williams) and a Ph.D. program in culture and communication were developed at Temple.

With funding from the National Science Foundation, and under the auspices of PIEF, Temple, and the Anthropology Film Center, a Summer Institute in Visual Anthropology (SIVA) was held in Santa Fe, June–August, 1972, hosted by Carroll Williams and Joan Williams at the Film Center and at St. John's College. Karl Heider, Jay Ruby, Carroll Williams, and Sol Worth were the resident faculty at SIVA, and several important researchers in visual anthropology came as visiting lecturers or discussants for several days each, including Edward T. Hall, Ray Birdwhistell, Alan Lomax, Paul Ekman, John Adair, John Collier, Jr., Don Rundstrom, Ron Rundstrom, and Timothy Asch. The twenty official participants ranged from published associate professors O. Michael Watson, Phoebe Diebold, and Larry Gross, to advanced graduate students and recent Ph.D.'s such as Rudolfo Serrano, Buck Schieffelin, and Bambi Schieffelin, to second year graduate students Steven Feld, Thomas Blakely, and Laura Greenberg. Alphonso Ortiz and other scholars informally joined the discussions from time to time, and Fred Eggan observed that these twelve concentrated weeks were the equivalent of a two year course that did not yet exist anywhere else. SIVA had a great impact on the thinking of the participants individually, and influenced subsequent research designs and even the career choices of some, but it also served as a intensive forum for wide ranging discussions on options for the institutional future of visual anthropology in the United States.

During the following AAA annual meeting in fall 1972, at a session chaired by Sol Worth (and attended by Margaret Mead, other leading visual anthropologists, and many others interested in the subject), energetic discussions were held concerning the establishment of a new professional society and affiliated journal. The Society for the Anthropology of Visual Communication (SAVICOM) officially came into existence at the 1973 AAA meetings, and in the ensuing years became a major affiliated society within the American Anthropological Association. In the fall of 1974, Volume 1, Number 1 of the Society's journal, *Studies in the Anthropology of Visual Communication*, was published under the editorship of Worth. Starting in 1980, after several years of successful publication and following Sol Worth's death, Jay Ruby, Larry Gross, and Tobia Worth edited the journal—under the new title *Studies in Visual Communication*—until 1985. During the latter years, the journal was published by the Annenberg School of Communications at the University of Pennsylvania. From 1973 to 1984, SAVICOM also published the *SAVICOM Newsletter* (successor to the *PIEF Newsletter*), under the successive editorships of Jay Ruby (1973–1978, at Temple; Carroll Williams co-editor), Ira Abrams (1979–1980, at the University of Southern California), and Jack Rollwagen (1980–1984, at SUNY-Brockport). During this period, serving as SAVICOM President were Jay Ruby, Sol Worth, Jay Ruby again, John Adair, Carroll Williams, and Jack Rollwagen. A cumulative index to *PIEF Newsletter* and *SAVICOM Newsletter* articles and other items of enduring interest has recently been published (Chalfen and Dalderup 1988).

In 1984 at the Denver AAA meeting (following a couple of years of intermittent discussions), after SAVICOM had been for several years outside the official AAA umbrella, it was reorganized, renamed the Society for Visual Anthropology (SVA), and became an official Unit within the reorganized American Anthropological Association. Serving successively as SVA President have been Jack Rollwagen, Thomas Blakely, and Karl Heider, with Richard Chalfen the current President-Elect. Allison Jablonko was Secretary/ Treasurer from 1984–1987, with Joanna Scherer the present officeholder. Timothy Asch has been the *SVA Newsletter* editor since its inception in 1985 (as the successor to the *SAVICOM Newsletter*, though with a new series of volume numbering), assisted by managing editor Daniel Marks. A monthly column in the *Anthropology Newsletter*, edited for several years by Allison Jablonko and now by Richard Chalfen, provides news about SVA events, SVA members' activities, visual anthropology publications, and profiles of visual anthropologists.

Joan Williams currently is the Film Screenings organizer for the AAA annual meeting (following several successful years by Peter Allen). She also has organized the SVA/AAA Film and Video Festival for the 1986, 1987, 1988, and 1989 AAA meetings (and has hosted the Festival's jury each spring in Santa Fe). Building on an idea discussed by visual anthropologists at national and international meetings for several years (and harkening back to a conference organized at the Smithsonian Institution in 1973 by Richard Sorenson), since 1985 Tom Blakely (with Allison Jablonko twice and Karl Heider once) has annually organized a Visual Research Conference, held in the day or two just prior to the start of the scientific program of the AAA annual meetings. Also at the AAA meetings, Tim Asch and Nancy Lutkehaus regularly give a workshop on teaching with ethnographic film, Emilie de Brigard and Edward T. Hall have hosted discussions moving toward the revitalization of the Anthropological Film Research Institute (AFRI), and each year brings interesting new paper sessions and panel discussions. In general, the number and quality of scientific sessions and special events on visual anthropology at the AAA annual meetings in recent years have been growing robustly.

The *SVA Newsletter* publishes, along with many other items, news of programs and courses in visual anthropology. In the U.S., for example, there continues to be a very active master's program in visual anthropology and Ph.D. in culture and communication at Temple University directed by Richard Chalfen. The Anthropology Film Center coordinates with Temple, and also runs a year-long program of its own on the technical and theoretical bases of documentary and social science film production (Joan Williams and Carroll Williams). The University of Southern California, through its Center for Visual Anthropology (in cooperation with the Department of Anthropology, the School of Cinema/Television, and the School of Broadcast Documentary Journalism), has a vibrant master's program in visual anthropology under the direction of Timothy Asch, and now also can admit Ph.D. students on a tutorial basis. Jerome Mintz teaches students in Ethnographic Film on a tutorial basis in the Indiana University Anthropology Ph.D. program. At New York University, Faye Ginsburg heads a certificate program in Ethnographic Film and Video for students at either the master's or Ph.D. level, offered in conjunction with the NYU Department of Cinema Studies. In other countries, in addition to the new Granada Center at the University of Manchester directed by Paul Henley, there are also programs or courses in France, Australia, Italy, India, Finland, Holland, Switzerland, Austria, Canada, West Germany, Yugoslavia, and elsewhere around the world.

In the last few years, under the energetic direction of Asen Balikci, the Commission on Visual Anthropology of the International Union of Anthropological and Ethnological Sciences (in cooperation with increasingly active regional visual anthropological organizations) has grown considerably in activities, in membership, and in *CVA Newsletter* readership. The range of festivals, conferences, workshops, and other visual anthropological events reported in the *CVA Newsletter* from a great variety of countries continues to increase impressively—further testimony of the great vitality of visual anthropology worldwide. The Commission has also importantly facilitated the creation of a major international journal in this subdiscipline, *Visual Anthropology*, edited by Jay Ruby in collaboration with an international group of visual anthropologists serving on the board of editors, as associate editors, and as book and film reviews editors.

The Directory of Visual Anthropology takes a further step toward more systematically gathering and disseminating knowledge about people who are engaged in visual anthropological research, writing, production, teaching, or practice—and has a goal of encouraging the development of broader and stronger professional networks and a sharing of knowledge and experience among people interested in visual anthropology. A book-length history of visual anthropology is currently being written by Anja Dalderup of Temple University, and the Directory Listings note several other historical works in progress. The time has come for scholarly overviews and histories to be written about the ideas, research methods, personages, professional and social networks, and institutional forms in this growing field. Why not also do oral history research (in any medium) with the men and women who have helped shape the diverse facets of visual anthropology, as is being done with women anthropologists in the Southwest by Barbara Babcock, Nancy Parezo, Jennifer Fox and collaborators (Babcock and Parezo 1988)? Let us all lend support and encouragement to those who engage in these important tasks.

Thomas D. Blakely

Works Cited:

Babcock, Barbara and Nancy J. Parezo (1988). Daughters of the Desert: Women Anthropologists and the Native American Southwest 1880–1980. Albuquerque: University of New Mexico Press. [Illustrated exhibition catalog, including all photographs and captions from the original museum exhibition. The traveling exhibition is scheduled through 1990. A one-hour presentation video (co-authored with Jennifer Fox) won a Commendation for Excellence, AAA/SVA Film and Video Festival, 1986. There is also an archive of many hours of videotaped interviews with women anthropologists.]

Chalfen, Richard and Anja Dalderup (1988). Selective Index of Visual Anthropology Newsletters 1970–1983. SVA Newsletter (Fall):34–40.

Chiozzi, Paulo (1986). Anthropologia Visuale: Riflessioni sul Film Etnografico con Bibliografia Generale. Florence, Italy: La Casa Usher.

Gardner, Robert (1970). Program in Ethnographic Film (PIEF)—A Review of Its History. PIEF Newsletter 1(1):3–5.

Jablonko, Marek and Allison Jablonko (1987). Review of Paolo Chiozzi, Anthropologia Visuale: Riflessioni sul Film Etnografico con Bibliografia Generale. Visual Anthropology 1(1):71–73.

DIRECTORY LISTINGS

Abramowitz, Alan W.
P.O. Box 45121, Seattle, WA 98145. Home: 619 Western Avenue, Seattle, WA 98104. *Phone:* (206) 621-0710. *Profession:* Photographer. *Interests:* Documentaries, ethnographic still photography. *Training:* M.A. Anthropology. Film workshop, M.I.T. *Work in progress:* "Children Fight Against Leukemia: A Life After," photo essay. *Geographic focus:* Worldwide. *Languages:* Spanish, Hebrew.

Visual productions: "Blue Collar Workers," photo essay from a project on industrial health and safety. "Amongst the Shoshone, Banock, Idaho," photo essay.

Abrams, Ira R.
Department of Radio-TV-Film, CMA 6.118, University of Texas at Austin, Austin, TX 78712. Home: 5609 Palisade Court, Austin, TX 78731. *Phone:* (512) 471-4071; home (512) 451-8385. *Profession:* Associate Professor of Radio-TV-Film; film and television producer/writer; social anthropologist. *Interests:* The production of television series about culture and anthropology, anthropological documentaries, ethnographic film and video training, interpretation of cultural and scientific information for public television audiences, film development and business (feature production). *Training:* Ph.D. Social Anthropology/Social Relations, Harvard University, 1973. *Work in progress:* Documentary on the Huichol of Mexico. Documentary on an artist whose work bridges the U.S. and Latin American cultures. Also producing a feature length motion picture film. *Geographic focus:* Mesoamerica, Southeast Asia, Indonesia. *Languages:* Spanish (fluent), some Maya and Indonesian. *Technical expertise:* Directing, cinematography, and production management; archaeological survey and excavation. *Other information:* Member of the Producers Guild of America.

Visual productions: "The Three Worlds of Bali" (producer and director; with J. Stephen Lansing), Odyssey Series (PBS), CINE Golden Eagle 1982. "Shadow Worlds of Bali" (producer and director; with J. Stephen Lansing), 60 min. film. "Faces of Culture" (series producer and writer), 26-part series for KOCE-TV; Emmy, Ohio State Award. "Planet Earth" (producer), two episodes, WQED. "The Ghosts of Cape Horn" (associate producer). "Indonesia Indah" (writer and production manager), IMAX feature. Film researcher for "Ripley's Believe It or Not," Columbia Television. "Chiefs and Kings of Indonesia" (cinematographer; with J. Stephen Lansing), 60 min. documentary film broadcast in The Explorers series by the Disney Channel, 1983.

Adra, Najwa
43 Mist Lane, Westbury, NY 11590. *Phone:* (516) 334-6386. *Profession:*
Anthropologist, free lance consultant. *Interests:* Anthropology of dance.
Training: Ph.D. Culture and Communication, Temple University, 1982.
Work in progress: "Bar'a Brauado: Yemen Dance and the Tribal Concept."
Geographic focus: Middle East, North Africa, Yemen Arab Republic.
Languages: Arabic (native), French (speaking and writing), Turkish
(speaking), and Italian (reading).

Aibel, Robert
7905 Hidden Lane, Elkins Park, PA 19117. Office: Annenberg School of
Communications, Philadelphia, PA 19104. *Phone:* (215) 635-6109; office
(215) 898-4475. *Profession:* Professor, filmmaker. *Interests:* Ethnographic
and documentary filmmaking. The study and use of ethnographic and documentary films. The study of visual communication in all of its many forms:
art, film, video, photography, clothing, etc. as socio-cultural behavior. Social
communication. *Training:* M.A. and Ph.D. Annenberg School of Communications, University of Pennsylvania. *Work in progress:* Film on collectors
and collecting in America. Film companion for "A Country Auction."
Papers concerning the social and communicative functions of amateur art.
Geographic focus: U.S.A. *Other information:* Produced a study guide for the
film "A Country Auction."
   Visual productions: Films: "A Country Auction," and "Can I Get You a
Quarter?"

Alegria, Ricardo E.
Centro de Estudios Avanzados de Puerto Rico y el Caribe, Apartado S-4467,
Viejo San Juan, Puerto Rico 00904. Home: San José 101, Viejo San Juan,
Puerto Rico 00904. *Phone:* 723-4481. *Profession:* Educator (anthropology).
Affiliation: AAA. *Interests:* Ethnographic filmmaking. Slides for teaching
Puerto Rican archaeology and folk arts. *Training:* M.A. Anthropology,
University of Chicago. Ph.D. Anthropology, Harvard University. *Work in
progress:* Films on Puerto Rican folk arts. *Geographic focus:* West Indies
(Puerto Rico). *Languages:* Spanish, English, French (reading).
   Visual productions: Archaeological films: "La Buena Herencia" and
"Indios de Boriquen." Folklore film: "La Fiesta de Santiago Apostol en Loiza,
Puerto Rico, 1948." Folk art films: "La Vida de Cristo Segun El Santero F.
Caban," "D. Tomas Rivera, El Alfarero," "Las Mascaras de Ponce, Puerto
Rico," "La Cesteria Popular," and "Los Sombreros de Paja de Cabo Rojo."
Series of slides on Puerto Rican archaeology and folk art.

Albers, Patricia C.
Department of Anthropology, University of Utah, Salt Lake City, UT 84112.
Home: 1000 Princeton, Salt Lake City, UT 84105. *Phone:* (801) 581-5757;

home (801) 485-4123. *Profession:* Anthropologist. *Interests:* Historical analysis of ethnographic photographs and prints reproduced on postcards. Impact of tourism on ethnographic photography. Application of critical theory to photographic analysis. *Training:* Ph.D. Anthropology, University of Wisconsin, Madison. *Work in progress:* A book on history of American Indian postcard imagery. Study of impact of tourism on postcard imagery of American Indians in the Southwest. Study of changing ethnographic images of Mexico on the postcard. Also working on listings of postcards published on American Indians and other ethnic groups. *Geographic focus:* American Indians, Mexico. *Languages:* Spanish (r,w,s), French (reading).

Allen, Peter S.
Department of Anthropology, Rhode Island College, Providence, RI 02908. Home: 98 Transit Street, Providence, RI 02906. *Phone:* (401) 456-8005; home (401) 274-2397. *Profession:* Anthropologist. *Interests:* Cultural anthropology, teaching with ethnographic film, archaeological film, film reviewing, ethnographic and archaeological filmmaking. *Training:* A.B. Middlebury College, 1966. A.M. Anthropology/Archaeology, Brown University, 1968. Ph.D. Anthropology, Brown University, 1973. *Work in progress:* Preparing a proposal for an ethnographic film on a modern Greek healing shrine/ritual. *Geographic focus:* Mediterranean, Europe. *Languages:* Modern Greek (good speaking, reading, fair writing), Italian (fair speaking, reading, poor writing), French (fair reading). *Additional expertise:* Certified in scuba diving. *Other information:* 1977 to present, Film Review Editor for Archaeology Magazine. 1982 to present, Film Reviews Editor for the journal American Anthropologist.

Alpers, Michael Philip
Papua New Guinea Institute of Medical Research, P.O. Box 60 Goroka EHP Papua, New Guinea. *Phone:* 721469. *Profession:* Epidemiologist. *Interests:* Ethnographic filmmaking, epidemiologic filmmaking. *Work in progress:* Kuru film documentation. Salt making, sophisticated traditional technology in Papua New Guinea. *Geographic focus:* Papua New Guinea Highlands. *Languages:* English, Tok pisin.

Andrews, Jan
341 West Pierpont Avenue #1, Salt Lake City, UT 84101. *Phone:* (801) 355-3612; office (801) 538-6113. *Profession:* Independent producer and filmmaker, anthropologist. *Interests:* Ethnographic and documentary filmmaking and photography to illustrate and dramatize aspects of human behavior within an anthropological context, particularly the diversity of mankind, yet how and where similarity occurs through time and space. *Training:* M.A. Anthropology. 16mm film production. Independent film production through university courses and outside sources. *Work in progress:* "Lysistrata, Lysistrata: A

Mystery in the Making," film based on the Greek play by Aristophanes which explores the relationship between men and women, war and peace (funded by the Independent Filmmaker Program, American Film Institute). *Languages:* French (advanced in all categories); Arabic (standard speaking). *Additional expertise:* Training and research in cultural experiences of health and medicine among Southwest Indians. Anthropology of development in the Middle East (Egypt).

Visual productions: "Seduction," 8 min. 16mm film, a cross-cultural look at women and adornment. "Anasazi," 1986, 8 min. 16mm color film on preservation and protection of ancient sites and artifacts in southern Utah. "Exiles: Between Two Worlds," 1988, 25 min. 16mm b/w film on Southeast Asian political refugees in Utah.

Arlen, Shelley A.
University of Oklahoma Library LL 206, 401 West Brooks, Norman, OK 73019. Home: 1311 Spruce Drive, Norman, OK 73072. *Phone:* (405) 325-1888; home (405) 364-0443. *Profession:* Librarian (acting head, acquisitions department). *Interests:* Photographic archives. Analysis of visual symbolic form. Photographs as a means of interpreting social organization. Iconography. *Training:* M.L.S. Library Science. M.A. Anthropology. M.A. English. Seven years experience as photographic archivist, now humanities librarian. *Work in progress:* Interpretation of Native American social organization from still photographs. *Geographic focus:* North America. *Languages:* Reading knowledge of Spanish. *Technical expertise:* Experience in cataloging and preserving photographic materials. *Other information:* Also interested in Renaissance iconography.

Aron, William S.
1227 South Hi Point, Los Angeles, CA 90035. Office: Department of Anthropology, University of Southern California, University Park, Los Angeles, CA 90089-0661. *Phone:* (213) 934-0426; (213) 743-7100. *Profession:* Instructor of Visual Anthropology, photographer. *Interests:* Documentary photography. Still photography as an aesthetic and ethnographic tool of expression. *Training:* M.A. and Ph.D. Sociology, University of Chicago, 1972. Post doctoral training in community sociology/psychology, Albert Einstein College of Medicine, New York, 1974–1976. *Work in progress:* Diversity of the Jewish community in Los Angeles. The homeless in L.A. *Geographic focus:* Ethnic groups and neighborhoods. *Languages:* Hebrew (fair), Turkish (good). *Technical expertise:* Still camera; darkroom chemistry.

Asch, Patsy
Department of Anthropology, Research School of Pacific Studies, Australian National University, Canberra, ACT 2601 Australia. Department of Anthropology, University of Southern California, Los Angeles, CA 90089-0661.

Phone: 61-49-2162 (49-7368); California (213) 743-7100. *Profession:* Ethnographic filmmaker. *Interests:* Ethnographic filmmaking. *Training:* M.A.T. Education. M.A. Anthropology. *Work in progress:* Three films on eastern Flores: a film on a peasant cremation in Balinese; a film on a bride-wealth negotiation on Roti, eastern Indonesia; two videotapes on a spiritual leader in East Java. *Geographic focus:* Indonesia.

Visual productions: Editor and producer: "A Balinese Trance Seance," 1979; "Jero on Jero," 1981; "The Medium is the Masseuse," 1983; "Jero Tapakan: Stories from the Life of a Balinese Healer," 1983; "The Water of Words," 1983. Sound person for "Sons of Haji Omar."

Asch, Timothy

Department of Anthropology, University of Southern California, Los Angeles, CA 90007. *Phone:* (213) 743-7100 *Profession:* Anthropology, ethnographic film. *Interests:* Ethnographic film and ethnography. *Training:* Anthropology, ethnographic filmmaking, photojournalism. *Work in progress:* Research and film from the studies of the Ata Tana Ai from eastern Flores in eastern Indonesia (with Doug Lewis and Patsy Asch). A Balinese cremation (with Linda Connor and Patsy Asch). *Geographic focus:* Southern Venezuela, East Africa, Afghanistan, Indonesia. *Languages:* French (intermediate level), Indonesian (intermediate level). *Technical expertise:* Movie camera, still camera, sound, carpentry, electricity, mechanical repairs, gardening, and skin diving. *Other information:* Run a master's degree program in ethnographic film in the Department of Anthropology at the University of Southern California in collaboration with USC's School of Cinema and Television and its School of Journalism.

Visual productions: "The Feast," 1970. "The Ax Fight" and "Tapir Distribution," 1975. "A Balinese Trance Seance" and "Jero on Jero: A Balinese Trance Observed," 1979. "The Medium is the Masseuse: A Balinese Massage," 1983. "Jero Tapakan: Stories From the Life of a Balinese Healer," 1983. (All distributed by DER, 101 Morse Street, Watertown, Massachusetts 02172.)

Aschenbrennen, Joyce

Anthropology Department, Box 1451, Southern Illinois University at Edwardsville, Edwardsville, IL 62026. Home: 8711 Lucas-Haul Road, St. Louis, MO 63136. *Phone:* (618) 692-2744; home (314) 867-5672. *Profession:* Professor of Anthropology. *Interests:* Research with video, videotaped oral histories. Videotaped documentary using oral histories. *Training:* Ph.D. Anthropology. *Work in progress:* Video film on family changes in metro area. *Geographic focus:* Local-metro St. Louis area. *Languages:* German (read), Spanish. *Additional expertise:* Kinship and family. *Other information:* Interviewed on Channel 2 (KTVI-St. Louis) Turnabout Series in 1984, some video sequences included.

Visual productions: Video/lecture presentation on family economies and changes of gender roles, 1986.

Ascher, Robert

Department of Anthropology, Cornell University, Ithaca, NY 14853. Home: 524 Highland Road, Ithaca, NY 14850. *Phone:* (607) 255-5137; home (607) 257-7943. *Profession:* Anthropologist. *Interests:* Filmmaking (cameraless animation), visible language. Courses taught: Visual Anthropology; Myth on Film; Native Americans on Film; Seminar on Film (above are graduate and undergraduate). *Training:* Ph.D. Anthropology, University of California, Los Angeles. *Work in progress:* "In the Garden of Pomegranetes," film based upon Kabbalah. Myth/dream/film, paper in progress. *Geographic focus:* North America, South America, Middle East. *Languages:* Spanish (r,w,s), German (read). *Technical expertise:* Techniques of animation.

Visual productions: "Cycle: From the Wulamba," a cameraless animated film of Australian myth.

Ayres, Barbara

Department of Anthropology, University of Massachusetts, Harbor Campus, Boston, MA 02125. *Phone:* (617) 929-8145; office (617) 929-8150. *Interests:* Teach a course on anthropological film.

Balikci, Asen

Department of Anthropology, Université de Montréal, P.D.B. 6128 Station A, Montréal, Québec, Canada H3C 3Y7. Home: 467 Outremont Avenue, Outremont, Québec, Canada H2V 3M3. *Phone:* (514) 343-6565; (514) 273-7422. *Profession:* Visual anthropologist. *Affiliation:* Commission of Visual Anthropology (IUAES), c/o Department of Anthropology, University of Montreal. *Interests:* Ethnographic filmmaking. Teaching courses on visual anthropology. Various organizational activities related to the Commission on Visual Anthropology. *Training:* Ph.D. in Anthropology, Columbia University, 1962. *Work in progress:* Organizational activities related to the Commission on Visual Anthropology, IUAES. *Geographic focus:* Arctic, Afghanistan. *Languages:* French, English, Bulgarian.

Visual productions: Netsilik Eskimo Film Series, National Film Board of Canada. "Sons of Haji Omar," Smithsonian Institution, an ethnographic film.

Bán, András

1124 Budapest, Somorjai 11/B, Hungary. *Phone:* (361) 661722. *Profession:* Historian of art. *Affiliation:* Müvelódéskutató Intézet (Institute for Cultural Research), Budapest, Hungary. *Interests:* Family visual archives; visual speechact. *Training:* History of art and mathematics, ELTE (University of Budapest), approximately M.A. level 1969–1975. *Work in progress:* Family archives in Hungary—a visual anthropological research project, Müvelódéskutató Intézet, Budapest. Visual speechact—theoretical frameworks, for Ph.D. level. *Geographic focus:* Hungary. Cross-cultural research projects in Italy and U.S. *Languages:* English, French, Hungarian. *Technical expertise:* Photographical practice. *Other information:* Family Photography and Values (A családi fotó és az érték), lecture, Tömegkeommunikáciosc Kutatóköpont, Budapest, 1985; Research on Private Photographs (Privát fotó kutatás), lecture at University of California at Davis, 1985.

Bannister, Jerry B.
Chair, Department of Social Sciences, Western Connecticut State University, 181 White Street, Danbury, CT 06810. *Phone:* (203) 797-4094. *Profession:* Associate Professor of Anthropology and Sociology. *Interests:* Professional interests in visual anthropology are in teaching about world cultural areas, primarily South Asia, through the media of photographic slide/videotape. *Training:* M.A. Social Sciences (anthropology/sociology and South Asia area studies), Syracuse University, 1969; Syracuse University internship with U.S. Agency for International Development, New Delhi, India, 1971; Fulbright Study-Travel Grant, India, 1981; Fulbright Study-Travel Grant, Pakistan, 1983. *Work in progress:* Pakistan: slide/videotape (with Christina Carver Pratt), 1/2 hour. Philippines: slide/videotape, 1/2 hour. *Geographic focus:* South Asia, Asia.

Visual productions: "India: Images From the Cultural Past," 1985 (photography, narrative, with Christina Carver Pratt; Marie O'Brien director, George Theisen producer), 50 min. color slide/videotape, VHS format, AV/TV Center, Western Connecticut State University. "Images of Villages and Cities," 1986 (photography, narrative with Christina Carver Pratt, Sal Cordaro and Linda L. Lindsey; Marie O'Brien director, George Theisen producer), 50 min. color slide/videotape, VHS format, AV/TY Center, Western Connecticut State University.

Banta, Melissa
Home: 66 Mount Vernon Street, Arlington, MA 02174. *Phone:* (617) 646-5146; (617) 926-8200 ext 150. *Profession:* Photographic archivist, exhibition curator. *Affiliations:* Earthwatch, 680 Mount Auburn Street, Watertown, MA 02272; Harvard University Library, Wadsworth House, Cambridge, MA 01238. *Interests:* Study and use of anthropological photography for teaching, exhibition, publication, and film; archival photograph collections. *Training:* B.S. Anthropology, M.S. Communications. *Work in progress:* "The Invention of Photography and Its Impact on Learning" exhibit, Harvard University Library, 1989. *Languages:* French (r,w,s).

Barker, John H.
Department of Anthropology DH-05, University of Washington, Seattle, WA 98195. *Phone:* museum (206) 543-5590; department (206) 543-5240.

Profession: Anthropologist. *Affiliation:* also Thomas Burke Memorial Washington State Museum, University of Washington, Seattle, WA 98195. *Interests:* Tapa cloth and other indigenous art forms of Melanesia. The portrayal of anthropologists in films. *Training:* Ph.D. Religious Change in Papua New Guinea, University of British Columbia, 1985. *Geographic focus:* Melanesia.

Visual productions: Participant and subject in "Papua New Guinea: Anthropology on Trial," 1983, Nova Films, Boston.

Barrow, Anita M.
Department of Anthropology, William Paterson College, Wayne, NJ 07470. *Phone:* (201) 595-2180; (201) 595-2274. *Profession:* Anthropologist. *Interests:* Teaching with ethnographic film, producing anthropological visuals, ethnographic and/or anthropological media analysis. Family and kinship, development, migration. *Training:* Ph.D. Anthropology, University of California at Berkeley, 1984. Affiliation with CAF Productions, an independent film production company. *Work in progress:* Educational videotape on infectious disease from a bio-cultural perspective. *Geographic focus:* Brazil, the United States, Caribbean. *Languages:* Portuguese.

Visual productions: Research consultant to CAF Productions for two films: "Carifesta" and "Nigeria Now."

Baskauskas, Liucija
Department of Anthropology, California State University at Northridge, 18111 Nordhoff Street, Northridge, CA 91330. Home: 130 Fraser Avenue, Santa Monica, CA 90405. (On leave in Sweden until January 1990.) *Phone:* (818) 885-3331. *Profession:* Anthropologist, professor. *Interests:* Teaching with ethnographic film. Oral histories via video. *Training:* Ph.D. Anthropology, UCLA. *Geographic focus:* Contemporary U.S.A., urban, ethnic, U.S.S.R. *Languages:* Lithuanian (excellent), Spanish (poor).

Visual productions: "Visual Culture," 1986, available by film loan from Intercampus Connection, Instructional Media Center, Northridge, CA.

Bass, George F.
Institute of Nautical Archaeology, Texas A&M University, College Station, TX 77843. *Phone:* (409) 845-6695; department (409) 845-5242. *Profession:* Professor, archaeologist. *Interests:* Involvement in films on nautical archaeology. Visual methods of documentation and analysis in underwater archaeology research. Ancient Near Eastern material culture, art, and iconography. *Training:* M.A. Near Eastern Archaeology, Johns Hopkins University, 1955. Ph.D. Classical Archaeology, University of Pennsylvania, 1964. *Geographic focus:* Underwater archaeology in Turkey. *Languages:* French (reading and speaking), German (reading), Turkish and modern Greek (some speaking of both).

Visual productions: Assisted in privately produced film on my underwater excavations off Yassi Ada, Turkey in 1961–1962; narrated the film for an hour-long BBC-TV showing as well as for National Geographic lecture series. Assisted in TRT (Turkish Radio and Television) film on my underwater excavation at Serce Limani, Turkey, in 1977–1978. Assisted in the Odyssey program "The Ancient Mariners" on PBS-TV—the film included segments from both of the previous two, as well as new footage from Bodrum, Turkey. Assisted in KUHT production of 1987 PBS documentary "Voyage to Antiquity" on my excavation of a Bronze Age shipwreck near Kas, Turkey.

Beatty, John
2983 Bedford Avenue, Brooklyn, NY 11210. Office: Department of Anthropology and Archaeology, Brooklyn College, Bedford Avenue and Avenue H, Brooklyn, NY 11210. *Phone:* (718) 338-1544; (718) 780-5507. *Profession:* Anthropologist (also hold private investigator's license). *Interests:* Symbolic anthropology, linguistics, ethnographic filmmaking and analysis, kinesics, proxemics, performing arts/dance. *Training:* Ph.D. Anthropology. Courses in film at Brooklyn College. *Work in progress:* Japanese funeral ceremonies, the Highland fling, The Gaelic College at Ostaig, Chinese New Year and the Lion Dance. *Languages:* German, Spanish, Japanese, Mohawk. *Additional expertise:* Surveillance photography. *Other information:* Have taught courses in Anthropology of American Indian Dance, Anthropology of Performing Arts, and The American Indian in Documentary Films. Co-organized ethnographic film festival at Brooklyn College.
Visual productions: "Iroquois Social Dance," with Nick Manning and Junichi Takahashi. "Festival of Chariots—Hare Krishna in New York."

Becker, Karin E.
August Sodermans v. 5, 126 54 Hagersten, Sweden. *Phone:* 46-8-885431. *Profession:* Professor, researcher. *Interests:* Photojournalism, history and pratice. Ethnographic photography, especially for American studies/folklore studies. Cross-cultural and historical analysis of photography as cultural forms. Documentary photography, theory, practice, and history. *Training:* B.A. Sociology, Wellesley, 1968. M.A. Journalism, Indiana, 1972. Ph.D. Mass Communication, Indiana, 1977. *Work in progress:* "Telling Picture Stories: The Rise of the Photo Essay in Germany, England and the United States, 1928–1940" (with Hanno Hardt), book manuscript submitted to publisher. Fieldwork among U.S. newspaper photographers and picture editors. Comparing theory and practice of cultural documentation as seen in photographic archives of Nordic Museum and Swedish folklife research through Institut for Folklivsferskning, Stockholm. *Geographic focus:* U.S. and West Europe. *Languages:* German (fair reading, fair writing, some speaking), Swedish (fair reading, some speaking and writing). *Technical expertise:* 35mm b/w and color photography; some past experience shooting 16mm film

and video. *Other information:* Fulbright Professor, Institut für Kommunikations Wissenschaft, University of Munich, 1983. Research grants from DAAD, ACLS.

Bednarek, Fred
7 Pond Hill Drive, Boonton, NJ 07005. Office: Country College of Morris, Route 10 and Center Grove, Randolph, NJ 07869. *Phone:* (201) 335-9487; office (201) 361-5000 ext 400. *Profession:* Professor of Sociology/Anthropology. *Interests:* Teaching mainly—however, I wish to make a video or film of a woven label mill in Paterson, New Jersey as they change to the modern machines and new technology. When the old looms are destroyed this will be a lost cultural artifact. *Training:* M.A. Educational Anthropology, New York University, 1962. Ph.D. equivalent (ABD) in General Anthropology. *Languages:* Spanish (poor).

Behar, Ruth
Department of Anthropology, University of Michigan, 1054 LSA, Ann Arbor, MI 48109. Home: 1133 Lincoln, Ann Arbor, MI 48104. *Phone:* (313) 764-9940; department (313) 764-7275; home (313) 747-9197. *Profession:* Assistant Professor, Postdoctoral Scholar. *Interests:* Ethnographic photography, teaching with ethnographic film, history of ethnographic and documentary filmmaking and photography, and approaches to the photo essay. *Training:* Ph.D. Anthropology, Princeton University, 1983. Photo student with Emmett Gowen and Joel Meyerowitz (1977–1979). *Work in progress:* A book of life history texts and photographs of the women of Mexquitic (San Luis Potosí, Mexico). A preliminary version of this work was shown in an October, 1987 exhibition at Rachhain Graduate Studies Center, University of Michigan. *Geographic focus:* Spain, Mexico. *Languages:* Bilingual in Spanish and English. Reading knowledge of French, Italian, and Portuguese.

Belk, Russell W.
Graduate School of Business, University of Utah, Salt Lake City, UT 84112. Home: 155 St. Moritz Strasse, Park City, UT 84060. *Phone:* (801) 581-7401; home (801) 649-6731. *Profession:* N. Eldon Tanner Professor of Business Administration. *Interests:* Ethnography of contemporary American consumption, consumers, and small-scale sellers. Semiotic analysis of art related to these topics. Analyses of verbal and non-verbal communication through consumption artifacts and impression formation based on such artifacts. Historical museum myth-making and analysis of historical photos for consumption meanings. Teaching qualitative research, including reliance on video and photography. Production of ethnographic videos. *Training:* Ph.D. Consumer Psychology, University of Minnesota, 1972. B.A. English and American Studies. *Work in progress:* "The Sacred and the Profane in Consumer Behavior: Theodicy on the Odyssey," co-authored paper. "Posses-

sions and the Extended Self," paper. Edited book with photos on contemporary American consumption. Co-authored paper: "Sacred and Profane Aspects of Money." Photo-aided ethnography: "The Art Show" and "The Making of a Museum." Photo- and video-aided ethnographic work with pet owners, sports fans, music lovers, collectors, visitors to PTL and Newport homes, and tattooed persons. Video: "The Automobile in Contemporary American Culture." *Geographic focus:* North America; limited work with small-scale markets in Papua New Guinea, Bali, and Brazil. *Languages:* Spanish (minimal speaking), French (minimal speaking). *Technical expertise:* Work in 35mm photography, 3/4" and 1/2" video production and editing, fieldwork methods, computer-aided analysis, archive preparation. *Other information:* Organized and led a multi-disciplinary research team from 15 universities on a coast-to-coast "Consumer Behavior Odyssey," June–August, 1986. This project produced an archive of 4000+ slides, 130+ 3/4" videos, 1000+ pages computer-based fieldnotes, and miscellaneous artifacts (all housed in an institutional archive), and has or is resulting in numerous papers, articles, videos, and multi-media presentations, as well as a book.

Visual productions: "Deep Meaning in Possessions," 1987 (co-producer), video, with written summary, distributed by Marketing Science Institute, Cambridge, MA.

Benedict, Burton
Department of Anthropology, University of California, Berkeley, CA 94720. *Phone:* (415) 642-5468; (415) 642-3391. *Profession:* Anthropologist, Professor and Associate Director of the Lowie Museum of Anthropology. *Interests:* Filmmaking, teaching with film. *Geographic focus:* Mauritius, Seychelles.

Visual productions: "1915 Panama Pacific Fair, " 1985, 28 min. video cassette.

Benthall, Jonathan
Royal Anthropological Institute, 56 Queen Anne Street, London, WIM 9LA, UK. Home: 212 Hammersmith Grove, London, WG 7HG, UK. *Phone:* 01-486-6832; 01-749-5339. *Profession:* Director, Royal Anthropological Institute, and Editor, Anthropology Today. *Affiliations:* Member of AAA, SVA, and Association of Social Anthropologists of the Commonwealth. *Interests:* Study of ethnographic film and educational uses of ethnographic film. Study of anthropological photography, anthropology of the body, and the home video camera.

Bertocci, Peter J.
Department of Sociology/Anthropology, Oakland University, Rochester, MI 48309. Home: 326 Orchardale, Rochester, MI 48309. *Phone:* department (313) 370-2420; personal (313) 370-2423; home (313) 651-9417. *Profession:* Anthropologist and college professor. *Interests:* Teaching with ethnographic

film. *Training:* Ph.D. Anthropology, Michigan State University, 1970. *Geographic focus:* South Asia, Middle East (Islamic societies). *Languages:* French, Spanish (conversational fluency; read and translate professional materials), Bengali (working knowledge developed in fieldwork). *Other information:* I have developed and taught for over ten years a course entitled Culture and Society Through Film. The course utilizes ethnographic and other documentary films, as well as certain classics of the "realist" film genre to introduce cultural anthropology as a field, illustrate the use of film in the documentation and analysis of cultural and social systems, and develop students' critical abilities in comprehending cinematic material.

Bick, Mario J. A.
Bard College, Annandale-on-Hudson, NY 12504. Home: 26 South Street, Rhinebeck, NY 12572. *Phone:* (914) 758-6822 ext 217; home (914) 876-6036. *Profession:* Anthropologist. *Interests:* Advise student work which includes ethnographic film/video photography. Interested in indirect forms of identity creation in urban areas. Plastic arts and provincialism. *Work in progress:* Analysis of urban image—Brazilian city—through post cards. Urban space as indicant of cultural, economic, and social transformations. Problem of provincial art. Problem of conditions under which abstract art vs. representational art occurs. *Geographic focus:* Brazil. *Languages:* Portuguese (read, speak), French (speak, read), Russian (speak, understand).

Biella, Peter
4917 Hazel Avenue, Philadelphia, PA 19143. Office: Department of Anthropology, Temple University, Philadelphia, PA 19122. Office: Moore College of Art, 20th and Parkway, Philadelphia, PA 19143. *Phone:* (215) 748-4097; Temple (215) 787-7775; Moore (215) 568-4515, ext 1210. *Profession:* Cultural anthropologist, ethnographic documentary filmmaker/videomaker. *Affiliation:* also President, Contemporary Historians, Inc., (non-profit) and President, Documentary Film (both companies for production and dissemination of ethnographic media). *Interests:* Ethnographic film and video production; scholar/teacher of ethnographic film and video theory and practice. *Training:* B.A. and M.A. in Film Production, San Francisco State University; M.A. and Ph.D. in Cultural Anthropology, Temple University. *Work in progress:* Maasai Film Project: three experimental ethnographic films (shot in 6x7cm negatives and Widelux camera accompanied by simutaneously recorded sound—7,000 negatives shot). Explores Maasai pastoralist and Wakwere (Bantu-speaking) farmer dispute settlement, changing roles of Maasai women and children, and epistemology of ethnographic film production (to be released in 16mm, b/w cinemascope, 90 minutes). Pennsylvania Artist Project: two 12 min. 3/4" video productions which are designed to bring a cultural perspective on the work of two artists, funding given by Pennsylvania Council on the Arts. *Geographic focus:* Fieldwork in East Africa, Costa Rica,

and some in Egypt and Trinidad. *Languages:* French (good speaking and reading), Spanish (good reading, poor speaking). *Technical expertise:* Extensive experience in film and video production overseas—wrote manual for this type of work (1985). Ran camera for some sixty 16mm and 3/4" videotapes. Considerable editing experience (about 3 hours final screen time). *Other information:* Ethnographic companion to Maasai Film Project films. Particularly interested in finding ways to lower production budgets in order to increase productivity and reduce theoretical limitations which result from astronomical production and post-production costs. Seeking to create networks among radical ethnographic film and videomakers.

Visual productions: "Priscilla, My Daughter," 1975, 38 min. 16mm b/w and color documentary on lesbianism and the relationship between mother and daughter. "Maasai Solutions," 1981, film about East African dispute settlement. "Ka Tei: Voces de la Tierra," 1986 (co-director, camera), 90 min. 3/4" video on Costa Rican Cabecar Indian land rights, assimilation, ethnocide, emphasis on the articulation of modes of production. "An Immoveable Feast: Celebration of an Egyptian Saint," 1986 (editor, first camera), 28 min. 16mm color film on syncretism in a yearly festival.

Birdwhistell, Ray L.

1417 East Shore Drive, Brigantine, NJ 08203. *Phone:* (609) 266-2514. *Profession:* Cultural anthropologist. *Affiliation:* Emeritus Professor, Annenberg School of Communications and Department of Folklore and Folklife, University of Pennsylvania. *Interests:* Communicative patterns in social organization. Multi-generational communication. Communication theory. Kinesics: body motion communication. Ethnographic methods in communication research. Interpersonal communication codes. Communication as social interaction. *Training:* A.B. Sociology, Miami University of Ohio. M.A. Anthropology and Sociology, Ohio State University. Ph.D. Anthropology and Human Development, University of Chicago. *Geographic focus:* Native Americans, Appalachians, U.S., comparative ethnic styles. *Languages:* French, Italian, Spanish, Portuguese, German (reading, some speaking). *Additional expertise:* Woodcarving. Restoration of oriental carpets. *Other information:* Professional correspondance and papers deposited in The Archive of Folklore and Folklife, Department of Folklore and Folklife, University of Pennsylvania.

Visual productions: "Letters from Sosu," 1945–46, radio series on race relations, Canadian Broadcasting Co., Toronto, Canada. "Birdwhistell Notes," 1953–54, weekly discussion of anthropology, WHAS-TV and WAEV-TV (Louisville, Kentucky), sponsored by University of Louisville, Division of Adult Education. "Kinesics," 1964 (with Jaques D. Van Vlack), a 16mm filmed lecture, distributed by Pennsylvania State University Audio-Visual Services. "Micro-cultural Incidents in Ten Zoos," 1969 (with Jacques D. Van Vlack), 16mm, produced by Eastern Pennsylvania Psychiatric Institute, distributed by PSU Audio-Visual Services. "Natural History of An Interview," 1971 (with Henry Lee Smith, Jr. and Norman A. McQuown), one hour television tape, Department of Linguistics, SUNY, Buffalo.

Bishop, John

461 Eliot Street, Milton, MA 02186. Office: Documentary Educational Resources, Watertown, MA 02172. *Phone:* (617) 696-0231; office (617) 926-0491. *Profession:* Film/video producer, camera, editor; photographer, writer. *Interests:* General film and video production with special interest in animal behavior, primate behavior, American folklife and music, ethnographic film, low budget alternatives in production, film archiving and preservation, home movies and home videos. *Training:* Field experience working with anthropologists in Nepal, East Africa, Puerto Rico, Micronesia, and the United States. *Work in progress:* Research footage on cow-yak hybrid pastoralism in Himalayas. *Geographic focus:* Have camera—will travel! *Languages:* Mediocre French (reading, speaking). *Technical expertise:* Extensive experience and knowledge of all levels of film and video production, editing, and archiving. *Other information:* I have a complete 16mm Aaton camera system and Nagra sync recorder.

   Visual productions: 16mm films: "New England Fiddles," regional music of New England, distributed by DER; "Rhesus Play," description and analysis of monkey play, distributed by UCEMC; "YoYo Man," portrait of professional Filipino yoyo demonstrator, distributed by DER; "Hand Play," local tradition of hand figures by 10 year old American boys; "New England Dances," square, contra, and set dancing among the Irish, French, and Yankee populations of the Northeast United States. "Land Where the Blues Began," PBS special on musical and socio-economic origins of the Blues in Mississippi.

Blackman, Margaret B.

Department of Anthropology, SUNY College, Brockport, NY 14420. Home: 291 Main Street, Brockport, NY 14420. *Phone:* (716) 395-5705; department (716) 395-2682; home (716) 637-2931. *Profession:* Anthropologist. *Interests:* Photographic ethnohistory (the use of historical photographs in ethnohistorical studies). Native American art, historical and contemporary. *Work in progress:* The Studio Indian: Documenting Archival Photographs from B.C. Archivaria. *Other information:* Unpublished papers presented at meetings: "Tzum Seeowist ('Face Pictures'), British Columbia Natives in early Victoria Studios," presented at a conference on "The Photograph and the American Indian," Princeton University, September 18–21, 1985.

Blakely, Pamela A. R.

University Museum, University of Pennsylvania, 33rd and Spruce, Philadelphia, PA 19104. Home: Faculty Fellow, Van Pelt College House, 3909 Spruce Street, Philadelphia, PA, 19104. *Phone:* (215) 243-5024. *Profession:*

Folklorist, ethnographer, college teacher. *Affiliation:* also Folklore and Folklife Department, University of Pennsylvania. *Interests:* Ethnoaesthetics, African visual art and ritual dance, festival, performance, art as communication, material culture including vernacular architecture, women's folklore, visual fieldwork methodologies. *Training:* Ph.D. candidate, Folklore Institute, Indiana University (minors in Art History and African Studies); M.A. Folklore, Indiana University; A.B. Fine Arts, Radcliffe College, Harvard. *Work in progress:* "Performing Dangerous Thoughts, Women's Artistic Action in Central African Funerary Events" (dissertation); "*Bílóngwé*: Hêmbá Material Culture" (book ms.); "Hêmbá Headrests" (article); "Social Dimensions of Hêmbá Portraiture" (article). *Geographic focus:* Africa, U.S., Scandinavia. *Languages:* Kiswahili (r,w,s); Kíhêmbá (r,w,s); French (r,w,s); Danish (read). *Technical expertise:* 35mm still photography. Sound recording. *Other information:* Archive (with Thomas D. Blakely): 60,000 photographs, 400 rolls of super-8, 600 hours audiotape, 35 hours video, cross-referenced to extensive fieldnotes on several years of ethnographic research in eastern Zaïre (1974–79, 1982, 1985).

Visual productions: Curator, "Boast Flags of the Fante Asafo" exhibit, October–November 1986 (with Doran Ross, UCLA Museum of Cultural History), Religion in Africa conference, Brigham Young University, Provo, Utah.

Blakely, Thomas D.

Folklore and Folklife Department, University of Pennsylvania, Philadelphia, PA 19104. Home: Faculty Fellow, Van Pelt College House, 3909 Spruce Street, Philadelphia, PA 19104. *Phone:* (215) 243-5024; messages (215) 898-7353 or 898-7461. *Profession:* Anthropologist, folklorist. *Affiliation:* also Department of Anthropology, University of Pennsylvania. *Interests:* Proxemics, semiotics, visual research methodologies, ethnography of communication, performance theory, analysis and interpretation of visual texts, speech and gesture, narrative and discourse, visual arts, intercultural communication, teaching with ethnographic film, visual aspects of the professional practice of anthropology ("applied visual anthropology"), ethnographic film and video production. *Training:* B.A. Social Relations, Harvard College. Summer Institute in Visual Anthropology (Anthropology Film Center, Santa Fe, 1972). Certificate in African Studies and M.A./Ph.D. Anthropology, Northwestern University. Post-doctoral work in Folklore. *Work in progress:* "Social Dimensions of Hêmbá Portraiture" (article, with Pamela A. R. Blakely). Papers on visual communication in face-to-face interaction, on ethnographic methods, on eliciting with photographs and video, on "Visual Anthropology and Ethnosemantic Analysis," and on "Interlocutor–Guided Microanalysis." Longitudinal research on the interrelation of visual signs and verbal art in important central African events: negotiation, conflict resolution, dispute settlement, healing ritual, and funerary festival.

Geographic focus: Africa, East and Central Africa, Zaïre; urban and rural U.S. *Languages:* French (r,w,s), Kiswahili (r,w,s), Kíhêmbá (r,w,s). *Additional expertise:* Microanalysis of photo, film, and video records. Ethnographic photography, filming, and sound recording. *Other information:* Director of an ethnographic field school. Also teach visual anthropology, ethnography of communication, and intercultural communication courses, an anthropology films lab, and visual ethnography units in other courses. Organizer, SVA/AAA Visual Research Conference (held Tuesday/Wednesday at the AAA meetings each year).

Visual productions: "Faces of the City," 1969–70 (writer, director, producer), educational television series on urban issues, fifteen 1/2-hour shows, Channel 11 KTWU Television, Topeka, Kansas. "African Carving: A Dogon Kanaga Mask", 1974 (with Eliot Elisofon), Harvard Film Study Center, Cambridge (distributed by Phoenix Films and also by Pennsylvania State University Audio-Visual Services).

Blanc-Szanton, Cristina
Southern Asian Institute, Columbia University, New York, NY 10027. Home: 5204 Delafield Avenue, Bronx, NY 10471. Office: New School for Social Research, 65 Fifth Avenue, New York, NY. *Phone:* home (212) 601-8233; Columbia (212) 280-3616; New School (212) 741-8963. *Profession:* Anthropology. *Interests:* Teaching with ethnographic and commercial films with a focus on Southeast Asia (Thailand, Philippines). I am teaching one course on media and use of media in Southeast Asia. Interested in the analysis of visual symbolic forms; the structuring of reality as denoted by visual productions and artifacts; anthropological teaching with visual media; using media in cultural feedback; and the study, production, and use of ethnographic, archaeological, or other anthropological film, video, or photography. *Other information:* Do film reviews on films focusing on Thailand or the Philippines (especially interesting or useful commercial films).

Blaustein, Richard
Director, Center for Appalachian Studies and Services, East Tennessee State University, P.O. Box 19,180A, Johnson City, TN 37614. Home: 1303 Buffalo Street, Johnson City, TN 37601. *Phone:* (615) 929-5348; home (615) 928-5819. *Profession:* Folklore. *Interests:* Fieldwork with video, teaching with video, also production of video, film, and slide/tape programs for general audiences. Main topics: folklore, esp. music. *Training:* Ph.D. Folklore, Indiana University, 1975. *Work in progress:* Consulting work on "Long Journey Home," film-in-progress dealing with Appalachian migrants, Appalshop, Whitesburg, KY. Re-dubbing slide-tape show, "Country Music in the Tri-Cities," to 1/2" VHS video. *Geographic focus:* Southern Appalachians. *Languages:* French (r,w,s), Mandrarin Chinese (r,s, some w).

Technical expertise: Scripting, editing, audio sound-track production, also interviewing. *Other information:* Project director and consultant on various media grants, 1974 to present. Have been doing a lot of radio production as well as visual media work.

Blount, Clinton M.
TCR/BioSystems, 8526 Rolling Green Way, Fair Oaks, CA 95628. *Phone:* (916) 961-7325. *Profession:* Consulting anthropologist, cultural resource management. *Interests:* Ethnographic video recording, analysis of subsistence technology (Native American) using video, ethnohistorical research using photo archives, public interpretation using photographic and video media. *Training:* M.A. Anthropology, California State University, Sacramento. Graduate work in anthropology at University of California, Riverside. *Geographic focus:* California (Native American societies and California history). *Technical expertise:* Videography, video editing, sound recording, still photography.

Visual productions: "The Extension of Tradition," videotape for the Croctar Art Museum, Sacramento. "An Oral History Sampler," videotape for the U.S. Army Corps of Engineers. "A Walk Through Yesterday," an oral history video program for the Vacaville Museum.

Blystone, Peter
Museum of Northern Arizona, Route 4, Box 720, Flagstaff, AZ 86001. *Phone:* (602) 774-5211. *Profession:* Anthropology, filmmaking, exhibit design. *Affiliation:* also Northern Arizona University. *Interests:* Filmmaking and videomaking related to the Southwest and its native, natural, and modern history. *Training:* B.A. and M.A. Anthropology, Northern Arizona University. *Work in progress:* Videotapes: "Young Hopi," "Archaeology of Northern Arizona," "Paleontologists at Work," "White Mind, Native Mind: Art versus Craft." *Geographic focus:* The Colorado Plateau and the general Southwest region. *Languages:* Spanish (r,w,s). *Technical expertise:* Lighting, sound, editing. *Other information:* On the video team at the Museum of Northern Arizona, inaugurating a new era of interpretation and research for a museum that is engaged in research, publications, and exhibits.

Visual productions: "The Children of Changing Woman" (David Baxter writer, producer, director; assisted by Richard Sims and Peter Blystone), videotape. "Young Navajo" (co-producer, with Richard Sims), videotape.

Bogue, Nila
2868 Shasta Road, Berkeley, CA 94708. *Phone:* (415) 848-1411; office (415) 540-4898. *Profession:* Visual anthropologist, ethnographic filmmaker. *Interests:* Ethnographic filmmaking (directing, editing, and sound). Teaching with ethnographic film. *Training:* M.A. program, Center for Visual Anthropology, USC, 1984. B.A. Sociology/Anthropology, Oberlin College, 1982.

Undergraduate and graduate course work at the University of Michigan, Ann Arbor. *Geographic focus:* China, Taiwan (and immigrant communities in the U.S.A.). *Languages:* Mandarin (practical control of written and spoken language), Spanish (same as Mandarin). *Technical expertise:* Editorial skills: trained on Steinbeck and Moviola video. Camera woman: 16mm, super-8, and video (1/2", 3/4" formats). Sound: trained on Nagra. *Other information:* Fieldwork includes grade-school settings in Ohio, Massachusetts, Michigan and China-towns in Los Angeles.

Visual productions: "The Urban Pow Wow," 1985 (camera, editor; co-director with Thomas Fleming), 16mm color ethnographic film on the process of changing secular public areas into sacred areas for Native American Pow Wows in Los Angeles. "Addressless," 1986 (editor; Scheerer and Millstein directors), 16mm color ethnographic film on the homeless and handicapped in Los Angeles. "The Heavenly Voice of China," 1987 (director), 3/4" video on Peking opera in Los Angeles.

Borchert, Jim
History Department, Cleveland State University, Cleveland, OH 44107. Home: 11811 Lake Avenue #903 Lakewood, OH 44115. *Phone:* (216) 687-3935; messages (216) 687-3920; home (216) 521-3384. *Profession:* Associate Professor of History. *Interests:* Historical photo-analysis (behavior and material culture). Anthropological photography. Material culture and social space. *Training:* Ph.D. American Studies, with one area in anthropological photography. *Work in progress:* Social Landscapes of an American Community; Lakewood, Ohio, 1889–1989 (book). *Geographic focus:* Urban U.S.

Bosko, Dan
72-36 112th Street, Apt. 511, Forest Hills, NY 11375. *Phone:* (718) 575-8363. *Profession:* Anthropologist (sociocultural), video editor. *Affiliation:* Professional Association of Anthropologists, New York City. *Interests:* Utilizing powerful computer controlled editing systems. Video editing (documentary). *Training:* Film study at State University of New York at Stony Brook, 1973. Six years' experience as a video editor for broadcast. *Work in progress:* Writing/producing a documentary on the world's largest water project to be undertaken in southern Africa. *Geographic focus:* Southern Africa. *Languages:* Sesotho (fluent), Hungarian (speak passably well), Czech (understand). *Technical expertise:* I am able to use the special effects devices used in video production and post production.

Visual productions: Documentary on "The Van Cliburn International Piano Competition," 1985 (editor), 90 minute program broadcast on PBS, June.

Boyer, David
Sociology Department, Marietta College, Marietta, OH 45750. Home: 1000 Warren, Marietta, OH 45750. *Phone:* (614) 374-4768; home (614) 373-5924. *Profession:* Sociology. *Interests:* Teaching with ethnographic film. Eventually, I'd like to try my hand at ethnographic 'videomaking', especially in schools, sports teams, churches.

Brandt, Elizabeth A.
Department of Anthropology, Arizona State University, Tempe, AZ 85287. *Phone:* (602) 965-6213. *Profession:* Sociocultural anthropology, sociolinguistics. *Interests:* Using video to document oral history. Training Indian people to use video to document their own history, culture, and language. Producing video documentaries of Indian culture. *Training:* B.A., M.A., and Ph.D. in Anthropology and Linguistics. Some training in ethnographic film and still 35mm photography. *Work in progress:* Completion of three tapes, two which feature San Carlos Apache elders on location discussing the history associated with certain areas of the reservation, other on the role of the godmother in the Apache puberty ceremony, which shows the godmother and her camp. *Geographic focus:* U.S. Southwest, American Indians, Apache. *Languages:* German (r,w,s), Spanish (reading and comprehension), Apache (reading and comprehension). *Technical expertise:* Editing.
Visual productions: Three different videotapes of the Apache puberty ceremony among the San Carlos Apache, color 3/4" and 1/2". Exhibit "Photography in Anthropology" (still photograph unit on changing Taos Pueblo).

Brooks, Bruce C.
417 1/2 N. 3rd, Hamilton, MT 59840. *Phone:* (406) 363-5719. *Profession:* Professional archaeologist. *Affiliations:* University of Montana and the U.S. Bureau of Land Management. *Interests:* Archaeological photographer, artist. *Training:* B.A. Anthropology, University of Montana. *Work in progress:* A pictorial report on all the pictographs in the Bitterroot Valley of Montana. *Geographic focus:* Western United States, including Alaska and Hawaii. *Languages:* Some Spanish and French. *Technical expertise:* Computer.

Brown, Donald N.
011 Classroom Building, Oklahoma State University, Stillwater, OK 74078. Home: 524 West Harned, Stillwater, OK 74075. *Phone:* (405) 744-6108; home (405) 372-7958. *Profession:* Professor of Anthropology. *Interests:* Documentary programs for public television. Development of visual materials for classroom use. Use of still photography in ethnographic research. *Training:* B.A. Harvard. M.A., Ph.D. Anthropology, University of Arizona. *Geographic focus:* Oklahoma, southwestern U.S.

Visual productions: Documentaries for public television: "Nations Within a Nation: Sovereignty and Native American Communities," 1986, 60 min.; "Always There Comes a New Spring: Vietnamese Adaptations to Oklahoma," 1983, 30 min. Slide-tape programs transferred to videotape for classroom use: "Molas: Needle Art of Cuna Indian Women," 1988, 13 min.; "The Ethnic Experience in Oklahoma," 1981, 19:30 min.; "The Ponca Indian Experience," 1981, 22 min.; "The Black Experience in Oklahoma," 1981, 18:37 min.; "The German-American Experience in Oklahoma," 1981, 26:48 min.; "The Mexican-American Experience in Oklahoma," 1981, 20:23 min.; "The Vietnamese Experience in Oklahoma," 1981, 25 min.

Bruner, Edward M.
Department of Anthropology, 607 South Matthews, University of Illinois, Urbana, IL 61801. Home: 2022 Cureton Drive, Urbana, IL 61801. *Phone:* (217) 333-6233; home (217) 384-6383. *Profession:* Professor of Anthropology. *Interests:* Performance and narrative, especially tourist performances, which are primarily visual rather than verbal. Teaching with ethnographic film. Post-structuralist and post-modern anthropology. *Training:* Ph.D. University of Chicago, 1954. *Work in progress:* Comparative study of tourist performances, heavy visual content and interpretation. *Geographic focus:* Indonesia primarily, comparative work in Bali, Kenya, Egypt, and Israel. *Languages:* Indonesian. *Other information:* Photography has long been a serious hobby and professional tool, but now moving to more systematic examination of the visual component of performance.

Bugos, Paul E.
255 Rochelle Avenue, Philadelphia, PA 19128. *Phone:* (215) 483-2047. *Profession:* Film editor. *Interests:* Ethnographic filmmaking, teaching with ethnographic film. *Training:* Ph.D. Anthropology, Northwestern. *Geographic focus:* South America. *Languages:* Spanish (reading, speaking). *Technical expertise:* 16mm and video editing, ethnography. *Other information:* Three years ethnographic field research among the Ayoreo (Bolivia/Paraguay).
    Visual productions: "The Ax Fight" (editor). "The Myth of Naro as Told by Dedeheiwa," "Myth of Naro as Told by Kaobowa," "Moonblood," "Tapir Distribution," "Jaguar," "Bride Service" (series editor; production manager).

Burns, Allan F.
Department of Anthropology, 1350 Turlington Hall, University of Florida, Gainesville, FL 32611. *Phone:* (904) 392-0299; department (904) 392–2031. *Profession:* Anthropologist. *Affiliation:* also Universidad Complutense de Madrid. *Interests:* Ethnographic film and video, participant photography, still photography. *Work in progress:* "Kosrae Ethnography Study", funded by Micronesian Endowment for Historic Preservation to train Micronesians in video documentary in historical and archaeological preservation. Grant from

"Dialogues in Anthropology," videotaped oral history of discipline funded by Wenner-Gren. "La Rioja—Work and Identity," Spanish videotape of northern Spain. "Vision Quest," book on still and video for the social sciences. "Participant Photography among Chinese, Venezuelan, and U.S. Students," article. *Geographic focus:* Yucatan, Mexico, southwestern U.S., southeastern U.S., northern Spain. *Languages:* Spanish (fluent), Yucatec Mayan (r,w,s). *Other information:* I regularly teach visual anthropology at the University of Florida and have been an exchange professor at the Universidad Complutense in Madrid, Spain, where I taught and developed visual anthropology interest in the anthropology program.

Visual productions: "An Evening of Talent," 1984, 30 min. video for black women's health co-op, Monticello, Florida. PBS programs: "Maya in Exile," 1985, 30 min. on Guatemalan refugees in U.S.; "Maya Fiesta," 1988, 24 min. on the Fiesta of San Miguel celebrated by Mayan refugees in Florida.

Button, Gregory

3 Monmouth Street, Somerville, MA 02143. *Phone:* (617) 628-6196. *Profession:* Ph.D. candidate, college teacher. *Affiliation:* Brandeis University. *Interests:* Ethnographic filmmaking. *Training:* 6 years as a public radio and television producer. Have produced over 400 public radio productions as well as several public TV productions. Have held NPR Training Grants. Have studied both filmmaking and video production. *Geographic focus:* North America and China. *Languages:* Spanish (reading). *Technical expertise:* Radio and video production. *Other information:* Have reviewed film for public radio stations and have conducted two regional foreign film festivals with support from the N.Y. State Council on the Arts.

Buxbaum, Edwin C.

P.O. Box 3746, Greenville Station, Wilmington, DE 19807. Office: Academy of Lifelong Learning, 2800 Pennsylvania Avenue, Wilmington, DE 19806. *Phone:* (302) 994-2663; office (302) 573-4433. *Profession:* Anthropologist. *Affiliation:* Fellow, AAA; Professor Emeritus, University of Delaware, Department of Anthropology. *Interests:* Teaching with ethnographic film. *Training:* Ph.D. University of Pennsylvania. *Languages:* German, French. *Geographic focus:* Mediterranean, Greece, ethnic groups in U.S.

Byers, Paul

Box 115, Teachers College, Columbia University, New York, NY 10027. Home: 18 East 18th Street 2E, New York, NY 10027. *Phone:* (212) 678-3185; (212) 678-3192; home (212) 675-6519. *Profession:* Anthropologist/teacher. *Interests:* Organization of behavior—esp. place of rhythms; teaching; new research paradigms. *Training:* Ph.D. Anthropology, Columbia. *Work in progress:* A book on the place of rhythm/synchrony in self-correcting/self-organizing systems.

Byrne, William G.
Olive-Harvey College, Social Science Department, 10001 S. Woodlawn Avenue, Chicago, IL 60628. *Phone:* (312) 568-3700 ext 434. *Interests:* Teaching with ethnographic film—main interest is in effects. *Training:* Ph.D. Northwestern University, 1979. University of Chicago, 1962–63. *Languages:* French (reading–poor).

Cabezas, Sue Marshall
Documentary Educational Resources of Massachusetts, Inc., 101 Morse Street, Watertown, MA 02172. Home: 37 Gayland Road, Needham, MA 02192. *Phone:* (617) 926-0491; home (617) 449-3965. *Training:* B.A. Sociology, LeMoyne College, 1972; M.A. Sociology, Boston College, 1974, specializations in Socialization and Criminal Justice. Teaching and research assistantships in Anthropology and Criminal Justice; researcher, assistant editor for Benedict S. Alper's "Prisons: Inside Out." *Expertise:* Acquisition, negotiation, and administration of federal and private grants and contracts; selection and contract negotiations for film acquisitions; complete management of film production and distribution; accounting and financial reporting; design and implementation of plans for market research and analysis; presentation of symposia and workshops; planning, editing, and supervision of materials publication; data base, spreadsheets, word processing.
     Visual productions: Co-producer, "N!ai, the Story of a !Kung Woman" (production manager and coordinator of two crews filming in Namibia for this production), aired 1980 in PBS Odyssey series. "Airborn" (associate producer; a film by David Gulick). Production assistant: "Margaret Mead: A Portrait by a Friend," "Moonblood," "A Yanomamo Creation Myth," "Bride Service," "If It Fits," "A Balinese Trance Seance." Special credits on "The Navigators: Pathfinders of the Pacific," "New England Fiddles," "Yoyo Man," "The Pearl Fisher." Current production and grant administration on "Airborn," "Connick Glass Works," "New England Dances," "Sherman's March," "The Tourist."

Caldarola, Victor J.
Annenberg School of Communications, University of Pennsylvania, 3620 Walnut Street, Philadelphia, PA 19104. Home: 4317 River Road Apt. 1, Washington, DC 20016. *Phone:* (202) 362-9319. *Profession:* Communications. *Interests:* Theory and practice of ethnographic film and photography. Cross-cultural studies of filmic and photographic communication. Ethnographic approaches to the study of communicational processes. Transnational mass media and its impact on local pictorial communication. Production practices of the visual mass media. *Training:* Ph.D. candidate, Annenberg School of Communications, University of Pennsylvania. *Work in progress:* Dissertation research concerning photographic practices, pictorial experience, and transnational visual media in South Kalimantan, Indonesia. *Geographic focus:* Southeast Asia, Indonesia. *Languages:* Intermediate to advanced

competence in Indonesian-Malay (r,w,s). *Technical expertise:* Still photography, 16mm filmmaking.

Visual productions: "Working for Profit: Agrarian Enterprise in South Kalimantan," 1987 (with Patricia J. Vondal), 50 minute video.

Callaghan, John W.

117 Mateo Circle, Santa Fe, NM 87501. *Phone:* (505) 988-2620. *Affiliation:* Anthropology Film Center. *Interests:* Documentary and Research Films. *Training:* Ph.D. Behavioral Sciences, University of Chicago; Anthropology Film Center course. *Geographic focus:* Hopi and Navajo.

Visual productions: "The Hopi Center for Human Services." "The Home on the Range for Boys." "Navajo Childhood."

Campos, Yezid

Temple University, Department of Anthropology, Philadelphia, PA 19122. Permanent: Calle 86 N 16-14, Bogota 8, Colombia. *Phone:* (215) 787-7775; Colombia (57) (1) 236-2198. *Profession:* Anthropologist. *Interests:* Ethnographic filmmaking. Use of media within the context of participatory research approach. *Training:* M.A. Visual Anthropology (film and video training); Ph.D. student, Cultural Anthropology, Temple University. *Work in progress:* Photographic study of the Arhuaco culture. *Geographic focus:* Colombia. *Languages:* Spanish (native language), English (fluent).

Visual productions: Ethnographic 3/4" video: "Guirkanu: The Sacred Mountain," 9 min. Experimental 3/4" video: "Pulse," 8 min. Photographic exhibition, "Indian Communities from Colombia."

Cancian, Frank

School of Social Sciences, University of California, Irvine, CA 92717. *Phone:* (714) 856-6570; department (714) 856-7602; home (714) 640-8072. *Profession:* Professor of Anthropology. *Interests:* Social and economic anthropology, social stratification. Also teach Exploring Society Through Photography course. *Training:* Ph.D. Social Anthropology, Harvard, 1963. *Geographic focus:* Mexico. *Languages:* Spanish (good).

Carucci, Laurence M.

Department of Sociology, Montana State University, Bozeman, MT 59717. *Phone:* (406) 994-5255; department (406) 994-4201. *Profession:* Anthropologist. *Interests:* Ethnographic filmmaking, teaching with ethnographic film, photographic records (cross-cultural), proxemics, semiotic approaches to communication. *Training:* B.A. Anthropology, Colorado State University. M.A. Social Science, Ph.D. Anthropology, University of Chicago. *Work in progress:* Book, Marshall Island Christmas ritual, including spatial, gestural, and visual symbolic analysis and interpretation. *Geographic focus:* Oceania, Micronesia. *Languages:* French (read), Spanish (read), Marshallese (r,w,s).

Cedrini, Rita
Via S. Meccio 22, 90141 Palermo, Italy. Office: Rita Cedrini, Laboratorio Antropologico, Universitario Facolta di Lettere e Filosofia, Viale delle Scienze 90142 Palermo, Italy. *Phone:* 091-589254; office 091-590774. *Profession:* Ricercatore [researcher]. *Affiliation:* Direttore Laboratorio Antropologico Universitario. *Interests:* Anthropological research, teaching, methodology, theory, and practice. Analysis of visual symbolic forms. Study of cultural, historical, folkloristic, semiotic points of view. Forms of social organization involved in planning, producing, and using visual signs and systems of signs. Visual approaches to the ethology of human and other life forms. Anthropological teaching with visual media. Visual analysis and methods in the professional practice of anthropology. Study, production, and use of ethnographic and other anthropological film and video. *Training:* Segretario generale della Società Italiana di Antropologia Audio-visuale. *Work in progress:* Video; Antropologia e fotografia (book). *Geographic focus:* Sicilia (Italy). *Additional information:* Editor of the section entitled Immagini, in the quarterly journal Nuove Effemeridi (Palermo: Guida).

Visual productions: Videos (3/4" Umatic): "Il Signore delle fasce," "Il Mastro di Campo," "La festa in mostra," "Ero in festa," "Nasce un paladino," "Il sale del vento," "Himera," "La passione a Delia," "I patti dei sensali," "Gli archi votivi a S. Biagio Platani," "L'isola ritrovata (su una mostra)," "U triumfu," "Trapani, città dei coralli," "Canti dei carretieri in Sicilia," "L'albero in festa," "Il dolore e la senza." (The finished videos and also all the unedited tapes are in the Laboratorio Antopologico della Facolta di Lettere e Filosofia, Universita di Palermo.)

Chalfen, Richard M.
Department of Anthropology 025-21, Temple University, Philadelphia, PA 19122. Home: 916 Pine Street #9, Philadelphia, PA 19107. *Phone:* (215) 787-1413; home (215) 592-1722. *Profession:* Professor, professional consultant, researcher. *Interests:* The home mode of pictorial communication, "sociovidistics," native generated imagery, pictorial folklore, communications theory, teaching with visual media. *Training:* Annenberg School of Communications, University of Pennsylvania. Anthropology Film Center, Santa Fe, NM. *Geographic focus:* North America. *Languages:* French (reading). *Technical expertise:* Still photography, 16mm motion picture production.

Visual productions: "Cinema Naiveté: A Study of Home Moviemaking as Visual Communication," 1975. "Human Images: Teaching the Communication of Ethnography," 1977. "Context Film for 'The Navajo Film Themselves'," 1978. "Tourist Photography," 1980. "A Sociovidistic Approach to Children's Filmmaking: The Philadelphia Project," 1981. "Turning Leaves: The Family Albums of Two Japanese American Families," 1987, NEH museum exhibition.

Chin, Daryl
141 Wooster Street, Apt. 6D, New York, NY 10012. *Phone:* (212) 473-6695. *Profession:* Writer, curator, editor. *Interests:* The study of art and performance from social, historical, political, semiotic, and aesthetic points of view; using media in cultural feedback; visual theories; the exhibition and dissemination of minority (Asian-American, Afro-American, women's) art and media; film/video/photo archiving. *Training:* Co-founder of Asian-American Film Festival; co-founder of the Asian-American Video Festival; co-curator, "The Altered Photograph" (including ethnographic and anthropological slide-shows) at P.S. 1 (Institute of Art and Urban Resources, Long Island City) in 1979. *Work in progress:* Curating a history of Asian-American film and video for the Whitney Museum of American Art in fall 1988 (completed) and fall 1989. *Geographic focus:* United States, Japan, India, France. *Other information:* Also playwright and director.

Chiozzi, Paolo
Istituto di Antropologia, University of Florence, Via del Proconsolo, 12, 50122 Firenze, Italy. Home: Via Strozzi, 91/c, 50047 Prato, Italy. *Phone:* (55) 214049; home (574) 33038. *Profession:* Anthropology. *Interests:* Ethnographic film and video production. Teaching visual anthropology. Bibliography and film/videography of ethnographic film and video. Film archives. Ethnographic film festivals. Urban anthropology, political anthropology, human ecology. *Work in progress:* "Ethnic Groups in Florence" and "Antropologia del paesaggio" (videos). "Parole, suoni e rumori nella documentazione audio-visiva in anthropologia" (for Sociologia delle comunicazioni, special issue on visual anthropology and visual sociology). Revised edition of Anthropologia visuale (Florence: Edizioni Scientifiche Fiorentine, first edition 1984). "Visual Anthropology: Notes on Ethnographic Film with a General Bibliography" (for the journal Visual Anthropology). *Geographic focus:* Europe, Italy. *Languages:* Italian, English, French. *Other information:* Director, Ethnographic Section, Festival dei Popoli (International festival on documentary film), Florence. Director, Summer School on Visual Anthropology, International Institute for the Study of Man, Cortona, Italy.
Visual productions: "La campagna nela citta," 1984, 15 min. color Umatic; "La carta a mano," 1985, 30 min. color Umatic; "La cartiera ad acqua," 1985, 30 min. color Umatic, "The Dawn of Visual Anthropology in Italy," 1988, 25 min. b/w Umatic, "Anthropos," 1988, twelve part program on visual anthropology (each part 48 min., color), broadcasted October–December.

Cho, Hae Joang
Department of Sociology, Yonsei University, Seoul 120, R.O.K. *Phone:* 392-0131 ext 2180. *Profession:* Anthropologist. *Affiliation:* AAA member. *Interests:* Ethnographic filmmaking. Teaching with ethnographic film. *Training:* UCLA filmmaking course in summer 1975. *Work in progress:*

"The Descendants of the Yangban: Cultural Continuity and Change." *Geographic focus:* Korea. *Languages:* Korean, English.

Visual productions: "Sex-role Patterns of the Female Diver's Community on the Cheju Island of Korea." "Devotees of Hare Krishna in the 20th century U.S.A."

Clements, Emilia González

8010 Lillibridge, Lincoln, NE 68506. *Phone:* (402) 483-5754. *Profession:* Applied anthropologist. *Interests:* Teaching and advocacy using visual media in cross-cultural issues, women's economic development, and peace and justice issues. Project planning and design. *Training:* M.A. and post graduate in Cultural Anthropology. *Work in progress:* Micro-economic development projects in Peru and Mexico. An untitled video on the La Joya project. *Geographic focus:* Latin America. *Languages:* Spanish (native speaker), English (excellent), French (fair, reading).

Visual productions: Photo essays/slide programs: "Feminization of Poverty," "Panchita—Third World Woman," "U.S. Foreign Policy in Central America," "The Role of Women in Development," "Grassroots Development in Nicaragua," "Self-Help Development: La Joya, Northern Mexico," "The Role of Beneficiaries in Development Projects," and "Participatory Development: A Model."

Coggeshall, John M.

Department of Sociology, Clemson University, Clemson, SC 29634. *Phone:* (803) 656-3822; department (803) 656-3238; home (803) 653-6008. *Profession:* Anthropologist. *Interests:* Material culture, folk culture, and ethnic architecture. Primarily interested in using 35mm photography to document types of ethnic architecture, and then relating material culture to other ethnic criteria. *Training:* Ph.D. Anthropology, Southern Illinois University. Four years' fieldwork experience in American subcultures. *Work in progress:* Compiling slides of photograph collection. "The Power of Images: Issues in Ethnographic Photography," book project with R. Tindall. *Geographic focus:* United States subcultures and ethnic groups. *Languages:* Reading ability in French, German, Latin. *Technical expertise:* 35mm photography, self-taught.

Visual productions: "With Devotion: Southern Illinois Religious Arts and Artists," 1985, photographic and ethnographic exhibit with gallery notes, University Museum, Southern Illinois University, Carbondale. Cover photograph, Journal of American Folklore 99(2), 1986.

Collier, John, Jr.

Muir Beach, Star Route, Sausalito, CA 94565. Laboratory: 339 A 5th Street, San Francisco, CA 94118. *Phone:* (415) 388-1188; lab (415) 751-2393. *Profession:* Professor Emeritus, Anthropology; teacher of photography. *Affiliations:* San Francisco State University, San Francisco Art Institute.

Interests: Photography and film for anthropological research. In collaboration with Cornell University, research assistant in developing photography for behavioral sciences (fieldwork in Nova Scotia, among the Navajo Indians, and on the Peru-Cornell Hacienda Vicos in the Andes of Peru). *Work in progress:* Equal Opportunity for Human Difference (book). Research text based on film research of schools in Alaska, Rough Rock on the Navajo reservation, and multi-ethnic classrooms in San Francisco (publication pending). *Geographic focus:* Colombia, Peru, Canada, and in the American Southwest. *Languages:* Working skill in Spanish. *Additional expertise:* Documentary photography for the Farm Security Administration. Industrial photography for Fortune, Ladies Home Journal, Farm Quarterly, and Scientific America. Photographic designing. *Other information:* Fine art trained—ten years of fine art painting. Appointment at San Francisco State in Anthropology and Education: taught photography, communication, anthropology, and education. Taught the Foundation of Education and carried out ten years of film research in Alaskan Eskimo schools, Navajo community Rough Rock school, and multi-cultural education in San Francisco public schools. Prepared a book on education for ethnic diversity.

Collier, Malcolm

370 4th Avenue, San Francisco, CA 94118. School office: Asian American Studies, San Francisco State University, 1600 Holloway Avenue, San Francisco, CA 94132. *Phone:* (415) 387-8084; office (415) 338-1480. *Profession:* Teacher, photographer, consultant. *Affiliation:* San Francisco State University, Department of Asian American Studies. *Interests:* My interests fall in a number of areas including: the use of film, photography and video for research purposes; use of photography and other visual media as forms of documentation and expression in ethnic communities by ethnic people; use of visual records in teaching, particularly in ethnic studies; applied usage of information gained in visual research, mainly in area of cross-cultural education and teacher training. These interests have involved work with proxemics, kinesics, and related variables in film, video, and still photography. Also interested in process of communication knowledge through visual combined with verbal forms including visual books, films, and video. Considerable experience with photographic layout and use of visual research records in subsequent communication of research findings. Some experience in use of computers to handle data from visual research. *Training:* M.A. Anthropology, SFSU— primary research related to degree involved film in study of cross-cultural communication. *Work in progress:* Paper/articles: "Photographic Exploration of Asian America" and "Asian American Communities: Redefinitions and New Forms" (based on photographic explorations carried out by Asian American Studies students and staff at SFSU. *Geographic focus:* California, San Francisco Bay Area—Asian American communites, ethnic communities, new immigrants, education; New Mexico/Arizona—Spanish speaking and Indian communites;

Alaska; Latin America—Mexico, Peru. *Languages:* English; Spanish (colloquially spoken New Mexico variant, fairly fluent, learned in childhood, moderate written command). *Other information:* Have various photo exhibits and study guides for use in teaching of visual anthropology and courses in Asian American Studies (not available for distribution). Extensive experience in teaching of field methods in visual anthropology as well as in basic photographic skills—both field recording and production.

Visual productions: "A Film Study of Classrooms in Western Alaska," 1979, Center for Cross Cultural Studies, University of Alaska, Fairbanks. "Nonverbal Factors in the Education of Chinese American Children: A Film Study," 1983, Asian American Studies, San Francisco State University (also ERIC).

Cone, Cynthia A.

Department of Anthropology, Hamline University, St. Paul, MN 55104. *Phone:* (612) 641-2247; department (612) 641-2295. *Profession:* Professor. *Interests:* Cross-cultural comparative aesthetics, teaching with ethnographic film, behavior and the built environment. *Training:* Ph.D. University of Minnesota, 1976. M.A. University of Minnesota, 1971, thesis title "Art and Value: Defining Art for Anthropology." *Work in progress:* Use of video techniques in community development. *Geographic focus:* Mexico, Native Americans, U.S. *Languages:* Spanish.

Conklin, Harold C.

Department of Anthropology, Yale University, 2114 Yale Station, New Haven, Connecticut 06520. *Phone:* (203) 432-3667; department (203) 432-3700. *Profession:* Anthropologist. *Interests:* Ethnography enhanced to maximum with graphic, illustrative, pictorial, diagramatic, colormetric, photographic, cartographic imagery—not limited to structures, processes, and techniques of our Western art. Color and b/w still photography, aerial photography, film, sketching-painting-modeling (especially by locals), graphs, 2- and 3-dimensional models, etc. Archiving, cataloging, and indexing of visual records. Writing systems and their diverse forms and uses. Vision, perception, and cultural aspects of shape, size, distance, density, color, and number. Art and technology. *Work in progress:* Ifugao technology. Hanunóo writing. Material-resource technology in cultural context. Environment and culture. Language and environment. The ethnography of seeing. *Geographic focus:* Pacific, Southeast Asia, Philippines. *Languages:* Tagalog, Hanunóo, Ifugao, Indonesian, French, Spanish, Dutch, and German. *Additional expertise:* Fieldwork, museum work, teaching, publication related to academic work in anthropology, linguistics, and ecological research.

Visual productions: "Hanunóo," 1958 (filmed and taped in 1953), 17 min. 16mm color sound film, distributed by Pennsylvania State University and Washington State University.

Coplan, David B.

Comparative Humanities, Box 210, SUNY College at Old Westbury, New York, NY 11568. *Phone:* (516) 876-3115. *Profession:* College teacher. *Interests:* Audio-visual instructional materials and programs; ethnographic films, especially on performing arts. *Training:* Ph.D. Anthropology/ Ethnomusicology at Indiana University. Preparation and technical processing of audio-visual instructional materials in Britain, South Africa, and U.S. Anthropologist on film projects. *Geographic focus:* West Africa, southern Africa. *Languages:* French (good reading), Sotho (fair speaking and reading). *Technical expertise:* Sound work for film, script writing.

Visual productions: Various projects on southern African black performing arts, including slide-tapes, broadcast scripts and broadcast programs. Anthropologist/consultant for "Songs of the Adventurers," 1987, film on Basotho migrant workers and women of Lesotho, southern Africa (Constant Springs Productions, Devault, PA).

Crowdus, Gary

Vice President, The Cinema Guild, 1697 Broadway, Room 802, New York, NY 10019. *Phone:* (212) 246-5522. *Profession:* Film distributor, magazine editor. *Affiliation:* also Editor, Cineaste Magazine. *Training:* BFA, Motion Picture Production, Institute of Film and Television, New York University. *Work in progress:* "A Political Companion to Film," book.

Cuéllar, José B.

Stanford Geriatric Educational Center, School of Medicine, 703 Welch Road #1, Stanford University, Stanford, CA 94305. *Phone:* (415) 723-7063; home (415) 322-1329. *Profession:* Anthropologist. *Interests:* Ethnophotography, use of films and slides in teaching, filmmaking and slide-tape productions. *Training:* M.A. and Ph.D. in Anthropology (UCLA). *Work in progress:* Cholismo: The Development and Diffusion of an International Mexican Barrio Subculture. Project on Mexican-American families and alcohol. 30 minute slide presentation on ethnicity and aging. *Geographic focus:* U.S.–Mexico borderland; Mesoamerica. *Languages:* Spanish (native). *Additional expertise:* Grantsmanship.

Dakowski, D. Bruce

22 Butler Close, Woodstock Road, Oxford OX2 GJG, England. *Phone:* 865 53008. *Profession:* Anthropologist/broadcaster. *Affiliation:* Oxford University, Institute of Social Anthropology. *Interests:* Ethnographic filmmaking, psychological anthropology, theories of mind. *Training:* Medical Doctor- M.B., B.S. London, Diploma in Social Anthropology. *Work in progress:* D. Phil., Oxford, on the dialogue between psychoanalytic theory and social anthropology. *Geographic focus:* The head! *Languages:* Bedroom French.

Visual productions: Six part television series: "Strangers Abroad," on the lives and work of six great anthropologists.

Dallalfar, Arlene

2240 Virginia Street, Berkeley, CA 94709. *Phone:* (415) 848-3381. *Profession:* Sociology/Film. *Affiliation:* UCLA. *Interests:* Sociology—theory, history, social change, women, and ethnicity. Ethnographic film—teaching with ethnographic film. *Training:* M.A. Sociology, UCLA, 1982. *Languages:* Arabic (r,w,s), Persian (r,w,s), French (r,w,s).

Damon, George H. Jr.

Media Communications Department, Framingham State College, Framingham, MA 01701. *Phone:* (508) 626-4667. *Profession:* Professor, educator, photographer. *Interests:* Autobiographical photographic research, intercultural and cross-cultural communication, semiotic theory and photography, analysis of visual symbolic forms, relationship of visual and verbal symbols in context, interpretation and transformation of messages through the media. *Training:* M.Ed. in Educational Communication and Technology. Peace Corps (Morocco). Doctoral candidate in Intercultural Communication and Education. *Work in progress:* "Class, Culture, and Perception: Photographing to Reveal an Intercultural Process," doctoral dissertation. *Geographic focus:* North Africa and the Middle East. *Languages:* French (intermediate reading, speaking, and writing), Arabic (intermediate speaking). *Technical expertise:* Professional photographer, audio and video productions. *Other information:* Fulbright Professor, Morocco, 1984-86.

Visual productions: "Morocco: A Living Mosaic," multi-image show and color prints.

Davidson, Margaret Blancy

27 Champney Street, Brighton, MA 02135. *Phone:* (617) 782-4382. *Profession:* Freelance producer, video editor. *Interests:* Ethnographic filmmaking (including photography and video). *Training:* M.A. Radio-TV-Film (visual anthropology emphasis), Speech and Dramatic Arts, University of Missouri.

Visual productions: "Missouri Archeology: Discovering Our Heritage," videotape. "Missouri Archeology: The First Missourians," videotape.

d'Azevedo, Warren L.

Department of Anthropology, University of Nevada, Reno, NV 89557. *Phone:* (702) 784-6704. *Profession:* Anthropologist. *Interests:* Use of photography in ethnographic fieldwork and teaching. Problem of organization of extensive private slide collection. *Training:* Graduate studies at University of California, Berkeley and Northwestern University. *Geographic focus:* Liberia, West Africa: religion, artistry, social organization. Western North America, Great Basin: ethnology. *Languages:* French (read); German (read).

de Brigard, Emilie
FilmResearch, 8 Christian Hill Road, Higganum, CT 06441. *Phone:* (203) 345-2338. *Profession:* Archivist, visual anthropologist. *Affiliation:* Institute of Living, Hartford, and Department of Anthropology, Yale University. *Interests:* African and Japanese film, music, medicine, visual education, film/video/photo archiving, organization of information, costume and textiles. *Training:* M.A. Theatre Arts, UCLA, 1972. B.A. Harvard College, 1963. *Work in progress:* "Jean Rouch: A Portrait by a Friend" to appear in Visual Anthropology. *Geographical focus:* West Africa, Latin America. *Languages:* French, Spanish, Portuguese, German, Japanese. *Additional expertise:* Welding; wolves.

Visual productions: "Margaret Mead: A Portrait by a Friend," 1978 (producer), 16mm film. "Dance and Human History," 1974, (footage research; Alan Lomax and Forrestine Paulay directors), 16mm film.

De Friedmann, Nina S.
Apartado Aéreo 100.375, Bogotá, Colombia, South America. *Phone:* 2 58 68 97. *Profession:* Social anthropologist. *Affiliation:* ETNO, Bogotá, Colombia. *Interests:* Film and photography in anthropological research and publications. *Training:* Social anthropology. *Work in progress:* Gente al sol: Negros en Colombia (book). *Geographic focus:* Colombia, Caribbean Black peoples and ethnic relations. *Languages:* Spanish (r,w,s), English (r,w,s), French (reading, speaking).

Visual productions: 16mm films: "Rivers of Gold," 1974, 20 min. b/w; "Villarrica," 1973, 22 min. b/w; "Congos," 1978, 20 min. 16mm color. Super-8 film: "La fiesta del indio en Quibdó," 1971, 13 min. (All four films: Instituto Colombiano de Antropología.)

Dekin, Albert A. Jr.
Department of Anthropology, State University of New York, Binghamton, NY 13901. Home: P.O. Box 505, 44 Maple Avenue, Newark Valley, NY 13811-0505. *Phone:* (607) 777-2737; home (607) 642-8512. *Profession:* Anthropologist, Associate Professor. *Interests:* Production of instructional media (film, slides, tape). Use of film media in teaching. *Training:* Ph.D. Michigan State University, 1975. A.B. Anthropology, Dartmouth College, 1965. *Work in progress:* Slide set on excavations at the Utqiagvik Site, Barrow, Alaska for Pictures of Record. Videotape on excavations at Barrow, etc., for the University of Alaska, Anchorage (consultant). *Geographic focus:* Alaska, northeastern North America. *Languages:* French (reading-good, writing-poor, speaking-fair). *Additional expertise:* Archaeology, cultural resource management, project management.

Visual productions: "Techniques for Recovering the Past," 1973, 20 min. b/w film on archaeological investigations.

de Peña, Joan F.
Department of Anthropology, University of Manitoba, Winnipeg, Manitoba, Canada, R3T 2N2. *Phone:* (204) 474-6327. *Profession:* Anthropologist. *Interests:* Ethnographic filmmaking, teaching with ethnographic visual aids including film. *Training:* Ph.D. Anthropology, Indiana University, 1958. Assisted some in film editing. *Work in progress:* Re-editing of work prints of film footage on Inuit populations from eastern Canadian arctic. *Geographic focus:* Eastern Canadian arctic, specifically Igloolik and Hall Beach, N.W.T. (film taken during International Biological Program Studies 1969-72). *Languages:* English (r,w,s), Spanish (reading), German (reading).

Visual productions: Film Studies from Igloolik, N.W.T., parts I and II, each is a 25 min. b/w silent film. Films held by Distribution Group, University of Manitoba.

Desmond, Lawrence G.
51 Yerba Buena Avenue, San Francisco, CA 94127. *Phone:* (415) 681-5174. *Profession:* Archaeologist. *Affiliations:* California Academy of Sciences; University of Colorado, Mesoamerican Archive and Research Project. *Interests:* Stereo photogrammetry, archaeological applications. Photo archives, development and organization. Computer applications to storage and retrieval of photographs in archives. Data management of photo collection, computer storage of photographs. Ethnographic photography. 19th century photographic processes. *Training:* Ph.D. Anthropology, University of Colorado, 1983. Professional photographer with training by Ansel Adams and Pirkle Jones. *Work in progress:* Interpretive text to accompany a catalogue of 750 Le Plongeon archaeological photographs taken in the 1870's in northern Yucatan (I have completed the duplication of the Le Plongeon negatives and cataloging of the collection)—provides a case study of the interaction of photography and the development of archaeology in the 19th century. Use of stereo photogrammetry at Chichen Itza to evaluate stereo photogrammetry as a method for archaeological documentation and to measure loss in detail in bas-reliefs over past 100 years by comparing Le Plongeon photos with stereo photogrammetry. *Geographic focus:* Mesoamerica. *Languages:* Spanish (excellent reading, fair writing and speaking).

Visual productions: Designed and developed the Mesoamerican photographic archives of the Mesoamerican Archive and Research Project of the University of Colorado, Boulder (director David Carrasco). Archives consists of more than 7,000 photos of the Templo Mayor archaeology site in Mexico City. Photos show process of excavation over a four year period. Photos of current condition by Desmond, with majority from institutions and persons associated with the project. Numerous other ethnographic and archaeological photographs in professional journals and other publications.

Dewey, Alice G.
Department of Anthropology, University of Hawaii, 2424 Maile Way, Honolulu, HI 96822. Home: 2828 Kahawai Street, Honolulu, HI 96822. *Phone:* (808) 948-7578, (808) 988-6451, department (808) 948-8415. *Profession:* Anthropologist. *Interests:* Social anthropology, economic anthropology, kinship, anthropology of art—especially aesthetics. *Training:* Ph.D. in Anthropology. *Work in progress:* Continuing interest in cognitive patterns of Javanese. *Geographic focus:* Southeast Asia, especially Javanese culture. *Languages:* Moderate spoken Indonesian; poor reading ability in Spanish, French, Dutch; poor speaking Javanese.

Diaz-Granados, Carol
7433 Amherst Avenue, St. Louis, MO, 63130. Campus Box 1114, Department of Anthropology, Washington University, St. Louis, MO 63130. *Phone:* university (314) 889-5252; home (314) 721-0386. *Profession:* Archaeologist, educator, designer. *Affiliation:* also Mark Twain Summer Institute, St. Louis. *Interests:* Art as language; graphic symbolism and communications in prehistory; theories in the beginnings of aesthetics, interpretations, and uses of art in prehistory; teaching anthropology; anthropology through the arts. *Training:* Ph.D. coursework completed, 1982. M.A. in Anthropology, Washington University, 1980. B.F.A. in Graphic Design, Washington University, 1964. *Work in progress:* "Norms of Graphic Response." "Design Seriation and Interpretation of the Petroglyphs of Missouri." *Geographic focus:* Midwestern United States and Colombia, South America (in particular the northwest coastal region). *Languages:* Spanish (r,w,s). *Technical expertise:* Photography, graphics, signing.

DiMichele, Donna Longo
[in Bibliography: see **Longo, Donna A.**]
1863 Old Meadow Road #203, McLean, VA 22102. Office: Smithsonian Archives, Arts and Industries Building rm 2135, Washington, DC 20560. *Phone:* (703) 356-2494; (202) 357-3364. *Profession:* Anthropology. *Affiliation:* Photo Survey Project, Smithsonian Institution Archives. *Interests:* Still photography, especially historical photographs of North American Indians, semiotics, analysis of visual forms, communication theory, reflexivity, the role of photography in cross-cultural relations and perceptions. *Training:* M.A. Anthropology, The American University, Washington, DC, 1985. B.A. Anthropology, University of Rhode Island, Kingston, RI, 1978. *Geographic focus:* North American Indians: U.S. Southwest Pueblos. *Other information:* Illustrations researcher for the Handbook of North American Indians, vol. 4, History of Indian–White Relations (1988, Washington, DC: Smithsonian Institution).

Di Sparti, Antonio
via G. Cimabue 41, I-90145 Palermo, Italy. Office: Instituto Filologia E
Linguistica, Viale delle Scienze, I-90128 Palermo, Italy. *Phone:* 091/408484
Profession: Professor of Semiotics and Linguistics at University of Palermo.
Affiliation: Societá di Linguistica Italiana (SLI), Associazione Italiana Studi
Semiotici (AISS), International Association for Semiotic Studies (IASS),
SVA. *Interests:* Semiotics and linguistics of mass communications, advertising, computational linguistics. *Training:* Humanities and linguistics,
computer programming. *Work in progress:* Sign processing and cerebral
hemispheres, nonverbal comunication and TV commercials, semiotics and
computer. *Languages:* English, French, Italian. *Additional expertise:* I have
directed for five years at a local TV station.

Dornfeld, Barry
3816 Hamilton Street, Philadelphia, PA 19104. *Phone:* (215) 386-3102.
Profession: Independent filmmaker. *Affiliation:* Annenberg School of
Communications. *Interests:* Ethnographic and documentary filmmaking,
performance studies (ethnomusicological research), production of culture and
representation in documentary. *Training:* Ph.D. candidate in Communi-
cations, M.A. Communications, Annenberg. B.A. Anthropology, Tufts.
Training at the Anthropology Film Center, Santa Fe, NM. *Geographic focus:*
West Africa, Appalachia. *Languages:* French (rusty intermediate). *Technical
expertise:* Sound recording, still photography, cinematography.
   Visual productions: "Dance Like a River: Odadaa! Drumming and
Dancing in the U.S.," 45 min. color 16mm documentary film, distributed by
Indiana University Audio Visual Center. "Years Away From Laos: The
Hmong in Philadelphia," 25 min. video documentary. "Powerhouse for God,"
one-hour documentary film about an Appalachian Baptist church (co-director,
with Jeff Titon and Tom Rankin).

Doughty, Paul L.
2155 NW 3rd Place, Gainesville, FL 32603. Office: Department of Anthropology, Turlington Hall, University of Florida, Gainesville, FL 32611.
Phone: (904) 392-2031. *Profession:* Professor of Anthropology and Latin
American Studies. *Interests:* Photography as a teaching and research tool for
the analysis of socio-cultural change, to evaluate development projects, to
document historical materials relevant to anthropological analysis, as illustration of human social interaction, particularly inter-class and inter-ethnic
behaviors, for teaching and lecturing about international and intercultural
relations, and for presenting thematic exhibitions on human life ways, social
change, social problems, aesthetic culture and "pop culture." *Training:* Ph.D.
Cornell University, 1963; several years of residence and work in Latin America particularly. *Work in progress:* A computerized archive of photographs for
teaching and research, University of Florida. *Geographic focus:* Latin America:

Peru and Andean areas, Mexico, Guatemala, El Salvador, Costa Rica, Spain, Nicaragua. *Languages:* Spanish (r,w,s). *Technical expertise:* Basic darkroom skills. Still photography in color and b/w. *Other information:* Several hundred photographs published in popular magazines and professional publications as illustrative material.

Visual productions: "Andean Cultural Ecology," 1969–70, photo essay, Indiana University Museum. "The Unknown Indiana," 1970, photo essay on the sculpture and architecture of Indiana University. "Living Through Tragedy: The Peruvian Earthquake of 1970 and Its Aftermath," 1982, photo essay for Grinter Galleries, University of Florida.

Drewal, Henry John
Art Department, Cleveland State University, Cleveland, OH 44115. *Phone:* (216) 687-2090 ext 2105. *Profession:* Professor/researcher in African Art. *Affiliation:* also The Metropolitan Museum of Art. *Interests:* Ethnographic filmmaking, especially performance (ritual, dance, masquerades, etc.) *Training:* M.A./Ph.D. Anthropology/Art History/History, Columbia University. Study under Margaret Mead, several films produced in super-8 and 16mm. *Work in progress:* "The Meaning of Oshugbo Art Among Ijebu Yoruba: A Reappraisal," in B. Engelbrecht and R. Gardi, eds. Festschrift, Ethnologisches Seminar, Universitat Basel, Basel, Switzerland. *Geographic focus:* Africa, Afro-America, Afro-Brazil. *Languages:* French (fluent); Yoruba (fair in r,w,s); Spanish (fair in r,w,s); Portuguese (poor in r,w,s). *Other information:* Consultant for NEH film entitled "Sons of the Moon," by Deirdre Lapin and Francis Speed.

Visual productions: Super-8 color sound films: "Mardi Gras," 1969, 16 min., New Orleans; "Living Space: A Study of an Artist's Family Living in a Loft," 1970, 25 min., written commentary, New York; "Efe/Gelede Ceremonies Among the Western Yoruba," 1971, 29 min., written commentary, Benin (R.P.B.) and Nigeria. 16mm color film: "John Eboh: Portrait of a Traditional Yoruba Carver," 1980, 10 min., Benin (R.P.B.), produced for African Artistry exhibition.

Dry, Constance Crawford
Ethnovision Inc., 2112 South Street, Philadelphia, PA 19146. Home: 2207 Delancey Place, Philadelphia, PA 19103. *Phone:* (215) 735-2188; home (215) 732-5848. *Profession:* Videotape design and production. *Interests:* Ethnovision, Inc. is a videotape production company that produces programs for use by corporations and educational institutions in the areas of training, documentation, research and intergroup relations. *Training:* B.A. Mt. Holyoke College, 1965. M.V.A. Temple University, 1982. *Work in progress:* Production of videotapes for non-profit corporations. The use of videotape as a social document. *Geographic focus:* Philadelphia, PA. *Languages:* Spanish (r,w,s).

Dumont, Jean-Paul
Department of Sociology and Anthropology, George Mason University, Fairfax, VA 22030. *Phone:* (703) 323-2900. *Profession:* Professor of Anthropology. *Interests:* I have made films, written about films, and teach a course on Visual Anthropology. *Training:* Ph.D. Anthropology, University of Pittsburgh, 1972. *Geographic focus:* South American Lowlands, Philippine lowland Christians. *Languages:* French (native), Spanish (fluent r,w,s), Cebuano (reading, some speaking, no writing).

Duncan, Faith L.
726 38th Avenue, San Francisco, CA 94121. *Phone:* (415) 752-4040. *Profession:* Anthropologist, archaeologist, ecologist, palynologist. *Affiliation:* Presently an environmental educator, Marin Headland Campus, Yosemite National Institutes, BBNRA, Sausalito, CA 94965. *Interests:* Study of space and relationship between visual symbols via photographic analyses—urban streets, neighborhoods, and native American homes in an urban environment. The use of photography in the study of oral communication and history. Historical photographic analyses for the purpose of outlining land use and resource exploitation patterns. Application of visual data towards interpreting the past. Applications of photography in archaeological sciences. *Training:* Ph.D. candidate, and M.A. Anthropology and Geosciences, University of Arizona. B.A. Anthropology, San Francisco State University, 1978. Studied under John Collier 1975-1979, SFSU. *Work in progress:* Historical photographic analyses for the purpose of reconstructing past vegetation and resource management in Marin County, California (Ph.D. dissertation). Also working with photography as a tool in environmental education: school week programs in the ecological sciences for grades K-12, Marin Headlands Institute. *Geographic focus:* Far western North America. *Languages:* Spanish (reading and speaking fair), French. *Technical expertise:* Microscope photography (pollen morphology and analyses). 35mm photography: ethnography, archaeology, geosciences.
    Visual productions: "The Visualization of Oral History: A Study of a Woman's Life," 1977, slide-tapes. "Photographic Essay of Castro Street—Neighborhoods in San Francisco," 1978. "History of the Rocks: Tumamoc Hill," 1985 (with Madeline Cook), photographic essay for the Annual Global Arid Lands Conference, University of Arizona; a study of arid lands' cultural resources. All negatives and documentation on file with author.

Durrans, Brian
Museum of Mankind, 6 Burlington Gardens, London, WIX 2EX, England. Home: 6 Alexandra Road, Chiswick, London, W4IAX, England. *Phone:* (01) 437 2224. *Profession:* Anthropologist, Museum Curator. *Affiliation:* Deputy Keeper, Museum of Mankind (Ethnography Department of the British Museum. *Interests:* Museum exhibitions; cultural representations that take

visual forms; the character, variability, organization, documentation and interpretation of complex visual representation events; and categorizations of material culture. Mass, popular, and third-world traditions; innovations in visual symbolic systems; elite vs. mass taste in material culture; the social organization and conscious direction of visual symbolic systems. *Training:* Ph.D. in Cultural Anthropology (Oceanic canoe types); exhibition curating. *Work in progress:* Catalogue of Charles Hose Collection from Borneo in the British Museum (ethnography, colonial relations). Exhibition on rickshaw art from Bangladesh. Crafts and ideology in India (long-term project). *Geographic focus:* India, Borneo, worldwide. *Languages:* French (r,w,s well), German (read moderately well).

Visual productions: "Vasna: Inside an Indian Village," exhibition, part of the British Museum's contribution to the 1982 festival of India in Britain.

Edson, Paul

820 Merton Road, Apt. 210, Detroit, MI 48203. *Phone:* (313) 341-9631. *Profession:* Anthropologist, writer, critic. *Interests:* Primarily: images as both expressive culture and symbol systems, art as an indicator of culture contact. Secondarily: the built environment, museology, dance, 19th and 20th century design. *Training:* Ph.D. Anthropology, Indiana University, 1974. *Work in progress:* A study of formats in European figural art. *Geographic focus:* Europe and the Soviet Union, Africa. *Languages:* Reading knowledge of Latin, Romanian, French. *Technical expertise:* Sound recording, archiving.

Eisenbeis, Manfred R.

Berliner Strasse 77, 6050 Offenbach, West Germany. Office: Hochschule für Gestaltung, Department of Visual Communication, Group of Media Development and Research, Schlosstrasse 316050 Offenbach, West Germany. *Phone:* 069-88 29 29; 069-81 99 58. *Interests:* History and theory of visual communication/pictorial communication, ethnology of visual communication, aesthetics and its role in communications. *Training:* Hochschule für Gestaltung, Ulm: Visual Communication. Universities of Tubingen and Munich: Art History, Philosophy, Social Psychology, Sociology. German Institute of Film and TV, Munich: Filmmaking. Sorbonne and Ecole Pratique des Hautes Etudes, Paris: Anthropology, Mass Communication, Semiotics, Art History, Social Psychology. *Work in progress:* Works on the history of human communication, on aesthetics, and art and technology (new media). *Languages:* French, English, German (r,w,s). *Technical expertise:* Electronic media. *Other information:* Professor, consultant at UNESCO and the Council of Europe. Member of the German Commission of UNESCO.

Elder, Mary-Scovill

Syneraction, Inc, 2500 Johnson Avenue, Riverdale, NY 10463. *Phone:* (212) 884-7310; FAX no. (212) 601-2954. *Profession:* Midwife, doctorate near completion. *Affiliation:* Columbia University Teachers College, Department of Family and Community Education. *Interests:* Ethnographic video/filmmaking. Teaching with ethnographic video/film. Kinesic and other systematic study of body motion communication and gesture. Video microanalysis. Biological rhythm, interaction analysis/research. Video/film/photo archiving. *Training:* Doctoral candidate, Department of Family and Community Education, Columbia University Teachers College. C.N.M. and M.S. *Work in progress:* "Rhythm Sharing Among the Deaf," video microanalysis of interpersonal communication between a deaf-mute Puerto Rican father and Black American mother and their hearing infant—doctoral dissertation. *Geographic focus:* Fieldwork in Black and Puerto Rican communities, Bronx, NY.

El Guindi, Fadwa

El Nil Research, 1147 Beverwil Drive, Los Angeles, CA 90035. *Phone:* research office (213) 553-5645. *Profession:* Anthropologist. *Interests:* Ethnography, ethnographic filmmaking, teaching with ethnographic film. *Training:* Ph.D. Anthropology, University of Texas, Austin, 1972. *Work in progress:* Three ethnographic films: "El Moulid: Egyptian Religious Festival" (soon to be released, approx. 40 min), "Egyptian Ceremonial Crafts" (editing in progress), "Birth Ritual and Cosmological Beliefs in Egypt." *Geographic focus:* The valley Zapotec in Oaxaca, Mexico; Egypt; Nubians in Egypt; the Arab World. *Languages:* Arabic (r,w,s), Spanish (read, speak), French (r,w,s). *Other information:* Ethnographic slides on Zapotec life and ritual, on birth ritual in Egypt, 1986, and on male circumcision, religious festival, and ceremonial crafts in Egypt, 1987.

Visual productions: "'El Sobou': Egyptian Birth Ritual," 1986, 27 min. color 16mm.

Erdman, Joan L.

5415 South Cornell Avenue #2, Chicago, IL 60615. Office: Department of Liberal Education, Columbia College Chicago, 600 S. Michigan Avenue, Chicago, IL 60605. *Phone:* (312) 643-6245; office (312) 663-1600 ext 530. *Profession:* Writer, teacher, media consultant, anthropologist. *Affiliation:* also Research Associate, Committee on Southern Asian Studies, University of Chicago. *Interests:* Performance studies, South Asian culture and society, cultural change, artists and artisans, women in the visual and performing arts, ethnographic films and ethnographic texts, anthropology of performance. *Training:* Ph.D. Anthropology, University of Chicago, 1980. M.A. Anthropology, University of Chicago, 1975. B.A. Social Relations (magna cum laude), Radcliffe College, 1962. *Work in progress:* "A New Tradition: Modern Indian Dance," a study of the great dancer and choreographer Uday Shankar and his creation of Indian modern dance (book ms.). "Daring: The Autobiography of Zohra Segal," (book ms., co-written with Zohra Segal, dancer/actress). Co-author, Manganiyar Professional Folk Musicians of Rajasthan. Co-director of films "Advancing Women" and "Sacred Time." *Geographic focus:* South Asia. *Languages:* Hindi (r,w,s), French (r,w,s), some Sanskrit, Latin, and Bengali. *Technical expertise:* 35mm photography, taping and sound systems, musical instruments (tabla and piano).

Visual productions: Creative consultant on "India Speaks," 1985; and "Circles, Cycles, Kathak Dance," 1988.

Erickson, Frederick
Graduate School of Education, University of Pennsylvania, Philadelphia, PA 19104. *Phone:* (215) 898-5693, or 898-3273. *Profession:* Anthropology of education. *Interests:* Sociolinguistics, audiovisual microanalysis, ethnographic research methods. *Training:* Ph.D. Anthropology of Education, Northwestern University. *Geographic focus:* U.S. minority groups. *Other information:* Editor, Anthropology and Education Quarterly.

Eyde, David B.
Department of Sociology and Anthropology, University of Texas at El Paso, El Paso, TX 79968. Home: P.O. Box 100, UTEP, El Paso, TX 79968. *Phone:* (915) 747-5740. *Profession:* Associate Professor of Anthropology. *Interests:* Use of ethnographic film in teaching. Especially interested in symbolism, including visual symbols. *Training:* Ph.D. Anthropology, Yale University, 1966. *Work in progress:* Currently rewriting thesis for book on warfare and social structure among the Asmat of S.W. New Guinea (little direct relationship to visual anthropology, though the Asmat are among the world's great woodcarvers). I retain my interests in Mexico and Mexican Americans, especially with regard to the use of "santos" as symbols in churches. I'll probably do at least a bit more dealing with Korea. *Geographic focus:* Melanesia, Mexico and Mexican-Americans, Korea. *Languages:* Spanish (read, write, speak some), German (read haltingly), French (read haltingly).

Fabian, Rhonda J.
904 S. 47th Street, Philadelphia, PA 19143. *Phone:* (215) 724-1784. *Profession:* Television producer/consultant. *Affiliations:* R & R Productions; Annenberg School of Communications, University of Pennsylvania. *Interests:* Urban anthropology, anthropology of dance, ethnographic filmmaking. *Training:* M.A. Communications, Annenberg, 1989. B.A. Anthropology, University of New Orleans, 1986. Film Studies, University of Bridgeport, CT, 1975-78. *Work in progress:* "Newsroom," 30 min. broadcast documentary/ethnography of a southern network affiliate TV station. *Geographic focus:* New Orleans, Southern U.S., Caribbean, Latin America. *Languages :* Spanish (fluent), some French. *Technical expertise:* Professional broadcast video production, creation of visual stimulus objects for small group testing and discussion. *Other information:* Professional grant writer.

Visual productions: "The Latin Eye," a discussion of the work of two turn-of-the-century Central American photographers, 30 min. video. "Feet Can't Fail Me Now," 30 min. documentary exploring the role of dance in a black New Orleans community, including jazz funerals, social-club parades, tap dance, and Mardi-gras. Co-producer and editor of "A House Divided," an exploration of the history of desegregation in New Orleans through the eyes of the people who experienced it, 1988 New Orleans Press Club Award for best documentary, part of the Louisiana public school curriculum.

Fagan, Brian

Department of Anthropology, UCSB, Santa Barbara, CA 93106. *Phone:* (805) 961-2516. *Profession:* Archaeologist, professor. *Interests:* Teaching, archaeology and the wider audience. *Training:* Ph.D. Cambridge University.

Faris, James C.

Department of Anthropology U-158, University of Connecticut, Storrs, CT 06268. Home: 27 Centre Street, Mansfield Center, CT 06250. *Phone:* (203) 486-4512; home (203) 456-1012. *Profession:* Anthropologist. *Interests:* Social anthropology, critique of photography and film in anthropology, art and cognition, ideology. *Work in progress:* "Image, Document, Power: Anthropology and Photography Representations" (ms.). *Geographic focus:* Africa, Middle East, American Southwest. *Languages:* Kordofanian Nuba [Fungor] (speaking), Arabic (reading—poor), Spanish, French, German (reading—poor).

Visual productions: "Southeast Nuba," 1982 (anthropologist; C. Curling producer), 58 min., BBC-TV.

Farnell, Brenda M.

American Indian Research Studies Institute, 422 North Indiana Avenue, Bloomington, IN 47401. Field address: Box 944, Harlem, MT 59526. *Phone:* Indiana (812) 335-4086. Montana (406) 353-2590. *Profession:* Sociocultural anthropologist. *Affiliation:* Anthropology Department, Indiana University. *Interests:* The anthropology of human movement. Anthropology of the arts. Plains Indian sign language. Northern Plains dance styles. Gesture and storytelling performance. Labanotation, movement notation systems, literacy in human movement. Anthropology/philosophy of body-mind relations. *Training:* B.Ed. Dance and Physical Education, I.M. Marsh College, University of Liverpool, England. Advanced Diploma, Movement Studies and Dance Education, Laban Dance Center, London University. M.A. Anthropology of Human Movement, New York University. Ph.D. candidate, Department of Anthropology, Indiana University. *Work in progress:* The Visible and the Invisible: Anthropological Inquiry Into Movement and Meaning (forthcoming edited book, Metuchen, New Jersey: Scarecrow Press). Action and Meaning in Plains Indian Sign Language (Ph.D. dissertation). The Laban Script: An Ordinary Approach to Movement Writing (book with Drid

Williams). *Geographic focus:* North American Indians. *Languages:* German (r,w,s), French (read), Assiniboine (can make myself understood; cannot joke or gossip in it), PSL [Plains Sign Language]. *Additional expertise:* Labanotation Certification, The Dance Notation Bureau, New York.

Farrer, Claire R.
Department of Anthropology, Butte Hall–311, CSU-Chico, Chico, CA 95929-0400. Home: 15 Meadowlark Lane, Paradise, CA 95929. *Phone:* (916) 895-4646 or 6192; home (916) 872-2822. *Profession:* Associate Professor of Anthropology. *Interests:* Ethnographic film, aesthetic anthropology, folklore. *Training:* Ph.D. and M.A. Anthropology and Folklore, University of Texax, Austin. B.A. Anthropology, University of California, Berkeley. *Geographic focus:* U.S. Southwest (Indians, Hispanics, Anglos). *Languages:* Spanish and Italian (reading, writing, very limited speaking); Mescalero Apache (unwritten language).

Visual productions: "Geronimo's Children," 1975 (Michael Barnes producer, director) 60 min. color 16mm film, BBC Production.

Feest, Christian F.
Museum für Völkerkunde, A-1014 Wien, Austria. Home: Salztorgasse 7/21, A-1010 Wien, Austria. *Phone:* 43-222-934541 ext 516; home 6370803. *Profession:* Curator, Associate Professor. *Affiliation:* Museum für Völkerkunde, Vienna, Austria and Department of Anthropology, University of Vienna, Austria. *Interests:* Pre-photographic and photographic pictorial sources of ethnography, ethnographic illustration, material culture as visual arts, visual arts as material culture, iconography of cultures, archival storage and retrieval of visual information. *Training:* Ph.D. Anthropology, University of Vienna, 1969. *Work in progress:* "Jacques Le Moynes: Two Reattributions" (completed, unpublished). *Geographic focus:* Native North America. *Languages:* German, English (good reading, writing, and speaking of both); French, Spanish (fair reading, poor writing and speaking). *Other information:* Curator of photographic collections, Museum für Völkerkunde, Vienna.

Fernea, Elizabeth
3003 Bowman Avenue, Austin, TX 78703. Office: Center for Middle Eastern Studies, University of Texas at Austin, Austin, TX 78712. *Phone:* (512) 477-9348; (512) 471-3881. *Profession:* University lecturer, author, filmmaker. *Interests:* Ethnographic filmmaking (especially of women), teaching with ethnographic film, writing, and translating. *Training:* Graduate work, Mount Holyoke College, University of Chicago. B.A. Reed College. *Geographic focus:* Middle East. *Languages:* French (reading and speaking fluency), Arabic (speaking fluency). *Other information:* Have produced study guides for "A Veiled Revolution," "The Price of Change," "Women Under Siege," and "Saints and Spirits."

Visual productions: Producer-writer for the following 16mm films (also available in video): "A Veiled Revolution," 28 min. [also in Arabic]; "The Price of Change," 28 min. [also in Arabic]; "Women Under Siege," 28 min. [also in Arabic]; "Saints and Spirits," 28 min.; "Some Women of Marrakech," 28 min.

Fernea, Robert A.

Department of Anthropology, University of Texas at Austin, Austin, TX 78712. Home: 3003 Bowman Avenue, Austin, TX 78703. *Phone:* (512) 471-4206; (512) 477-9348. *Profession:* Cultural anthropologist. *Interests:* Teaching with ethnographic film; analysis of visual symbolic forms; the structuring of reality as denoted by visual productions and artifacts; the study of art and performance from social, cultural, historical, semiotic, and aesthetic points of view. *Training:* Ph.D. Social Anthropology, University of Chicago, 1959. *Geographic focus:* Middle East. *Languages:* French (good speaking and reading), Arabic (good speaking).

Field, Rachel

135 Eastern Parkway, Apt. 15C, Brooklyn, NY 11238. Office: WGBH-TV, 114 West Avenue, Boston, MA 01234. *Phone:* (617) 492-2777 ext 4310; home (617) 623-5440 or (718) 636–6026. *Professions:* Visual anthropology; broadcast journalism. *Affiliations:* also Communications Department, Marymount Manhattan College; Institute of Film and Television, New York University. *Interests:* Epistemological and ethical concerns in visual anthropology. Ethnographic film. TV and radio production. Women and anthropological film. Visual anthropology applied to medical anthropology and Latin American ethnography. *Training:* B.A. (languages, anthropology, film) New York University; M.F.A. Film and TV, New York University. Graduate work, New School for Social Research. Producer's Training Seminar, National Public Radio. *Work in progress:* The Mapuche Film Project (producer and director), 16mm documentary film on the largest indigenous group in Chile. The Columbus Project, PBS series on the legacy of the voyages of Columbus and the impacts on the Americas (associate producer). *Geographic focus:* Latin America, Central America, Brazil, Chile, U.S. *Languages:* Spanish (bilingual), Portuguese (fluent), French (fluent). *Technical expertise:* Audio engineering and sound recording. Cinematography, videography, and still photography. *Other information:* Chair, Board of Directors, The Association of Independent Video and Filmmakers (AIVF), 1987–89. Co-director, Symposium on Women and Ethnographic Film, Conference on Visual Anthropology (Philadelphia, Temple University) 1980.

Visual productions: Southwest Center for Education Television 13-part bilingual TV series, 1981 (associate producer, researcher), on cross-cultural exchange of teenagers of different ethnicities. "Abuelitas de Ombligo [Grandmothers of the Bellybutton]," 1983 (producer, director, videographer), 1/2 hour video documentary on the role of granny midwives in Nicaragua. "Chile: Decade of Dictatorship," 1984 (producer, director), independent video documentary and 1/2 hour radio feature for National Public Radio. Sound recordist for: "City News," 1980, WNET–TV American Playhouse Theatre; "Born in Flames," 1980 (Lizzie Borden producer, director), independent feature; "Sanctuary," 1982, 16mm docu-drama, U.N. High Commissioner on Refugees and World Council of Churches; "Target Nicaragua: Inside a Covert War," 1982 (director Saul Landau), 16mm documentary; Women in the Media, Inc. video documentary on the U.N. Decade for Women NGO Forum and Conference in Nairobi, Kenya, 1985 (also second camera); "Vara," 1986, Dutch Television 16mm film on Hopi/Navaho land dispute.

Finnegan, Gregory A.
Reference Department, Baker Library, Dartmouth College, Hanover, NH 03755. Home: RR2 Box 126, 2 Carpenter Street, Norwich, VT 05055. *Phone:* (603) 646-2868; (603) 646-2560; home (802) 649-1194. *Profession:* Librarian and anthropologist. *Affiliation:* Reference bibliographer for Anthropology and Sociology, Dartmouth College Library. Adjunct Associate Professor of Anthropology. *Interests:* Anthropological bibliography and filmography. Teaching with ethnographic film. Ethnographic film criticism and history. Use of ethnographic film for illustrating and analyzing social behavoir and structures. *Training:* Ph.D. Anthropology, Brandeis University, 1976. M.A. Library Science, University of Chicago, 1981. *Work in progress:* Paper analyzing the films of Robert Gardner. *Geographic focus:* West Africa (Sahel), Caribbean. *Languages:* Good French, passable German and Mooré (spoken by Mossi, West Africa). *Other information:* Editor for Audiovisual Anthropology, American Anthropologist, 1979–81. Book reviews editor, Visual Anthropology, 1988– .

Fleischhauer, Carl
American Folklife Center, Library of Congress, Washington DC 20540. Home: P.O. Box 413, Solomons, MD 20688. *Phone:* (202) 707-6590; home (301) 586-1277. *Profession:* Folklife specialist. *Interests:* Production of various media at the American Folklife Center: still photography, sound recording, motion picture film, and video. The materials we create are archived at the Library of Congress. Many items are selected for use in publication, exhibits, and the like. *Training:* MFA degree in film and photography, Ohio University, 1969. *Geographic focus:* United States.
Visual productions: "John Mitchell Hickman: Bluegrass Banjo Player," 1968, 16mm film. "How to Make Sorghum Molasses," 1971, 16mm film. "All Hand Work," 1971, 16mm film. "The Hammons Family," 1973 (co-editor), documentary phonograph record. "Blue Ridge Harvest," 1981 (co-editor), photographic book. "The Ninety-Six: A Cattle Ranch in Northern Nevada," 1985, laser videodisc.

Flowers, Nancy M.
154 Dean Street, Brooklyn, NY 11217. Department of Anthropology, Hunter College of the City University of New York, 695 Park Avenue, New York, NY 10021. *Phone:* (718) 858-0878; office (212) 772-5410. *Profession:* Cultural anthropologist, formerly photojournalist. *Interests:* Teaching with ethnographic film. Still photography. Visual observation for time allocation and social interaction study. Visual anthropology generally. *Training:* Ph.D. Anthropology, City University of New York Graduate School, 1983. Photojournalism major, Boston University 1959-60. *Work in progress:* Research on time allocation using various methods including visual observation. *Geographic focus:* Latin America, principally Brazil. Fieldwork in Central Brazil among Xavante Indians. Fieldwork focusing on agricultural workers in study of Brazilian development project. *Languages:* Portuguese (bilingual on all levels), Spanish (reading excellent, speaking and writing fair), French (reading excellent, speaking and writing fair). *Other information:* Member of SVA. Taught visual anthropology workshop course, Hunter College, spring 1985.

Visual productions: "The Yagua Blowgun," 1975, ethnographic photograph exhibit at the Conference on Visual Anthropology, Temple University.

Ford, Thomas M.
P.O. Box 5187, Louisville, KY 40205. Home: 2222 Woodbourne Avenue, Louisville, KY 40205. *Phone:* (502) 454-3179. *Profession:* Photographer, geophysical data analyst. *Interests:* Study and interpretation of human behavior utilizing still and motion picture photography. *Training:* B.A. Sociology/Anthropology, University of Louisville, 1949. *Geographic focus:* Latin and Oriental cultures. *Technical expertise:* Geophysical data acquisition, photographic data processing. *Other information:* Thirty years working in remote areas of the world, collecting and recording geophysical data.

Gardner, Robert G.
Film Study Center, Harvard University, 19 Prescott Street, Cambridge, MA 02138. *Phone:* (617) 495-3347 (or 3251). *Profession:* Filmmaker, teacher. *Interests:* Independent filmmaking (nonfiction and narrative). Human values, feelings, moral and ethical issues, existential questions of life. *Training:* M.A. Anthropology, Harvard University, 1958. *Work in progress:* Completing three films on the Afar of northeast Ethiopia. Preparing a narrative feature on a historical incident in the 19th century. Working on "End of the Road," a film about the people in "Dead Birds." *Languages:* French, Spanish.

Visual Productions: "Dead Birds," 1964, Phoenix Films. "The Nuer," 1971 (with Hilary Harris and George Breidenbach), CRM films. "Rivers of Sand," 1974, Phoenix. "Deep Hearts," 1981, Phoenix. "Forest of Bliss," 1985, Cantor Films. "Sons of Shiva," 1985, Center Productions, Boulder, Colorado. "Ika Hands," 1989, Museum of Modern Art.

Gatewood, John B.

Department of Social Relations, Price Hall 40, Lehigh University, Bethlehem, PA 18015. *Phone:* (215) 758-3810. *Profession:* Anthropologist. *Interests:* Videotape studies of social interaction and movement coordination. *Training:* Ph.D. in Anthropology, University of Illinois at Urbana-Champaign, 1978. *Work in progress:* Still photographs to supplement study of commercial fisheries in New Jersey. *Geographic focus:* North America. *Languages:* German (reading with difficulty), French (reading with difficulty), Basic, Pascal.

Gearing, Frederick O.

Department of Anthropology, SUNY Buffalo, Amherst, NY 14261. Home: 16 Candlewood Lane, Williamsville, NY 14221. *Phone:* (716) 636-2139. *Profession:* Cultural anthropologist. *Interests:* Interactional analysis: use of video records to map interpersonal synchronies with special focus on the functions of such synchronies on processes of interactional constraints. *Training:* Ph.D. University of Chicago, 1956. *Work in progress:* Sundry probes locally in urban situational settings. *Geographic focus:* North American Indians, village Greece, urban U.S. *Languages:* Greek (moderate proficiency in speaking).

Geary, Christraud M.

35 Sagamore Park, Medford, MA, 02155. Office: Humanities Program Coordinator, African Studies Center, Boston University, 270 Bay State Road, Boston, MA 02215. *Phone:* (617) 488-6033; office (617) 353-3673. *Profession:* Cultural anthropologist. *Interests:* Historical and ethnographic photographs, methodology, ethnohistory, study of art (esp. African art), photo archiving. *Training:* Doctorate in Cultural Anthropology, University of Frankfurt (West Germany). Cataloging of photographic collections in several archives: e.g. Basel Mission Archive, German National Archives. *Work in progress:* Study of African photographic holdings in archives in European, American, and African repositories. Preparation of a book on German colonial photography in Cameroon. *Geographic focus:* Africa, West Africa, Cameroon. *Languages:* German (native), French (fluent reading, good speaking, average writing level), West African Pidgin English (fluent speaking). *Technical expertise:* Field photography. *Other information:* Planning an interdisciplinary international conference on history and photography in Africa (tentative date: 1991).

Visual productions: "Images from Bamum: German Colonial Photography at the Court of King Njoya, Cameroon, West Africa 1902–1915," June–September 1988, museum exhibition, National Museum of African Art, Smithsonian Institution, Washington, D.C.

Geddes, William Robert

176 Hudson Parade, Clareville, New South Wales 2107, Australia. *Phone:* Sydney 918 2605. *Profession:* Social anthropologist. *Affiliation:* Emeritus

Professor, University of Sydney. *Interests:* Ethnographic filmmaking. Ethnography and general social and cultural anthropology. Methodology of ethnographic film. *Training:* M.A. New Zealand. Ph.D. Anthropology, London. Social anthropological field research in Fiji, Borneo, Thailand, and China. *Work in progress:* Ethnographic documentation of the Borneo films (see below). Survey of Hmong (Miao) communities in southern China. *Geographic focus:* Southeast Asia, Oceania, China. *Languages:* French (reading), Bidayuh [Dayak] (speaking). *Additional information:* Past Chairman of the Film Committee of the Australian Institute of Aboriginal Studies.

   Visual productions: Films: "The Opium People," 1959. "The Land Dayaks of Borneo," 1962. "Miao Year," 1968. "Vatulele: An Island in Fiji," 1975. "The Island of the Red Prawns," 1976. "The Ritual of the Field," 1980. "The Soul of the Rice," 1983. "Brides of the Gods," 1985.

Geertz, Hildred
Department of Anthropology, Princeton University, Aaron Burr Hall, Princeton, NJ 08544. *Phone:* department (609) 452-4537; office 452-4549. *Profession:* Anthropologist. *Interests:* Research in Bali and Indonesia on the analysis of visual symbolic forms, visual theories, relationships among different channels and modes of communication. Also the study of art, artifacts, and performance from social, cultural, historical, folkloristic, semiotic and aesthetic points of view; forms of social organization involved in planning, producing, and using visual signs and systems of signs; visual contexts of speech and verbal art. *Training:* Ph.D. Social Relations, Radcliffe College. *Work in progress:* Study of the arts in Bali (painting, carving, drama, dance, literature) and their changes in the 20th century in a specific village. *Geographic focus:* Bali. *Languages:* Indonesian (fluent), Balinese (speak fluently, read easily), Javanese (speak), Moroccan Arabic (speak), Dutch (read easily), French (read easily), Spanish (read), German (read).

Gidley, Mick
Director, Centre for American and Commonwealth Arts and Studies, Queen's Building, University of Exeter, Exeter EX4 4Q11 England. *Phone:* (0392) 264352; secretary (0392) 264263. *Profession:* University teacher of American Studies. *Interests:* History of anthropological photography. *Work in progress:* Biographical and critical study of Edward S. Curtis. *Geographic focus:* North America. *Languages:* Some French.

Gilbert, Loretta
3076 Woodhills Drive, Memphis, TN 38128. *Phone:* (901) 377-3439; messages (901) 323-8300. *Profession:* Graduate student, dancer. *Affiliations:* Memphis State University; Pyramid Dance Company. *Interests:* Ethnographic filmmaking, Middle Eastern dance, midwifery, teaching with ethnographic film, choreometrics. *Training:* M.A. candidate, Anthropology (visual). B.A.

Anthropology (medical). Undergraduate and graduate level courses in film and video production and editing. *Other information:* Founding member of Pyramid Dance Co., a professional (Middle Eastern) folkloric troupe.

Visual productions: Photo essay, 1985, documenting folklife traditions of the residents of Fayette County, Tennessee.

Ginsburg, Faye

Department of Anthropology, 25 Waverly Place, New York University, New York, NY 10003. *Phone:* (212) 998-8550. *Profession:* Anthropologist, documentary producer. *Interests:* History, method, and theory of ethnographic film, anthropology and broadcast media, women and film. Social movements, gender, social theory. *Training:* Ph.D. Anthropology, CUNY Graduate Center, 1986. Associate producer, WCCO-TV (CBS) Minneapolis, MN, 1982. American Association for the Advancement of Science Mass Media Fellow, 1981, documentary unit WCCO-TV (CBS) Minneapolis, MN. Film Study Center seminar with Jean Rouch, summer, 1979. *Geographic focus:* American culture. *Languages:* French (reading, speaking), Hebrew (speaking). *Other information:* I am currently the Director of the new Certificate Program in Ethnographic Film and Video, a joint program of the Anthropology and Cinema Studies Departments of New York University.

Visual productions: Documentaries/ethnographic films: "In Her Hands: Women and Ritual," 1979 (with D. Winston and L. Kharrazi), 20 min. b/w ethnographic video on ritual practice among Syrian Jewish women in Brooklyn, NY, funding by NEH, 1980 Global Village Documentary Award, distributed by Jewish Media Service; "In Praise of Camp Mooween," 1980, 20 min. b/w ethnographic video on camp reunions; "Farwell to Freedom," 1981, 47 min. color video documentary on Laotian Hmong, following one family from a refugee camp in Thailand to Minneapolis for WCCO-TV; and "Prairie Storm," 1982, 57 min. color video documentary on local conflict over the opening of the first abortion clinic in North Dakota for WCCO-TV.

Gmelch, George

Associate Professor, Department of Sociology and Anthropology, Union College, Schenectady, NY 12308. Home: 127 Font Grove Road, Slingerlands, NY 12159. *Phone:* (518) 370-6004; (518) 439-0817. *Interests:* Teaching with ethnographic film, uses of photography as a research tool, urban anthropology, cultural ecology, maritime anthropology, migration, and applied anthropology. *Training:* M.A. and Ph.D. University of California, Santa Barbara. B.A. Stanford University. *Geographic focus:* Ireland, Alaska, Caribbean. *Technical expertise:* Still photography.

Gonçalves, Antonio Claudio Brasil

Rua Nina Rodrigues No. 93/101, Jardim Botanico, 22461 Rio de Janeiro-RJ Brazil. Office: Rua Jardim Botanico 700/519, Jardim Botanico, 22461 Rio de

Janeiro-RJ Brazil. *Phone:* 021-226 6099; office 021-274 4040 or 239 6446. *Profession:* Filmmaker, journalist, anthropologist. *Affiliation:* Brazilian Association of Anthropologists, Brazilian Association of Foreign Correspondents. *Interests:* Social anthropology, TV documentaries, ethnographic film and video, African/Brazilian religions, teaching anthropology with film/video. *Training:* M.Sc. in Social Anthropology at London School of Economics, U.K. B.A. in Social Communications at Catholic University of Rio, Brazil. *Work in progress:* Research/production/direction of several documentaries about Brazil for Worldwide Television News (WTN, former UPITN), ITN/ Channel 4 in London, England, and ABC News/U.S.A. *Geographic focus:* Brazil, Latin America, and Africa. *Languages:* English, Spanish, French, and Portuguese. *Expertise:* Filmmaking, journalism, photography, video. *Other information:* Owner of Rio Cine Video, facilities and production house working with own video equipment in the Brazilian and American standards of professional expertise.

Visual productions: 16mm color films: "Erva Pariri/Amazonas," 1975, 15 min., Brazil; "Cassel Hospital, An Experiment within the National Health System," 1978, 40 min., London, U.K.; "The Seventh Enemy," 30 min., London, U.K.; "Brazil in the Eighties," 1980, 3 X 30 min., Brazil. Umatic color videos (Brazil): "The Brazilian Pantanal," 1982, 30 min.; "Brazil, Samba, and Soccer," 1986, 30 min.; "New Economy," 1986, 15 min.

Graburn, Nelson H. H.
Anthropology, U.C. Berkeley, CA 94720. Home: 14 Wilson Circle, Berkeley, CA 94708. *Phone:* (415) 642-3391, 642-2120; home (415) 845-1537. *Profession:* Anthropologist. *Interests:* Anthropology of art, anthropology of tourism, TV and fourth world peoples. *Training:* Ph.D. Anthropology, Chicago, 1963. M.A. Anthropology, McGill, 1960. B.A. Anthroplogy, Cambridge, 1958. *Work in progress:* "Carving is My Hunt Weapon: Inuit Art in Canada" (Berkeley: U. C. Press). Annotated bibliography of Eskimo art (Boston: G.K. Hall). *Geographic focus:* Circumpolar, Japan, tourists everywhere. *Languages:* French, Eskimo (fluent), German. *Other information:* member of the SVA.

Graves, Thomas E.
100 Pollack Drive, Orwigsburg, PA 17961. Office: 200 South Fourth Street, Minersville, PA 17954. *Phone:* (717) 366-3860; (717) 544-9123. *Profession:* Folklorist. *Affiliation:* Freelance folklife consultant and photographer. *Interests:* The symbolism (cultural, religious) of architecture, "the landscape" and folk art. The use of visual means to record the above. The interpretation of historical and cultural photographs and documents. The study of proxemics and kinesics in folkloric events. *Training:* M.A. and Ph.D. in Folklore and Folklife, University of Pennsylvania. *Work in progress:* Continued work in proxemics/kinesics/symbolism of folk medical ritual, and in symbolism of

folk art. Relating visual "mystical manuscripts" of 15–19th century to printed (non-visual) folk medical manuals. Exploring 19th century photographic stereographs as folkloric and ethnographic documents. Researching 19th century photos of coal mining in Centralia, PA for an exhibit at the Schuylkill County Center for the Arts, Pottsville, PA (with Don Yoder). *Geographic focus:* Ethnic groups found in Pennsylvania, especially Pennsylvania Germans, Gypsies, Ukrainians, Lithuanians. *Languages:* German, Spanish (reading), French (some). *Technical expertise:* Still photographer.

Visual productions: "Hex Signs Past and Present," (and) "Johnny Claypoole, Contemporary Hex Sign Painter," 1982, exhibits, Pennsylvania State University Berks Campus, sponored by the Pennsylvania Folklore Society, March 20–27. Videotape: (with Kathleen H. Jones, directors) "Tradition and Revival: Traditional Arts in the Life of the Congregation of St. Mary's Ukrainian Catholic Church, McAdoo, PA," 1982, Schuylkill County Council for the Arts, Pottsville, PA; and consultant for exhibition on this subject, fall 1982, held at Schuylkill County Arts and Ethnic center, Pottsville, PA. Consultant for "Ruthanne Hartung: Fraktur Artist," 1988, 30 min. video, Berks Community Television, Reading, PA. Director, "Berks County Gravestones," 1988, 60 min. video, Berks Community Television, Reading, PA. "The Pennsylvania German Hex Sign," traveling exhibit (with Don Yoder), sponsored by the Museum of American Folk Art, New York, NY, January, 1989 and continuing. "Craft and Community: Traditional Craft in Contemporary Society," traveling exhibit, sponsored by Balch Institute for Ethnic Studies and The Pennsylvania Heritage Affairs Commission, December, 1988 and continuing.

Griffin, Michael S.
1420 Raymond Avenue, St. Paul, MN 55108. Office: 111 Murphy Hall, 206 Church Street SE, University of Minnesota, Minneapolis, MN 55455. *Phone:* (612) 644-8177; office (612) 625-9824. *Profession:* College professor, documentary filmmaker. *Interests:* Research and writing in the following areas: anthropology and sociology of visual communication, forms of social organization involved in production of visual signs and systems of signs, media socialization of producers and audiences, history of ethnographic and documentary visual media forms, institutionalization of specific forms and/or codes for visual media work and the implications of such codes for access, informational content, and the propagation of ideology. *Training:* M.A. and Ph.D. Communications, the Annenberg School of Communications, University of Pennsylvania. (Studied with Sol Worth, Larry Gross, Dell Hymes, Paul Messaris, Steve Feld, and Amos Vogel). *Work in progress:* "Good Photography: Influences of Amateurs and Industry on Cultural Production" (book ms.). "Looking at TV News" (with Dona Schwartz). *Geographic focus:* U.S. *Languages:* French (reading), Spanish (reading).

Visual productions: "Handscapes" (with Jabari Coleman), 21 min., b/w

16mm film on graffiti wall painters in Philadelphia, made with the participation of the principal subjects, Pretty Boy and Boo.

Grimshaw, Allen D.
Department of Sociology, Indiana University, Bloomington, IN 47405. Home: 4001 Morningside Drive, Bloomington, IN 47401. *Phone:* office (812) 335-8536; messages (812) 335-2569; home (812) 336-3771. *Profession:* Sociology. *Interests:* Discourse analysis of sound-image records. *Training:* Degrees in Sociology and Anthropology, postdoctoral work in linguistics. *Work in progress:* What's Going on Here? Complementary Studies of Professional Talk, edited book, Norwood, NJ: Ablex. (Studies of the MAP soundimage record, in collaboration with several other scholars). Film (video) and audio records of MAP data will be published separately. *Geographic focus:* Primarily U.S., past work in India. *Languages:* Hindi (fair reading), Spanish (poor writing and speaking).

Gropper, Rena C.
65-07 110 Street, Forest Hills, NY 11378. Office: Hunter College, CUNY, Box 170, 695 Park Avenue, New York, NY 10021. *Phone:* (718) 275-4479; office (212) 772-5651; department office (212) 772-5410. *Profession:* Applied medical anthropologist. *Interests:* Proxemics. Teaching with ethnographic film. *Training:* Ph.D. Columbia University—trained by Ruth Fulton Benedict and Alfred Louis Kroeber. *Geographic focus:* Gypsies of the world, Tibet, India. *Languages:* French, German, Spanish, Romanes.

Gross, Larry
Annenberg School of Communications, University of Pennsylvania, Philadelphia, PA 19104. Home: 1916 Lombard Street, Philadelphia, PA 19146. *Phone:* Annenberg (215) 898-5620; home (215) 732-6887; Internet FLG@ ASC.UPENN.EDU *Profession:* Professor of Communications. *Interests:* Visual communication. Art, artists, and society. Mass media and society. Media and minorities. Pornography. *Training:* B.A. Psychology, Brandeis University, 1964. Ph.D. Social Psychology, Columbia University, 1968. *Work in progress:* "The Good Parts: Pornography, Sexuality, and Society" (working title, book). *Geographic focus:* U.S. *Languages:* Hebrew (fluent). *Additional information:* Editor, Studies in Visual Communication (1977–85).

Hagebölling, Heide
Berliner Str. 77, 6050 Offenbach/Main, West Germany. *Phone:* 69-819514. *Profession:* Professor of Video/TV and New Media. *Affiliation:* Fachhochschule Rheinland-Pfalz, Abt. Trier, Department of Communication and Design. *Interests:* Analysis of visual symbolic forms, study of art and new media, production of experimental and didactic videos and short documentaries. *Languages:* German, English, French. *Technical expertise:* Photography,

filmmaking, TV, visual design. *Other information:* Coordinator of Art and New Media: An International Workshop, Paris, December 1987, with professor Manfred Eisenbes, Offenbach (collaboration with UNESCO).

Hall, Edward T.
La Vereda #13, 707 Palace Avenue, Santa Fe, NM 87501. Office: 330 Garfield, Suite 205, Santa Fe, NM 87501. *Phone:* (505) 982-3203. *Profession:* Anthropologist, author, lecturer, consultant. *Affiliation:* Emeritus Professor of Anthropology, Northwestern University. *Interests:* Proxemics, intercultural communication, informatics. *Training:* Ph.D. Anthropology, Columbia University, 1942. M.A. Anthropology, University of Arizona, 1938. B.A. Anthropology, University of Denver, 1936. *Geographic focus:* Germany, Japan, France, U.S., Middle East, Latin America, worldwide.

Hall, Stephanie A.
3705 Adams Drive, Silver Spring, MD, 20902. *Phone:* (301) 946-5619. *Profession:* Ph.D. candidate, Department of Folklore and Folklife, University of Pennsylvania. *Interests:* Ethnographic photography/video, culture/folklore of deaf Americans, masquerade and festival costuming, videotapes made by community groups for their own use. *Work in progress:* Dissertation: "'The Deaf Club Is Like a Second Home': An Ethnography of Communication in American Sign Language." *Geographic focus:* U.S. *Languages:* American Sign Language, French (reading). *Technical expertise:* 35mm photography.

Halpern, Joel M.
Department of Anthropology, University of Massachusetts, Amherst, MA 01002. *Phone:* (413) 545-0028; department (413) 545-2221. *Profession:* Anthropologist. *Affiliation:* University of Massachusetts. *Interests:* Ethnographic filmmaking, teaching with ethnographic film, photography. *Training:* Ph.D. Columbia, 1956. *Geographic focus:* Southeast Europe, Southeast Asia, Arctic and urban U.S. *Languages:* French, Serbo-Croatian.
   Visual productions: "Yugoslavia, Old and New Ways," 1975, film strip, ISBN 0-03-091830-S, New York: Holt, Rinehart, and Winston, revised edition of 1972 production. "Southeast Asian Studies: Emerging Nations of Indochina," 1980, photographs, Educational Enrichment Materials Co., The New York Times, Inc. "The Halperns in Orasac," 50 min., production TV Belgrade, Yugoslavia, original in Serbo-Croatian, U.S. English version.

Hammond, Joyce D.
Department of Anthropology, Western Washington University, Bellingham, WA 98225. Home: 401 16th Street, Bellingham, WA 98225. *Phone:* (206) 676-3613; department (206) 676-3620; home (202) 647-0859. *Profession:* Professor of Anthropology. *Interests:* Visual arts, especially women's art forms; video (as created by informants themselves) and still photography by

and about others; performance; symbolic forms; film/video in teaching. *Training:* Ph.D. Anthropology (cultural), University of Illinois, Champaign-Urbana. *Geographic focus:* Polynesia and Polynesians in U.S. *Languages:* Reading and speaking knowledge of French, Tahitian. *Other information:* Examined home videos made by Tongan Islanders living in the Salt Lake City area of Utah in summer 1986.

Hanisch, Stuart

5018 Milward Drive, Madison, WI 53711. *Phone:* (608) 271-2848. *Profession:* Filmmaker. *Affiliation:* Ash Film Productions. *Interests:* Filmmaking, sound recording. *Training:* Graduate School, University of Southern California, Department of Cinema. *Work in progress:* Color 16mm films: "An African Artist in America," 27 min. "World Resources—Population," 60 min. *Technical expertise:* Electrical engineering, photography.

Visual productions: "The Last Menominee," 27 min. b/w 16mm film. "Have I Told You Lately That I Love You," 15 min. b/w 16mm film.

Haratonik, Peter L.

The New School, 2 W. 13th Street, New York, NY 10011. *Phone:* (212) 741-8903. *Profession:* Professor, Chair, Media Studies. *Interests:* Teaching with visual media. *Training:* Ph.D. Communication Theory, New York University. *Languages:* French.

Hardin, Kris

Department of Anthropology, 325 University Museum, University of Pennsylvania, Philadelphia, PA 19104. *Phone:* office (215) 898-4037; department (215) 898-7461. *Profession:* Anthropologist. *Interests:* Africa, arts, material culture, aesthetics. *Training:* Ph.D. Anthropology. *Work in progress:* "The Aesthetics of Action: Production and Re-Production in a West African Town," in review. African Material Culture (with Mary Jo Arnoldi, eds.) in preparation. *Geographic focus:* West Africa. *Languages:* French (reading), West African Krio (speaking).

Visual productions: "Fertility Choices: A Cross-Cultural Look at the Value of Children," 1987, slide-tape presentation written for the exhibition Generations, Smithsonian Institution.

Harper, Douglas

Sociology Department, SUNY C, Potsdam, NY 13676. Home: Rt. 1 Madrid, NY 13660. *Phone:* (315) 267-2569; home (315) 322-5594. *Profession:* College professor. *Interests:* Still photographs as ethnographic data, theory of visual communication, images in society, ethnographic film. *Training:* Mostly self-taught visually, participation in many conferences. *Geographic focus:* U.S. *Other information:* Editor: Visual Sociology Review. Editor: Book series, Visual Studies of Society and Culture, Temple University Press.

Visual productions: "Ernie's Sawmill," 1982, 25 min. color 16mm ethnographic film about a rural sawyer (co-director).

Hart, Lynn M.

Department of Education in the Arts, Faculty of Education, McGill University, 3700 McTavish Street, Montréal, Québec, H3A 1Y2, Canada. Home: 4233 Oxford Avenue, Montréal, Québec, H4A 2Y5, Canada. *Phone:* (514) 488-6426; home (514) 488-6426. *Profession:* Assistant Professor. *Interests:* Ethnographic filmmaking of graphic and plastic representational processes. Still photography in cross-cultural psychological fieldwork. Developing methods for analyzing visual data (film) to identify cognitive processes in graphic and plastic representation. *Training:* M.A. research in visual representation in young children. Ph.D. research, cross-cultural study of childrens' representation of the body in drawing and language. Honors B.A. in Fine Arts/Visual Art. *Work in progress:* Cataloging 4,000 slides and b/w photographs of Indian ritual art. Three year research project on the development of graphic and plastic representation among Inuit children and adolescents in northern Quebec. Developing methodology and techniques for analyzing videotapes of artists/children sculpting and drawing, to identify the cognitive processes and skills used by an artist during the production of a work of art. "Women's Ritual Art of Kumaon," article with many color and b/w photographs of the art. "Experts and Apprentices: The Acquisition of Soapstone Carving Skills among Inuit in northern Quebec," article (with T.O. Eisemon). *Geographic focus:* Indian Himalayas, Kumaon, Uttar Pradesh, northern Quebec. *Languages:* English and French (fluent), Hindi, Kumaoni, and Nepali (for research purposes). *Other information:* I have a collection of 4,300 color and b/w photographs I took during 20 months of cross-cultural fieldwork in the Indian Himalayas, including an extensive documentation of Kumaoni women's ritual art.

Hauck, Shirley A.

2440 E. Tudor Road #342, Anchorage, AK 99507. Department of Humanities, University of Alaska, 3211 Providence Drive, AK 99508-4670. *Phone:* home (907) 345-2699; office at Council on the Arts (907) 279-1588. *Profession:* Folk/Native Arts Director, college instructor, folk dance teacher. *Affiliation:* also Alaska State Council on the Arts. *Interests:* Choreology, choreometrics, art as visual communication, ethnomusicology in a visual medium, festival. *Training:* Ph.D. Anthropology, University of Pittsburgh. M.F.A. in Folk Arts of Eastern Europe, Duquesne University. *Geographic focus:* North American Natives, East European peasantry. *Languages:* German (fluent), Russian (beginner), Romanian (beginner). *Additional expertise:* Folk dance instructor and choreographer. *Other information:* Specialist in expressive culture, especially music, dance, festival and ritual, Alaskan Native plastic arts and folk crafts, costuming.

Heath, Dwight B.

Department of Anthropology, Box 1921, Brown University, Providence, RI
02912-1921. *Phone:* (401) 863-3251. *Profession:* Anthropologist. *Interests:*
Teaching with ethnographic film; studying social history via film, photos, and
other visual media; making ethnographic film. *Training:* Ph.D. Anthropology,
Yale University; considerable field experience and documentary research, some
filmmaking, Bolivia, 1963. *Work in progress:* Social history of alcohol use
as reflected in visual sources. *Geographic focus:* Worldwide (especially Latin
America, especially Bolivia). *Languages:* Spanish (read well, write fairly,
speak well). *Other information:* Consultant on all post-field phases of
Bolivian "Faces of Change" series (AUFS, Hubert Smith), and associated
study-guides. Study guide for "Viracocha," Hanover, New Hampshire: AUFS.
Pre-field consultant of "Living Maya" series (H. Smith); advisor for "Aymara
Leadership" 1984, by H. Smith.

Heidenreich, C. Adrian

1022 North 30th Street, Billings, MT 59101. Office: Native American
Studies/Sociology, Eastern Montana College, Billings, MT 59101. *Phone:*
home (406) 252-4216; office (406) 657-1673. *Profession:* Anthropologist,
college professor, and consultant. *Interests:* Visual anthropology: intercultural
images and cultural feedback, ethnohistory and visual media, analysis of
artifact and symbolic forms and cultural-visual media, teaching with visual
media (film/video, photographs, art, artifacts, exhibits, and performance); and
presentation of visual media for education and public programming. General:
cultural dynamics, ethnohistory, religion and worldview, history of social
thought, applied anthropology, multicultural education. *Training:* Postdoctoral
Fellow, Department of Anthropology, Smithsonian Institution, 1974-75.
Ph.D. Anthropology, University of Oregon, 1971. M.A. Anthropology, University of Oregon, 1967. B.A. Anthropology and English, Sacramento State
College, 1965. A.A. Social Science/Life Science, American River Junior
College, 1963. *Work in progress:* Study of Northern Plains Indian cultures
and ethnographic method/history through visual and written documents and
oral traditions, with emphasis on Native American cultural dynamics and
Indian-white relations. Study of Native American and Euro-American interpretations of the environment, landscape, and human-environment relations in
pictography, artifacts, oral tradition, and other representative symbolic modes.
Geographic focus: Native American cultures, esp. northern Plains. Pacific
island cultures. *Languages:* French (limited reading) and Spanish (limited
reading). *Technical expertise:* Photography (specializing in 35mm format),
video/film scripting/editing. *Other information:* In addition to numerous
general on-campus and extension courses in Anthropology, Native American
Studies, and Sociology, have taught Ethnographic Film, Intercultural Relations, Multicultural Education, Ethnohistory, and Literature of the American
Indian. Consulting and lecturing to many projects and organizations during

the past 19 years, including Billings Centennial, U.S. Bi-Centennial, and National Endowment for the Humanities Museum Exhibit Grants, schools, etc.

Visual productions: "Baasaxpilua: Northern Plains Celebration," 1982 (key cultural, picture, script, and editing consultant), 58 min. color educational videofilm, Crow Fair, produced by Denver Museum of Natural History, funded by Montana and Colorado Committees for the Humanities.

Heidenreich, Virginia L.

1022 North 30th Street, Billings, MT 59101. Office: Western Heritage Center, 2822 Montana Avenue, Billings, MT 59101. *Phone:* home (406) 252-4216; office (406) 256-6809. *Profession:* Museum educator and photographer. *Interests:* Museum education and visual media (film, video, slides, photographs, art, artifacts, exhibits, and performance); history and philosophy of photography; photographic education; visual media and oral history; study of visual media from socio-cultural, historical, and aesthetic viewpoints; visual media in communication; aesthetic and art criticism; rural environments and people; cultural dynamics and change. *Training:* M.A. Photography, Film, and Communication, George Washington University, 1977. B.A. Anthropology, Zoology, and Photography, University of Oregon, 1970. Other undergraduate work at UC, Davis and University of Philippines. *Work in progress:* Study of Montana peoples, landscapes, and cultures through visual and written documents and oral traditions. *Geographic focus:* North American rural cultures and environments, esp. the northern Plains/Rocky Mountain region. *Languages:* German (limited reading), Spanish (limited reading). *Technical expertise:* Photography (35mm and large-format), slide-tape and video/film scripting and editing. *Other information:* Consultant, lecturer, and free-lance photographer for many organizations and projects from 1970 to present, including Montana Institute of the Arts, U.S. Bureau of Land Management, Westmoreland Coal Company, National Endowment for the Humanities Museum Exhibit Grants, and public schools.

Visual productions: 1978-1984: Preparation of numerous slide-tapes and visual curriculum packets for the Yellowstone Art Center and Western Heritage Center, including: "The Yellowstone: River of Life," "Montana Landscape: One Hundred Years," "Edward Curtis: Photographer of the American Indian," "Eskimo Art," "Renaissance Art," and "Montana History." 1983-1986: "The Yellowstone River: Home, Thoroughfare, and Battleground" (consultant on aesthetics and interpretation), National Endowment for the Humanities Museum Exhibit Planning Grant to the Western Heritage Center, Billings, MT. 1985-1987: "Montana's Black Gold: Underground Coal Mining Communities 1880-1950," exhibit from April 1987 to Sept 1988 (curator of in-house and travelling exhibit), the Western Heritage Center, Billings, MT, funded by the Montana Coal Tax Cultural and Aesthetic Committee.

Heider, Karl G.
Department of Anthropology, University of South Carolina, Columbia, SC 29208. Home: 211 Southwood Drive, Columbia, SC 29205. *Phone:* (803) 777-6500; home (803) 799-1201. *Profession:* Anthropologist. *Interests:* Ethnographic film (making, using, theorizing). Scripted commercial film (use in teaching, use as cultural data on structure and behavior). Videotape analysis of naturally occurring behavior (children's emotions). Use of film and videotape clips for eliciting discussion of (emotion) behavior. *Training:* Ph.D. Anthropology, Harvard. *Work in progress:* Ethnography of emotion, including two years of fieldwork with Minangkabau and central Javanese, Indonesia (1983-1986) using various visual approaches. Theory of visual art manuscript on Good Form, in preparation. *Geographic focus:* Indonesia—Dani of Irian Jaya, Minangkabau of West Sumatra, Central Javanese. *Languages:* German, Dutch, French, Dani (Papuan), Indonesian, Minangkabau (Austronesian). *Technical expertise:* Low-level film and videotape.
Visual productions: Films: "Tikal," 1961. "Dani Sweet Potatoes," 1974; and "Dani Houses," 1974.

Henley, Paul
Granada Centre for Visual Anthropology, University of Manchester M13 9PL, UK. *Phone:* 61-275-3999. *Profession:* Anthropologist and documentary filmmaker, Director of the Granada Centre. *Interests:* Non-fiction filmmaking. Use of social documentary films and videos in anthropological teaching and research. *Training:* Ph.D. Anthropology, Cambridge University, Fellow at National Film and Televison School (1984-86). *Work in progress:* Article on teaching visual anthropology; article on difficulties of combining traditional research work with filming; various film projects at research stage. *Geographic focus:* Venezuela (Orinoquia and Caribbean coast). *Languages:* French, Spanish (speaking); Italian, Portuguese (reading).
Visual productions: "Reclaiming the Forest," 1986 (director, cameraman, editor), 57 min. 16mm film, produced by NFTS/RAI. "Cuyagua," (director, cameraman, editor), 108 min. 16mm film, produced by NFTS/RAI.

Hockings, Paul
Department of Anthropology (m/c 027), University of Illinois, Chicago, IL 60680. *Phone:* (312) 413-3570. *Profession:* Anthropologist. *Affiliation:* University of Illinois. *Interests:* Ethnographic filmmaking, history of ethnographic film. Social anthropology. Dravidian languages. Ethnography of medicine. *Training:* Ph.D. Anthropology, University of California, Berkeley. *Geographic focus:* Ireland, south India. *Languages:* French, German, Tamil, Badaga (all spoken and written, have given lectures in French and German, author of a book in Badaga). *Technical expertise:* Film and video editing, camera and sound work, still photography.

Visual productions: "The Village," 1968 (shot and edited with Mark McCarty), 70 minute 16mm b/w ethnographic film on an Irish community, Berkeley: UCEMC. Researcher for "The Man Hunters," 1969 (with Nicolas L. Noxon and F. Clark Howell), 69 minute color documentary on human paleontology and cultural origins, Culver City: MGM Documentary.

Holaday, Duncan Alan
Department of Communication Arts and Sciences, Lyndon State College, Lyndonville, VT 05850. Home: RFD 3 #45A, St. Johnsbury, VT 05819. *Phone:* (802) 748-1653. *Profession:* Professor. *Interests:* Ethnographic and other forms of filmmaking. Teaching about the use of film in social sciences. Teaching film history and theory. *Training:* Ph.D. Annenberg School of Communications. M.A. Anthropology, Cornell University. B.A. honors in Anthropology, Wesleyan University. *Work in progress:* "After Kuleshov," a teaching film for undergrauate film courses. The Camera Lesson—A New Perspective on the Diffusion of Communication Technology, Occasional Paper Series, Asian Mass Media and Information Research Center, Singapore. *Geographic focus:* Malaysia/Indonesia. *Languages:* Indonesian/Malay (excellent).
    Visual productions: Five hour video recording of masked dance drama of Cirebon, Java, 1979 (co-supervisor), Lincoln Center Dance Collection, NYC. Films: "Ngaben," 1981, 25 min. color/sound 16mm film, in Human Studies Film Archive, Smithsonian Institution. "Metos Jahhut," 16mm film about shamanistic rituals in a Malaysian hill society, Human Studies Film Archive, Smithsonian Institution. "Rina," 1987 (director), 40 min. dramatic TV play (pilot) made for Melasian television. "Sexual Harassment Series I and II," video, 10 minutes each. "Rehearsal," 1988 (video artist), rehearsal of the play Medea Material, co-production of Annenberg School of Communications and the University of Massachusetts, Department of Theatre.

Holleman, Linda C.
2241 Bay Street, San Francisco, CA 94123. *Phone:* (415) 563-8194. *Profession:* Anthropologist. *Affiliation:* Columbia University. *Interests:* Family studies. Ethnographic filmmaking. Cross-cultural health studies. *Training:* Ph.D. Anthropology, Columbia University, 1989. *Work in progress:* Indochinese healing practices. Drug use and its impact on families in the U.S., homelessness. *Geographic focus:* Indochina, urban U.S. *Languages:* French (philosophical reading level).

Holmes, Lowell D.
Department of Anthropology, Wichita State University, Wichita, KS 67208. Home: 2948 N. Terrace, Wichita, KS 67220. *Phone:* (316) 689-3195; home (316) 684-8297. *Profession:* Professor of Anthropology. *Interests:* Cultural anthropology, Samoan specialist; lecture on ethnographic filmmaking but do not have a separate course. *Training:* Ph.D. Anthropology, Northwestern

University, 1957. *Work in progress:* Presently working on feature length film titled "Island Treasures, Stevenson in the Pacific." This film deals with R. L. Stevenson and his relationship to Samoa and Samoans. *Geographic focus:* Polynesia. *Languages:* Speak some Samoan.

Visual productions: "Ea'a Samoa, The Samoan Way," 16mm color film. "The Coming of Old Age in Samoa," slides set with narration tape.

Homiak, John P. (Jake)

5812 LaVista Drive, Alexandria, VA 22310. Office: Human Studies Film Archives, E-307, National Museum of Natural History, Smithsonian Institution, Washington, DC 20560. *Phone:* (703) 922-5153; (202) 357-3349. *Profession:* Cultural anthropologist, film archivist. *Interests:* Analysis of visual symbolic forms, performance studies, ritual as social communication, speech behavior, gesture, emotion, Caribbean ethnography, diaspora studies, Afro-American expressive culture, ethnographic film and teaching. *Training:* Ph.D. Social Anthropology, Brandeis University, 1985. M.A. Human Behavior, U.S. International University, 1975. *Geographic focus:* Caribbean.

Hoskins, Janet Alison

Department of Anthropology, University of Southern California, University Park, Los Angeles, CA 90089-0661. *Phone:* (213) 743-7100. *Profession:* Assistant Professor of Anthropology. *Interests:* Ethnographic filmmaking, ritual communication, visual and verbal sign systems (oratory, gesture, dancing, sacrifice). *Training:* Ph.D. Anthropology, Harvard, 1984. *Work in progress:* Monograph on verbal and visual communication in Kodi ceremonial, concentrating on prestige feasts and calendrical rites. *Geographic focus:* Kodi district of West Sumba, Eastern Indonesia. *Languages:* Kodi, Indonesian, French, Swedish (also read Spanish, German, Dutch, and Italian)

Visual productions: "Feast in Dream Village," 35 min. 16mm (also on video cassette), with study guide, available from USC Center for Visual Anthropology. "Obligations to the Ancestors," "A Brideprice Negotiation," and "Dancing to Dedicate the Gong Stand," ethnographic video cassettes available from Human Studies Film Archive, Smithsonian Institution.

Howe, James

Anthropology/Archaeology Program, Room 20D-103, MIT, Cambridge, MA 02139. *Phone:* (617) 253-6954; department (617) 253-3065. *Profession:* Anthropologist, professor. *Interests:* Ethnographic still photography, visual symbolism, dealing with ethnographic film. *Geographic focus:* Central America.

Human Studies Film Archives

NHB E 307, Smithsonian Institution, Washington, DC 20560. *Phone:* (202) 357-3349. Anthropological film archives. Staff includes Director, Assistant

Director, Film Archivist for Preservation, Film Archivist for Information Management, Archives Technician. *Geographic focus:* International.

Husmann, Rolf

Greifswalder Weg 2, D-3400 Göttingen, West Germany. Office: Institut für Völkerkunde, Theaterplatz 15 D-3400, Göttingen, West Germany. *Phone:* 0551/39-7892. *Profession:* Anthropologist. *Affiliation:* Institut für Völkerkunde, University of Göttingen, Theaterplatz 15, 3400 Göttingen, West Germany. *Interests:* Ethnographic filmmaking, teaching with ethnographic film. *Training:* Ph.D. Göttingen University. *Geographic focus:* Africa. *Languages:* English, German (fluently); French, Spanish, Arabic (low to medium level). *Additional expertise:* Teaching filmmaking courses on ethnographic film since 1979. *Other information:* Organizer of three international symposia on visual anthropology in Göttingen (1983, 1985, 1987).

Hymes, Dell

Department of Anthropology, University of Virginia, Charlottesville, VA 22903-2022. Home: 205 Montvue Drive, Charlottesville, VA 22901-2022. *Phone:* (804) 979-5381; department (804) 924-7044. *Profession:* Anthropology, Linguistics, Folklore. *Interests:* Linguistic anthropology; ethnography of communication, ethnopoetics, visual transformations of oral traditions. *Training:* M.A., Ph.D. in Linguistics, Indiana University 1953, 1955, with minors in Anthropology and Folklore. *Work in progress:* Editions and analyses of Amerindian oral traditions in new formats and typographies, the latter in collaboration with the typographer Charles Bigelow. *Geographic focus:* North American Indian. *Languages:* French, a little German and Spanish, some acquaintance with a number of American Indian languages and New Testament Greek.

Iqbal, Syed Anwar

Department of Anthropology, Quaid-i-Azam University, Islamabad, Pakistan. Home: House 341 G-8/2, Islamabad, Pakistan. *Phone:* office 829913. *Profession:* Fieldwork supervisor and consultant anthropologist. *Interests:* Ethnographic filmmaking (especially video films) to explain Pakistani culture and society through photographs, collection of cultural artifacts, folk culture, ethnomusicology. *Training:* M.Sc. Anthropology, Quaid-i-Azam University, Islamabad, Pakistan, 1980; six years teaching and research experience. *Work in progress:* Video film: "The Marriage," ethnographic film which covers all traditional marriage ceremonies of a family living in an urban center. Video film and photographs on the life of Kalah people of Kafiristan, northern area of Pakistan. *Geographic focus:* Punjab and Sind Provinces of Pakistan. *Languages:* English (r,w,s); Urdu, Punjabi (fluently).

Visual productions: Video film: "The Shrine of Bari Imam," 45 min, ethnographic details of Urs annual festival.

Irvine, Dominique
221 Marmona Drive, Menlo Park, CA 94025. *Phone:* (415) 326-4524. *Profession:* Anthropologist. *Affiliation:* Fellow, Cultural Survival (Cambridge, MA). *Interests:* Teaching with ethnographic film. Ethnographic filmmaking. *Training:* M.A. and Ph.D. Anthropology, Stanford University, 1980 and 1987. M.F.S. Forestry and Environmental Studies, Yale, 1978. B.A. Anthropology, University of Pennsylvania, 1973. *Geographic focus:* Amazon. *Languages:* Spanish (excellent), French (good), Quichua (good to excellent).

Visual productions: "Runa: Guardians of the Forest," 1989 (with Ellen Speiser), in Quichua with subtitles in Spanish or English, 27:35 min. color, 16mm and video formats.

Jablonko, Allison
La Cima, 06069 Tuoro Sul Trasimeno, Perugia, Italy. *Phone:* 39-75-826-187; sister's phone in U.S. (206) 885–9433. *Profession:* Ethnographic filmmaker. *Interests:* Ethnographic filmmaking, intercultural communication using visual media, body movement studies and dance ethnology. *Training:* Ph.D. Anthropology, Columbia University, 1968. Certified movement analyst from Laban Institute for Movement Studies, NYC, 1967. *Work in progress:* "Fasnacht: A Singsing in Switzerland," a videotape exchange destined for a Papua New Guinea audience. "Alexander Technique: Tuning into the Body," a videotape. *Geographic focus:* Papua New Guinea, Central Europe. *Languages:* French, German, Italian (r,w,s).

Visual productions: "Kerepe's House," 1966, and "Maring in Motion," 1968, distributed in both film and video formats by Pennsylvania State University Audio-Visual Services. "To Find the Baruya Story," 1982, and "Her Name Came on Arrows," 1982, distributed in both film and video formats by Documentary Educational Resources. Maring: Documents of a New Guinea People, 1980, a series of eight 25 minute films: "1. Introduction," "2. Life with the Forest," "3. Individuality and Social Relationships," "4. Ritual Cycles," "5. Crops and Food Preparation," "6. Children," "7. Space and Time," "8. External Influences" (Scholastic and Educational Department of Channel 3 of RAITV, Italian National Television).

Jablonko, Marek
La Cima, 06069 Tuoro Sul Trasimeno, Perugia, Italy. *Phone:* 39-75-826-187. sister-in-law's phone in U.S. (206) 885-9433. *Interests:* Ethnographic filmmaking. *Training:* Summer at the Documentary Film Studio, Warsaw, Poland, 1966. Participated in the Festival Del Popoli, Florence, Italy, 1965-1968. Participated in the International Seminars for the Evaluation of Ethnographic Films, Florence, Italy, 1966-1968. Flaherty Seminar, 1967. Summer at the National Film School, Beaconsfield, Bucks, Great Britain, 1972. M.B.A. New York University, 1962. B.S. MIT, 1954. *Work in*

progress: "Maring research film II "—to be archived in Human Studies Film Archive, Smithsonian Institution, Washington, DC. *Geographic focus:* New Guinea. *Languages:* English, Italian, Polish, and Russian (excellent level of reading, writing and speaking of all four).

Visual productions: Research films: "Maring Research Film I, 1963-64," NIMH Archives (C. Gajdusek). "Polish Peasants at Work," summer 1966, research footage. "Mauritius—August 1968: An Exercise in Choreometrics." Films: "Kerepe's House: A House Building in New Guinea," distributed by Pennsylvania State University Audio-Visual Services. "Undala," special mention Festival dei Popoli 1968, Golden Cine Eagle 1966. "To Find the Baruya Story," distributed by DER, Watertown, MA. "Her Name Came on Arrows," distributed by DER. Maring: Documents of a New Guinea People, a series of eight 25 minute films made for Scholastic and Educational Department of Channel 3 of RAITV, Italian National Television (see listing for Allison Jablonko, above).

Jacknis, Ira
29 Red Ground Road, Roslyn Heights, NY 11577. Office: African, Oceanic, and New World Art, The Brooklyn Museum, 200 Eastern Parkway, Brooklyn, NY 11238. *Phone:* (516) 621-5152; office: (718) 638-5000 ext 280. *Profession:* Anthropologist. *Interests:* Museums, especially exhibition; history of visual anthropology; art and aesthetics. *Training:* Ph.D. Anthropology, University of Chicago, 1989. M.A. Anthropology, University of Chicago, 1976. *Work in progress:* George Hunt as a native photographer. Exhibition (co-curator with Diana Fane, Brooklyn Museum) of the North American Indian collections of Stewart Culin, to open at the Brooklyn Museum in 1990; accompanying catalogue "Objects of Myth and Memory: American Indian Art at the Brooklyn Museum" (with Diana Fane). *Geographic focus:* North American Indians, especially Northwest Coast. *Languages:* French (reading).

James, William R.
1000 Princeton, Salt Lake City, UT 84105. Office: Department of Economics, University of Utah, Salt Lake City, UT 84112. *Phone:* (801) 485-4123. *Profession:* Anthropologist. *Interests:* Historical analysis of ethnographic photographs and prints reproduced on postcards. Impact of tourism on ethnographic photography. Application of critical theory to photographic analysis. *Training:* Ph.D. Anthropology, University of Wisconsin, Madison. *Geographic focus:* American Indians, Mexico. *Languages:* French (reading), Spanish (r,w,s).

Jell-Bahlsen, Sabine
451 Broome Street, #PHW, New York, NY 10013. Summer: Aisching 1, 8211 Gstadt, West Germany. *Phone:* (212) 226-7854; office (212) 777-7275; in Germany 49-8054-302. *Profession:* Anthropologist, filmmaker, journalist.

Affiliation: Ogbuide, Ltd. Filmproductions, Ringier/Swiss Illustrated. *Interests:* The study, production, and use of ethnographic film, photography, and sound recordings, ambient sound, different and complementary channels of communication. The analysis of visual symbolic forms. Study of art and performance from a social and cultural viewpoint. "General audiences" and media, "minority" audiences, Third World media/TV. *Training:* Ph.D. Anthropology, The New School for Social Research, NY, 1980. M.A. Ethnology, Free University, Berlin, West Germany, 1974. The New School Film Department, 1982-85. Fieldwork: 1 year, Southeastern Nigeria (Igbo), 1978-79, and shorter return trips. *Work in progress:* "Mami Wata—An African Art of Making Sense," proposal for a 1 hour documentary film (16mm color, sound), developed in cooperation with the Nigeria TV Authority, Lagos, Nigeria. "On the Making of Eze Nwata—The Small King." *Geographic focus:* Africa, West Africa. *Languages:* German (fluent), French (read, write, speak; good–fair), Igbo (speak some), Spanish (read and speak fair).

Visual productions: "Divine Earth—Divine Water," 1981, 82 min. 16mm color and sound. "Eze Nwata—The Small King," 1982, 27 min. 16mm color and sound. "Caro-Caro," 1983, 3 min. slides and sound, available on video.

Johnson, David M.
4137 Pleasant Garden Road, Greensboro, NC 27406. Office: Department of Sociology and Social Work, North Carolina A & T State University, Greensboro, NC 27411. *Phone:* (919) 274-7032; office (919) 379-7894. *Profession:* Anthropology. *Interests:* Interested in human nonverbal behavior in general, use of still photography in research/teaching, analysis of visual forms. *Training:* Ph.D. Anthropology, minor: Mathematical Methodology, University of North Carolina, Chapel Hill, 1972. *Geographic focus:* Mostly North America. *Languages:* Some knowledge of Spanish and German. *Technical expertise:* Statistical techniques (teach statistics at college level), experience with micro computers, have own still photography business, some experience with super-8 filmmaking, videotape. *Other information:* Paper and slide show entitled "Representations of 'Nature': American Values and the Portrayal of Animals by Walt Disney Studios," presented to symposium "Making Exhibitions of Ourselves: The Limits of Objectivity in Representations of Other Cultures," The British Museum, London, England, February, 1986.

Johnson, Thomas Wayne
Department of Anthropology, California State University, Chico, CA 95929. *Phone:* (916) 895-6192. *Profession:* Professor. *Interests:* Teaching with ethnographic film, air photo interpretation, folk manipulation of the Japanese writing system. *Geographic focus:* Japan, Korea, the American West (Anglo culture). *Languages:* Japanese (good speaking, fair reading).

Johnson-Dean, Lynn
Box 3699, New Mexico State University, Las Cruces, NM 88003. *Phone:* (505) 646-2306. *Profession:* Television producer/director (sponsored research administrator). *Interests:* Utilizing and instructing others in the use and operation of portable video systems for specific purposes including the production of ethnographic and archaeological programs, video archiving, the promotion and study of cultural feedback and horizontal communication, and the transfer of technical information. *Training:* M.A. International Communication (Interdisciplinary), New Mexico State University, 1986. B.A. Radio, Television and Motion Pictures, University of North Carolina, Chapel Hill, 1970. *Work in progress:* Series of six 25 min. videotape programs on rural subsistence life in Honduras, prepared from material taken from an ethnographic examination of over 500 houses in northern Honduras, and to be used in teaching cultural anthropology and archaeology courses: types and forms of houses, the houselot (area around the house) and its features, the garden, women's activities, clay stoves, and other aspects of life in rural Honduras. *Geographic focus:* Central America and the world. *Languages:* Spanish (fluent: FSI 3—r,w,s), Arabic (beginning). *Additional expertise:* 13 years professional experience in television production. Three years in commercial broadcasting in Washington, DC, six years in developing countries. *Other information:* Advised faculty at three universities (England, Saudi Arabia, and U.S.) in the operation and utilization of video systems and the design of a cable television system and TV studio and facilities. Conducted workshops in developing countries on the use and operation of portable video systems.

Visual productions: "Utilización de Sistemas de Video Portatil en El Salvador," 1978, VHS. "Uses of Video at Loughborough University," 1979, 20 min. color Umatic, PAL. "Pollen, C-14, and Flotation Samples," 1984, series of five minute programs on sampling techniques, color VHS, NTSC. "Clay Stoves in Northern Honduras," 1987, 24:16 min. color VHS, NTSC.

Jones, Michael Owen
Folklore and Mythology, 1037 GSM-Library Wing, University of California, Los Angeles, CA 90024. *Phone:* (213) 825-4242. *Profession:* Professor of History and Folklore, and Director of Folklore and Mythology Center. *Interests:* Using still photography, film, and videotape in research of folk art and of organizational behavior including rituals, ceremonies, storytelling, and oral history. Teaching film and photography for folkloristic research. Teaching ethnographic film. *Training:* Degrees in Art, History, Folklore, and American Studies. *Work in progress:* Videotapes of organizational activities to edit into organizational histories. *Geographic focus:* United States. *Languages:* French and German (fair reading level). *Additional expertise:* Years of fieldwork experience plus teaching courses on research methods. *Other information:* Consultant to organizations regarding rewards, communication, history, and organizational development.

Kaplan, Flora S.
New York University, Graduate School of Arts & Sciences, Museum Studies Program, 19 University Place, Suite 308, New York, NY 10003. *Phone:* (212) 998-8080. *Profession:* Director, Museum Studies Program; Associate Professor of Museum Studies and Anthropology. *Interests:* Study of art and artifacts (Africa, Latin America); photography, interpretation of material culture, exhibitions, museology. *Training:* Ph.D. Anthropology, The Graduate Center, City University of New York, 1976. M.A. Anthropology/Archaeology, Columbia University. B.A. Hunter College. *Work in progress:* "In Splendor and Seclusion: Royal Women at the Court of Benin, Nigeria," book manuscript and traveling exhibition (currently being organized). "Making Exhibitions of Ourselves: Benin Art in Two Cultures." "Cognition and Style in Material Culture: An Urban Pottery Tradition in Puebla, Mexico" (book ms.). Also completing book length analysis of graffiti as a human phenomenon. *Geographic focus:* Nigeria, Mexico. *Languages:* Spanish, Portuguese, French. *Technical expertise:* Museum exhibitions, ethnographic film, photography.

Visual productions: "Photographic Murals," 1978 (photographer), Puebla State Museum. "Art of the Royal Court of Benin," 1981 (exhibition organizer, curator), New York University: The Grey Art Gallery. "Art of the Royal Court of Benin," 1985, exhibition, Benin City, Nigeria: Benin National Museum. Photographs selected from competitions: "Kiln Firing, Puebla, Mexico," 1979, American Anthropologist Appointment Calendar, Karl G. Heider, ed.; "Mother and Daughter Potters, Chiapas, Mexico," UNICEF 1986 Engagement Calendar, both editions; "Bronze Casting, Benin City, Nigeria," to appear in UNICEF 1991 Engagement Calendar.

Kealiinohomoku, Joann W.
Cross-Cultural Dance Resources, Inc., 518 South Agassiz Street, Flagstaff, AZ 86001. Department of Anthropology, CU Box 15200, Northern Arizona University, Flagstaff, AZ 86011. *Phone:* Home (602) 774-8108; department (602) 723-3180. *Profession:* Anthropologist, dance ethnologist. *Interests:* Primarily analyses and teaching; the performance arts—especially dance; cross-cultural culture change; expressive culture; empirical studies—fieldwork, interviewing; using visual means of description and analysis to study and interpret human (or humanly relevant) perceptions, behavior, interaction, or communication in context; the analysis of visual symbolic forms; visual theories; relationships among different channels and modes of communication; the visible expression of emotion; proxemic and other analyses of space and territory; kinesic and other systematic study of body motion communication, gesture, or dance; the structuring of reality; the study of art; performance from social, cultural, historical, folkloristic, semiotic, or aesthetic points of view; forms of social organization involved in planning, producing, and using visual signs and systems of signs; visual contexts of speech or verbal art; film/video/photo archiving; anthropological teaching with visual media; visual analyses

and methods in the professional practice of anthropology; using media in cultural feedback; the study, production, and use of ethnographic, archaeological, or other anthropological film, photography, or video. *Training:* Ph.D. Anthropology (cultural), minor in Folklore, focus on ethnomusicology and dance, Indiana University. M.A. Anthropology (cultural), focus on dance, and B.S.S. Speech and Theater, Northwestern University. *Work in progress:* Life history and analysis of hula dancer from last century. A study of various fixed-frame images of dancers. *Geographic focus:* Whole world, with special concentration on Pacific, American Southwest, and Black America. *Languages:* English is native, read Spanish, Hawaiian, and French.

Keefe, Susan E.
Department of Anthropology, Appalachian State University, Boone, NC 28608. Box 949, Blowing Rock, NC 28605. *Phone:* (704) 262-2295; 295-3978. *Profession:* Professor of Anthropology. *Interests:* Teach Anthropology Through Film. *Geographic focus:* U.S., Mexican Americans, Appalachia.

Kellers, James McW.
14 Beekman Road, Summit, NJ 07901. *Phone:* (201) 273-1910. *Profession:* Archaeologist (holistic) SOPA, photography (PCA), light microscopy, scientific illustrator. *Affiliation:* Terra Cognita, Inc., holistic studies. *Interests:* Filmmaking, teaching with ethnographic film, film and archaeology, still photography, motion picture, video. *Training:* Ph.D. New York University. M.A. University of Pennsylvania. B.A. Dartmouth College. Photo Lab, Commanders School—USAAF. *Geographic focus:* Anywhere asked to go. *Languages:* Spanish (now rusty), read French, and to a lesser degree Italian, German. I pick up field languages fairly rapidly (Arabic, Turkish, Russian, Greek) but as they are not used continually, they fall. *Technical expertise:* EDP utilization, SOPA. *Other information:* 1948-1956: advised graduate students at Yale going into field on photo matters and served as continuing advisor by mail and on return.

Kendall, David M.
1240 Summit, Lawrence, KS 66044. Office: KTWU/Channel 11, 301 N. Wanamaker Road, Topeka, KS 66604. *Phone:* (913) 749-0523; office (913) 272-8182. *Profession:* Public TV Producer. *Affiliation:* Summit Street Productions. *Interests:* Ethnographic filmmaking; teaching with ethnographic film; study of culture change, social and environmental issues. *Training:* M.A. Media Anthropology, University of Kansas, 1983. *Geographic focus:* American Midwest, Native Americans. *Languages:* Spanish (basic ability to read, write, and speak). *Technical expertise:* In-studio and remote directing, video photography, still photography, ENG photography. *Other information:* Teaching experience: Anthropology Through Films, undergraduate course at the University of Kansas. Grant-writing experience: funding secured from the

Kansas Committee for the Humanities, as well as Southwest Alternate Media Project. Member: Association of Independent Video and Film Makers and the American Film Institute. One year experience (1986-7) as news photographer for "The Lawrence Report," the evening news program in Lawrence, Kansas.

Visual productions: Documentaries (director, editor): "Another Wind Is Moving," 60 min., on past and present circumstances of Indian boarding schools in U.S.; "Tomorrow's Harvest" (also producer, writer), 60 min., on the role of the family farm in American society; "Return To Sovereignty," 45 min., on self-determination efforts of the Kansas Kickapoo; "The Flute-Maker," 20 min., about how a Kickapoo craftsman fashions a flute from sumac; "The Bustle-Maker" (also videographer), 20 min., on the creation of an Indian dance bustle; "The Herbalist," 20 min., on medicinal uses of wild plants as practiced by a Potawatomi; "Dr. Brinkley and the Sunshine Station," (also producer, writer), 60 min., on the life of an accused medical charlatan and the influence he commanded with his radio stations during the 1930's, produced in association with KTWU-TV, Topeka, KS, grant from the Southwest Alternate Media Project; and "Living With Alzheimer's," 30 min., incorporating documentary footage with a panel discussion. "Winfield Picker's Paradise," 1986, 90 min. documentary on the bluegrass festival associated with the national flat-pick guitar championship in Winfield, Kansas. "The Beijing Philharmonic in America," 60 min. documentary on the first major tour of the Chinese National Symphony. "Sunflower Journeys," 13-part series on people, places, and events in Kansas.

Kirkpatrick, Joanna
Bennington College, Division of Social Sciences, Bennington, VT 05201. *Phone:* home (802) 442-2344; office (802) 442-5401 ext 217. *Profession:* Cultural/social anthropologist. *Interests:* Ethnology and semiotics of folk and popular arts in South Asia. Uses of film and photographic documentation in field research and research discourse. *Training:* Ph.D. University of California at Berkeley, Anthropology. Non-terminal M.A. Yale University, Anthropology/Sociology. B.A. Stanford University, Anthropology. *Work in progress:* Book on the painted rickshas of Bangladesh. *Geographic focus:* South Asia, especially W. Bengal, Bangladesh, Punjab. *Languages:* Read French, Spanish, Hindi, Bengali. Some fluency in spoken Bengali. *Technical expertise:* Photography in the field. *Other information:* Have spent a lot of time in South Asia including Pakistan, India, Bangladesh, Nepal, Burma. Fieldwork in South Asia conducted over a period of 20 years, many trips, some longer than others (two of the trips: one year each).

Kolodny, Rochelle
5381 Jeanne Mance, Montréal, Québec, H2V 4K5 Canada. Office: Champlain Regional College, 900 Riverside Drive, St. Lambert, Québec, J4P 3P2 Canada. *Phone:* (514) 279-1205; office (514) 672-7360 ext 288. *Profession:*

College instructor, anthropologist. *Interests:* Analysis of social documentary photography (cultural aesthetic), analysis of art in cultural systems, use of visual media by anthropologists, ethical issues in production and use of visual media, philosophy of art. *Training:* M.A. Anthropology, McGill University, 1978. B.A. Anthropology, Hofstra University, 1971. *Work in progress:* "Pictures from Everyday Life: Mining the Archives" (with others). *Languages:* English (mother tongue), French (reading-good, writing and speaking-poor). *Other information:* Participant in "The Critical Eye" seminar, summer 1987, The Banff Centre, School of Fine Arts (Visual Arts), Banff, Alberta. Invited panelist for the international conference on art and photography, "Talking Pictures," in Toronto, Oct. 1987.

Koolage, William

452 University College, University of Manitoba, Winnipeg, Manitoba R3T 2N2, Canada. *Phone:* (204) 474-9120. *Profession:* Anthropology. *Interests:* Anthropological research, teaching, methodology and practice. Interaction and communication in context, relationships among different channels and modes of communication, proxemic and other analyses of space and territory, visual contexts of speech, cultural feedback, production and use of ethnographic video. *Work in progress:* Five productions on Native survival in southern (Canadian) health systems. *Geographic focus:* Northern and southern Canada.

   Visual productions: "Cultural Factors in Therapeutic Interaction," 1981 (with J. Kaufert, W. Koolage, and J. Conner), 20 min.

Koons, Adam

6524 First Street NW, Washington, DC 20012. *Phone:* (202) 722-4842. *Profession:* Advertising photographer, applied anthropologist (rural development). *Interests:* Use of photographs to teach technical practices (in agriculture). Analysis of visual demonstration of technical innovations through photos of change agents. Examining communication process between change agent and client in development, using photos to look at cases of interaction: proxemics and kinesics provide information about social status and communication style. Use of historic photographs for analysis of material culture and comparison to other cultures. *Training:* Photojournalist for four newspapers. Director of Photography, Logan Museum of Anthropology and Archaeology. Director of Photograpy, Cort Theatre, Beloit, WI. *Focus:* North America, West Africa. *Languages:* French (reading, writing, capable speaking, not fluent). *Technical expertise:* Large format (5X7 and 8X10) photography.

Kreamer, Chris Mullen

Department of Anthropology, National Museum of Natural History, Smithsonian Institution, Washington, DC 20560. Home: 1016 F Street NE, Washington, DC 20002. *Phone:* (202) 357-4733; home (202) 543-8161. *Profession:* Art historian, ethnographer. *Interests:* Visual arts, shrines, ritual, performance, aesthetics, proxemics, ethnographic photography, museum exhibits. *Training:* Ph.D. African Art History, Indiana University. *Work in progress:* Book on women's funerals in Africa; article on initiation. *Geographic focus:* West Africa, Togo. *Languages:* French (r,w,s), Moba (speak), Twi (some r,w,s), German (read). *Other information:* Teach pottery, metalwork, and art history field seminars in West Africa, Parsons School of Design.

   Visual productions: "Wild Spirits, Strong Medicine: African Art in the Wilderness," 1989 exhibition (traveling–1991), Center for African Art (NYC).

Krouse, Susan Applegate

3535 N. Humboldt Boulevard, Milwaukee, WI 53212. Office: Department of Anthropology, University of Wisconsin, Milwaukee, Box 413, Milwaukee, WI 53201. *Phone:* (414) 332-6358; office (414) 963-4019; department 963-4174. *Profession:* Anthropologist. Formerly Curator, New Hanover County Museum, Wilmington, NC, 1981-1986. *Interests:* Photographs/films as ethnohistorical documentation, esp. in Indian–White relations. *Training:* Ph.D. student, University of Wisconsin, Milwaukee; A.B., M.A. Indiana University. *Geographic focus:* North America/American Indians. *Languages:* French (read).

Kugelmass, Jack

YIVO Institute, 1048 5th Avenue, New York, NY 10028. *Phone:* (212) 535-6700. *Profession:* Anthropologist. *Interests:* Still photography, film. *Training:* Ph.D. Anthropology, New School. *Work in progress:* Photographs of contemporary Jewish life. *Geographic focus:* Jews, New York. *Languages:* Yiddish, French, German.

   Visual productions: "The Ghetto Ten," 1985 (author/photographer), 30 min. slide-tape, NBC. "The Miracle of Intervale Avenue," 1983, 12 min. slide-tape, The Jewish Museum. "The Miracle of Intervale Avenue," 1983, 66 min. documentary, BBC. "The Miracle of Intervale Avenue," 1983, photographic exhibition, The Jewish Museum.

Laban/Bartenieff Institute of Movement Studies, Inc.

31 West 27th Street, New York, NY 10001. *Phone:* (212) 689-0740. *Interests:* The Institute (also known as LIMS) is involved in education and research in the field of human movement studies. It is a center for the development and study of the principles of movement analysis formulated by R. Laban and further developed by his student and colleague, I. Bartenieff. LIMS offers a professional certificate program in Laban movement studies and four seasonal workshops in applications of movement analysis in such areas as dance, theater, non-verbal communication, anthropology, and the behavioral sciences. The Institute has been involved in research in applications of movement analysis on such topics as the analysis of cultural movement style, dance therapy, and non-verbal communication. LIMS also houses a library and media center in movement studies. *Other information:* Supports an alumni

organization of professional Laban movement analysts—American Association of Laban Movement Analysis (AALMA), and publishes a newsletter.

Lacy, Christabel

North Carolina School of the Arts, Winston-Salem, NC, 27101. *Phone:* (919) 770-3242; home (919) 788-8547. *Profession:* Anthropologist, college teacher. *Interests:* Relationships between linguistic and visual communication systems. Behavior and artifact as symbolic communication. Visual expression of fantasy. Teaching visual artifacts as cultural symbols. Kinetic art in sports. *Training:* Ph.D. Anthropology, minor emphasis Art History, University of Colorado, Boulder. M.A., B.A. Anthropology, minor Art History, University of Nebraska, Lincoln. *Work in progress:* Photo essay on competitive animal shows. *Geographic focus:* Classical Greece and Rome, contemporary North America. *Languages:* Reading ability in French, Latin, Greek (classic, modern), Spanish, German, writing ability in Greek. *Technical expertise:* 35mm photography.

Visual productions: "The Rural Schools of Cape Girardeau, Missouri," 1985, historical and contemporary photo exhibition, booklet, and slide/tape: a cultural study of the history of rural schools and communities in Cape Girardeau county, funded by Missouri State Endowment for the Humanities.

Lane, Bruce E. (Pacho)

309 Buckeye Trail, Austin, TX 78747. *Phone:* (512) 327-1357. *Profession:* Film Producer, director, camera, etc. *Interests:* Ethnographic film production and distribution, teaching film, completed films. *Training:* Doctoral studies, Film and Folklore, 1978–80, B.A. Political Science, 1963, University of Texas. M.A. Economics, 1966, University of Michigan. *Geographic focus:* Mexican Indian and Hispanic cultures. *Languages:* Fluent: Spanish, German, Portuguese. Semi-fluent: French, Russian, and Greek. *Technical expertise:* Camera, sound, editing, script writing, film research, all phases of video.

Visual productions: 16mm films: "The Tree of Life," 1976, 29 min. Mexican Indian ritual (NEA, CPB); "The Tree of Knowledge," 1982, 25 min., ethnic identity and ritual in a Mexican Indian community (NEA); "Stoney Knows How," 1982, 28 min.; "Tattooing as Folk Art," (NEA); "Battle of the Guitars," 1985, 17 min.; "Black and White Texas Blues," Dallas Art Museum. "Deep Ellum," 1985, 13 min.; "The Eagle's Children," 1986, 29 min., the spread of a Mexican Indian spiritual dance tradition to Mexican-Americans (NEA, TCH); "Texas Style," 1987, 29 min., Texas rural white music and culture (NEA); "The New Mexico Chile Film," 1987, 29 min. and 90 min., New Mexico society and culture through its chile cuisine (NMAD, private and corporate funds); "The Knights of Santiago," 29 min.—the influence of Islam in the Spanish conquest of the New World (NEA); "Deep Ellum," 60 min.— David "Fathead" Newman, Louis Johnson "The Wiz," and the Dallas Black Dance Company in a ballet on Dallas blacks in the 20's (corporate funds).

Distributor: University of Texas Film Library, Box W, Austin, TX 78712; phone (512) 471-3573.

Lansing, J. Stephen
Department of Anthropology, University of Southern California, University Park, Los Angeles, CA 90089-0661. *Phone:* (213) 743-7100. *Profession:* Anthropologist, Department Chair. *Interests:* Cultural anthropology, ethnographic film, systems ecology. *Geographic focus:* Southeast Asia. *Languages:* Indonesian, Russian, Balinese (speaking, reading). French, Dutch (reading).

Visual productions: "The Three Worlds of Bali" (writer—based upon my own research; Ira Abrams producer, director), 60 min. documentary film, broadcast over public television in the Odyssey series Nov. 17, 1981, awarded CINE Golden Eagle 1982, distributed by Documentary Educational Resources. "Shadow Worlds of Bali" (researcher, writer; Ira Abrams producer, director), 60 min. documentary film. "Chiefs and Kings of Indonesia," 1983 (director), 60 min. documentary film, broadcast in The Explorers series by The Disney Channel. "The Goddess and the Computer" (producer, director, cameraman; André Singer executive producer), produced by Channel 4, England and Center for Visual Anthropology, USC; to be broadcast on NOVA in 1989.

Lass, Andrew
Department of Sociology and Anthropology, Mount Holyoke College, South Hadley, MA 01075. Home: P.O. Box 334, South Hadley, MA 01075. *Phone:* (413) 538-2184; department (413) 538-2283; home (413) 533-4721. *Profession:* Assistant Professor of Anthropology. *Interests:* Analysis of symbolic systems, anthropology of history, phenomenology, speech and writing, concretization, the place of art in the politics of nationalism, (monuments and the representation of history), the presence of the past as fact and image (relics, forgeries, landscapes). *Training:* Ph.D. Social and Cultural Anthropology, University of Massachussetts, Amherst. M.A. Ethnography and Folklore, Charles' University, Prague. *Work in progress:* "Voice of Tradition" (tentative title of book in progress) takes a phenomenological, deconstructive view of the constitution of historical consciousness in the context of Czech nationalism by looking at the place 'folk' (as concept) occupies in the medievalist discourse of modern Czech scholars and artists. Initial stages of fieldwork focusing on the past and present experience of the newly invented histories of Ludwig I and Ludwig II of Bavaria. *Geographic focus:* Central Europe (Bohemia) and Germany (Bavaria). *Languages:* Czech (fluent), Slovak (passive), Russian (reading), German (reading), English (native). *Technical expertise:* Photography.

Lee, Thomas A., Jr.
Calle Chiapa de Corzo 78, San Cristobal de las Chiapas, Mexico 29200. *Phone:* 8-14-12. *Profession:* Archaeologist. *Interests:* Use of film for research,

teaching, and a medium for synthesizing results of archaeological research. Ethnographic filmmaking of social events, to record fast-disappearing human behavior, especially those that aid archaeological interpretation. Recording of complex archaeological excavation. Study of the origin and development of Mesoamerican writing systems. *Training:* M.A. Anthropology, 1966. *Work in progress:* "Nino Florero," color 16mm film of Chiapa de Corzo fiesta. Zoque religious ceremonialism. Tuxtla Gutierrez Copaya—class structure and hierarchical relations between two rank ordered communities. *Geographic focus:* Mesoamerica. *Languages:* Spanish (r,s—excellent, writing—good).

Visual productions: "Civilization in Chiapas" (co-producer), 28 min., color 16mm, English/Spanish versions, New World Archaeological Foundation, Brigham Young University.

Leeds, Anthony

62 River Place, Dedham, MA 02026. Department of Anthropology, Boston University, Boston, MA 02215. *Phone:* (617) 353-2195. *Profession:* Professor of Anthropology; photography, poetry, political activism. *Interests:* Teaching with ethnographic film, ethnographic filmmaking. *Training:* Ph.D. in Anthropology, technical photographic training from one of my graduate students and later at such places as the Cambridge Adult Learning Center, and others in Boston area. *Work in progress:* "Minha Terra, Portugal: Songs of Lamentation and Celebration" (the growth of an understanding and a commitment). *Geographic focus:* Latin America, U.S. (esp. Texas, Vermont), Europe (esp. Portugal, also Spain, England). *Languages:* Portuguese (r,w,s), Spanish (r,w,s), German (r,w,s), some French and Russian. *Additional expertise:* Considerable musical talent—sang in baroque chorus for 14 years, improvise complex folk- and Bach-based stuff, know much about technical aspects of music theory, a good deal of technical linguistics and of language use (e.g. rhetoric). Considerable farming technology.

Visual productions: Slide shows: "Portugal Perceived," accompanied by music (from records) and poems I wrote about my fieldwork in Minha Terra; Peruvian ecology; Brazilian urban settings; Vermont rural settings; the Yaruro; "Cycles I and II," dealing with visual logic (no words at all); and "Spaces" dealing with visual logic and 'psychological realities.'

Leininger, Madeleine

333 Covington 2D, Detroit, MI 48203. Wayne State University College of Nursing, 5557 Cass Street, Detroit, MI 48202. *Phone:* (313) 868-7158. *Profession:* Nursing and anthropology. *Interests:* Teaching, researching, filmmaking, research film and photography. Transcultural health care, culture of health professions, qualitative indicators of behavior, nursing care phenomena as comfort, suffering, support, touching, etc. *Training:* Ph.D. University of Washington. *Geographic focus:* Pacific Islands (Melanesia), U.S.A., Europe, South America. *Languages:* Read three languages but can only speak

fluent English. *Other information:* I have been using films and filming since 1960 when first studied people in New Guinea. I have studied ten cultures and have considerable filmic data (slides, movies, prints, etc.).

Lerch, Oliver

Sociology/Anthropology, Dowling College, Oakdale, NY 11769. Home: 130 Bayport Avenue, Bayport, NY 11705. *Phone:* (516) 589-6100; home (516) 472-1422. *Profession:* Anthropologist. *Interests:* Teaching with ethnographic film, ethnographic still photography. *Training:* Ph.D. Anthropology, Syracuse University, 1974. *Geographic focus:* France, especially Paris and Brittany; Long Island, NY. *Languages:* French (read easily with dictionary, write poorly, speak at advanced conversational level), German (read slowly, write stilted but grammatical sentences, simple conversation no problem).

Visual productions: Photo essay on the Carnival nomads of Brittany.

Lerner, Richard N.

Environmental Branch, U.S. Army Corps of Engineers, 211 Main Street, San Francisco, CA 94105. Home: 2335 Stuart Street, Berkeley, CA 94705. *Phone:* (415) 974-0440; home (415) 841-5362. *Profession:* Anthropologist. *Interests:* Environmental planning, social impact assessment, interpretive planning. *Training:* Ph.D. Anthropology, University of California, Berkeley, 1975. *Geographic focus:* California, India.

Visual productions: 16mm films (writer, producer, director): "The Environment and the Engineers at Lake Sonoma," 38 min.; and "Warm Springs, Building More Than A Dam," 27 min.

Lewis, E. Douglas

19 Mackie Road, Roleystone, Western Australia 6111 Australia. *Phone:* (09) 397-6663. *Profession:* Social anthropology. *Affiliation:* Australian National University. *Interests:* Ethnographic film, ethnology of Austronesia. *Training:* Ph.D. Anthropology, Australian National University. *Work in progress:* Production of films and documentary support on the rural life of the 'Ata Tana Ai of Eastern Flores, Indonesia. *Geographic focus:* Austronesia, Indonesia. *Languages:* Indonesian/Malay (fluent), Sara Sikka—Sikkanese language of Flores (fluent), Dutch, German, French, Portuguese (reading).

Linklater, Liza

475 Laurier Avenue West, Apt. 1007, Ottawa, Ontario KIR7X1 Canada. *Phone:* (613) 563-0768. *Profession:* Journalist, photographer. *Interests:* Documentary photography, photography in anthropology. *Training:* M.A. Social Anthropology and Photography, B.A. Social Anthropology, York University, Toronto. B.J. Journalism, Carleton University, Ottawa. *Geographic focus:* Asia, S.E. Asia (2 years in Bangkok, Thailand 1983-85). *Technical expertise:* Photography, film, video, magazine editing and production.

Visual productions: "Cultures in Contact," 1979 (coordinated audio-visual production, completed layout for photo-essay publication). "Where Do We Go From Here?," 1980 (co-producer), audio-visual presentation on Indo-Chinese refugee settlement issues in Toronto. Research for visuals used on "Counterparts," November 30, 1980, Multicultural TV, Channel 47, Toronto. Photo essay on Thai transvestites in Bangkok and Pattaya, Thailand 1984–85, published in Thailand and Australia, and exhibited in Toronto, Canada.

Lobo, Susan
333 Colusa Avenue, Kensington, CA 94707. *Phone:* (415) 527-5687. *Profession:* Anthropologist. *Affiliations:* Intertribal Friendship House, Community History Project (research coordinator since founding in 1978); Center for Latin American Studies, UC Berkeley (post-doctoral scholar). *Interests:* Still photography, video, migration, kinship, human rights and indigenous concerns, cultural survival. *Training:* M.A. and Ph.D. University of Arizona, Tucson, 1977. *Work in progress:* Community History Project: photographic community resource archives with ongoing collection and circulation of photographs of urban Indian community in San Francisco Bay area—Intertribal Friendship House, American Indian Center, Oakland, CA. "Generation to Generation," video, Susanville Rancheria, CA, funded by the California Arts Council, focusing on elders teaching youths traditional skills. *Geographic focus:* Indigenous people of North, Central, and South America. *Languages:* Spanish (good); Portuguese (fair). *Other information:* Co-founder and editor (until 1988) South and Central American Indian Information Center Newsletter. Founding member (spring 1985) of Bay Area Visual Anthropology Group (contact me for more information.)
Visual productions: "Quechan Singers," 1987, video, Intertribal Friendship House Community History Project.

Lockwood, William G.
Department of Anthropology, 1054 LSA, University of Michigan, Ann Arbor, MI 48109. Home: 1471 Kensington, Ann Arbor, MI 48104. *Phone:* (313) 764-7153; department (313) 764-7275; home (313) 662-3460. *Profession:* Professor of Anthropology. *Affiliations:* AAA, AES, past member of SVA. *Interests:* Teaching with ethnographic film, teaching about ethnographic film (Anthropology 457: The Film and Other Visual Media in Anthropology). *Training:* Ph.D. Anthropology, University of California at Berkeley, 1970. *Work in progress:* I am currently accumulating visual materials on Gypsies toward a future project I have in mind. *Geographic focus:* Eastern Europe primarily. Also Western Europe and contemporary USA. Gypsies (worldwide). *Languages:* Serbo-Croatian (fair), Spanish (fair reading and speaking, poor writing), French (poor reading). *Technical expertise:* Still photography: have shown in exhibits and have been published in a variety of publications (in addition to photos accompanying my own books and articles). *Other informa-*

tion: I am a charter member and very active in "Regards sur les Sociétés Européennes," a group of mostly European filmmakers and anthropologists interested in ethnographic and documentary film on European society and culture. We hold an annual meeting in Europe.

Lomax, Alan

Association for Cultural Equity, Inc., 820 West End Avenue, New York, NY 10025. *Phone:* (212) 666-5215. *Profession:* Anthropologist of expressive style. *Affiliation:* also Anthropology Department, Columbia University. *Interests:* Cantometrics, Choreometrics, Parlemetrics, Phonotactics. Cross-cultural studies of performance. Systematic analysis of the media for data on cultural traditions. Cultural activism, cultural equity. Writing, photography. *Training:* Education in anthropology and scientific methodology, 25 years of field recording and filming, and 50 years of media presentation of folk traditions in popular books, radio programs, recordings, television, films, and interactive computer media. My work is grounded in the insights of Ray L. Birdwhistell. *Work in progress:* "The American Patchwork," a series of one-hour programs on performance styles of American folklore (PBS—winter 1989/90). "The Urban Strain," a systematic study of American popular tradition of music and dance from song and film (in writeup). "The Treasury of Black Folk Music," a series of records of the Lomax recordings in the U.S. South and the West Indies. Film: "The Hot and the Cool." "The Global Jukebox," (working on prototype) to encompass the corpus of 4,000 cantometric analyses, 1,000 choreometric analyses, together with the cross-referenced systematic information on child-rearing, etc.: to be stored on an "electronic jukebox", and made available to the user in an interactive, exploratory style. *Geographic focus:* Field recording surveys of U.S., West Indies, Italy, Spain, and Great Britain. Worldwide comparative, systematic, multiscalar, computer organized analysis of singing style, movement style, speaking style, orchestral type, ensemble type, and phonotactic type of weighted cultural samples. *Languages:* French, Spanish, Italian. *Additional expertise:* Good sound recordist. *Other information:* Worked for 10 years creating the archive of folksong for the Library of Congress, 20 years as writer-producer on CBS, Mutual Broadcasting System, NBC, and BBC, and 25 years in collaboration with Conrad Arensberg, Edmund Erickson, Victor Grauer, Forrestine Paulay, Irmengaard Bartinieff, Norman Markell, and Carol Kulig on the Columbia Cross-cultural Study of Expressive Behavior.

Visual productions: Television: "The Land Where the Blues Began," 1979 (writer, director, producer; John Bishop camera and editor, Worth Long field researcher), Mississippi Educational Television, distributed by Phoenix Films. 16mm films (writer, director, producer, with Forrestine Paulay; all distributed by University of California Extension Media Center): "Dance and Human History," 1976; "Step Style," 1979; "Palm Play," 1979; "The Longest Trail," 1986, with 75 page teachers' guide.

Long, Joseph K.
Anthropology, Plymouth State College, Plymouth, NH 03264. Home: RFD 1, Campton, NH 03223. *Phone:* (603) 536-5000 ext 2424; messages ext 2335 or 2386; home (603) 726-4875. *Profession:* Anthropologist, professor. *Interests:* Medical anthropology, anthropology of consciousness, parapsychology and anthropology, teaching with ethnographic film, transpersonal anthropology. *Training:* Ph.D. Medical Anthropology and Epidemiology, University of North Carolina, Chapel Hill, 1973. M.S. Physical Anthropology, University of Kentucky, 1964. B.A. Comparative Literature, Southern Methodist University, 1959. *Work in progress:* Videotaping and analysis of spiritualist cults and folk healers in Jamaica, including divination/diagnosis. Documentary video of Robert Trivers (UCSB) and his work on the sociobiology of the Anolis lizards, esp. reciprocal altruism. *Geographic focus:* West Indies, Jamaica. *Languages:* Spanish (poor), German (poor), and Jamaican Patois.
Visual productions: "Introduction to Anthropology: A Program For Self-Instruction in the Science of Man," 1969, audio-tapes and filmstrips, 27 lectures, Carnegie Foundation and Articulated Instructional Media Program, University of Wisconsin, Madison.

Luehrsen, Thomas
Center for Visual Anthropology, USC Department of Anthropology, University Park, Los Angeles, CA 90089-0661. Home: 1141 West 27th Street, Los Angeles, CA 90007. *Phone:* (213) 743-7100; home (213) 747-2222. *Profession:* Filmmaker (ethnographic), visual anthropologist. *Interests:* Teaching with ethnographic film, ethnographic filmmaking. *Training:* M.A. Visual Anthropology, University of Southern California. B.A. Anthropology, University of California, Berkeley. *Work in progress:* "The Rocket Team," a documentary film project. *Languages:* German (fluent), Indonesian (beginning speaking). *Technical expertise:* Feature film experience in Los Angeles, West Germany, and Yugoslavia, documentary camerman and documentary and feature film sound. *Other information:* Fulbright Scholar, Westfalen Kolleg, Bielefeld, West Germany 1983–84.
Visual productions: "Zengbu After Mao," 1987 (producer, director; in collaboration with Drs. Jack and Sulamith Potter, U.C. Berkeley), 1/2 hour documentary/ethnographic film on 3/4" video about recent changes in a rural Chinese village, Academy of Television Arts and Sciences and National Educational Film Festival Awards. Have also been principally involved in variety of other award winning anthropological documentaries including "Addressless" and "Miles from the Border."

Lüem, Barbara
Bachlettenstrasse 64, 4054 Basel, Switzerland. Seminar für Ethnologie, Universität Bern, Schwanengasse 7, 3011 Bern, Switzerland. *Phone:* 061 54 31 55. *Profession:* Anthropologist (Scientific Assistant). *Interests:* Use of visual

material (film, video and photography) in teaching anthropology. Didactics of teaching visual anthropology. Visual media as a research tool. *Training:* Ph.D. Anthropology. *Work in progress:* Study of "Santa Barbara" cults in Switzerland using video as a research tool. *Geographic focus:* Europe, Indonesia (East Java). *Languages:* German (r,w,s), French (r,w,s), English (r,w,s), Spanish (r,w,s), Dutch (r,s), Bahasa Indonesia (r,s), Javanese (r,s).

Luskey, Judith
National Museum of African Art, Eliot Elisofon Archives, Smithsonian Institution, 950 Independence Avenue SW, Washington, DC 20560. Home: 2033 Belmont Road #622, Washington, DC 20009. *Phone:* (202) 357-4655; home (202) 234-1340. *Profession:* Anthropologist, archivist/curator of photographic collections. Consultant on photographic collections and films: e.g. National Museum of Natural History, National Anthropological Archives (NAA), Human Studies Film Archives, Heye Foundation Museum of the American Indian Photographic Archives, Filmed Explorations, Inc., Explorers Club, National Geographic Society. *Interests:* Ethnographic still photographs/films, photographic exhibitions and catalogues, photographic archives, videodiscs and computerization of visual data, history of photography, picture history publications. *Training:* M.A. Anthropology, Colorado, 1978, additional graduate studies in History of Photography and Photojournalism. Fieldwork: Archaeological expedition, University of Colorado Museum, Anasazi pueblo cultural remains; Smithsonian/U.S. Geological Survey. *Work in progress:* West African Museums Project, Rockefeller Foundation—exchange of photographs, films, and publications. Photographic exhibitions and ethnographic film festivals, picture histories using ethnographic still photographs. Writings: "Expeditions in North America and Africa (1850–1900)," author of book text and picture editor; "Capture the Golden Moment: Early Expeditionary Photographers of North American Indians," article; "Grand Endeavors: The Pictorialists and North American Indians," article. *Geographic focus:* North America and Africa; also South America, Asia, and Pacific. *Languages:* French (average reading, writing, difficulty with spoken). *Technical expertise:* Field photography; computerization of visual resource materials (film, photographs, artwork and maps); 19th century photography. *Other information:* Monitor and speaker for workshops and seminars on the communication of visual images, cataloging of anthropological photographic collections, history of anthropology, history of photography. Am on University of Colorado alumni staff as counselor to students interested in careers in anthropology, visual resource materials, and museums. In partnership, produced a software computer package for the documentation of artifacts and photographs which is available to museums, libraries, galleries, et al. with photographic collections. Smithsonian Award for Exceptional Service, 1985–1986, from Sylvia H. Williams, Director, NMAfA (for photographic exhibitions and publications, development of the Eliot Elisofon Archives).

Lutkehaus, Nancy C.
Department of Anthropology, University of Southern California, Los Angeles, CA 90089-0661. Home: 416 San Vicente Boulevard, Santa Monica, CA 90402. *Phone:* department (213) 743-7100; home (213) 458-0947. *Profession:* Cultural anthropologist. *Affiliation:* also Program for the Study of Women and Men in Society, USC. *Interests:* Teaching with ethnographic film, visual methods in research, gender studies, film theory, dispute settlement, music and performance, visual and aural history of anthropology. *Training:* B.A. Anthropology, Barnard College; M.A., Ph.D. Anthropology, Columbia University. *Work in progress:* Spencer Foundation project on the visual translation of culture: "Student's Responses to Filmic Images of the Other" (with Wilton Martinez). Visual documentation of the process of dispute settlement in highland New Guinea. *Geographic area:* Oceania, highland and island New Guinea, urban U.S. *Languages:* Tokpisn (r,w,s), Manam (r,w,s), French (r,w,s), Spanish (read), German (read). *Additional information:* Each year at the AAA meetings, Timothy Asch and I organize and chair an SVA workshop on teaching with ethnographic film—The Visual Translation of Culture: Workshop on the Use of Film and Text in Anthopology.

MacDougall, David
Director, Film Unit, Australian Institute of Aboriginal Studies, P.O. Box 553, Canberra, ACT 2601 Australia. Home: 12 Meehan Gardens, Griffith, ACT 2603, Australia. *Phone:* (062) 461-133; home (062) 952-002. *Profession:* Ethnographic filmmaker. *Affiliations:* also Visiting Lecturer, Department of Prehistory and Anthropology, Australian National University. *Interests:* Ethnographic filmmaking, film theory (documentary, ethnographic). *Training:* Ph.D. Harvard, 1961. M.F.A. University of California, Los Angeles, 1970. Graduate, UCLA Ethnographic Film Program, 1968. *Work in progress:* "Racing" (working title), film on Australian family in northern New South Wales. "Link-Up" (working title), film on Link-Up organization in Australia which attempts to reunite family members of Aboriginal families separated by policies of state and federal governments. *Geographic focus:* East Africa, Australia. *Languages:* French (intermediate), Turkana (basic).
    Visual productions: "To Live With Herds," 1972 (filmed in 1968). "Kenya Boran," 1974 (filmed in 1972). "Turkana Conversations" trilogy: "The Wedding Camels," 1977 (filmed in 1974); "Lorang's Way," 1979, (filmed in 1974); "A Wife Among Wives," 1981 (filmed in 1974).

MacDougall, Judith
Australian Institute of Aboriginal Studies, P.O. Box 553, Canberra, ACT 2601 Australia. Home: 12 Meehan Gardens, Griffith, ACT 2603 Australia. *Phone:* (062) 461-132; home (062) 952-002. *Profession:* Ethnographic filmmaker. *Interests:* Filmmaking. *Training:* M.F.A. University of California,

Los Angeles (ethnographic film program). B.A. Beloit College, Wisconsin.
Visual productions: "The Wedding Camels," 1977 (filmed in 1974).
"Lorang's Way," 1979 (filmed in 1974). "The House-Opening," 1980 (filmed
in 1977). "Takeover," 1980, (filmed in 1978). "A Wife Among Wives,"
1981 (filmed in 1974). "Three Horsemen," 1982 (filmed in 1978). "Collum
Calling Canberra," 1984 (filmed in 1982). "Stockman's Strategy," 1984
(filmed in 1982).

Magdanz, James S.
1300 College Road, Fairbanks, AK 99701. *Phone:* (907) 479-6211. *Profession:* Photographer. *Affiliation:* Department of Fish and Game, Division of
Subsistence—anthropological research arm employing approximately 25
professional researchers in anthropology, sociology, geography, and biology.
The Division uses photography in conjunction with major anthropological
research projects, principally in rural Alaska. A major goal has been to
describe socio-economic systems in village Alaska. *Interests:* Ethnographic
still photography. *Training:* University of Missouri, Columbia. *Work in
progress:* The subsistence economy of Brevig Mission, Alaska. Yukon river
salmon fisheries. *Geographic focus:* The Arctic. *Languages:* Saint Lawrence
Island Yupik [Eskimo] (elementary conversation), French (elementary reading).
Additional expertise: Arctic wilderness survival techniques. *Other information:*
1979 recipient of Alicia Patterson Foundation fellowship for journalism, and
Ellan Lyman Cabot Trust grant for teaching photography.
    Visual productions: "Shungnak," photo exibit documenting life in an
Alaskan Eskimo village; Alaska State Museum, Juneau.

Malcolm, Barbara
2635 Monmouth Avenue, Los Angeles, CA 90007. *Phone:* (213) 749-4965.
Profession: Visual anthropologist. *Interests:* Ritual, feminist and women's
issues. *Training:* M.A. Visual Anthropology, USC, 1989. *Work in progress:*
"Blessed Be," 3/4" video, on creation of new ritual and use of feminist witch-
craft in Los Angeles. *Geographic focus:* East Africa (Masai); Baja, California.
Languages: French, Swahili. *Technical expertise:* Cinematography, editing,
still photography.
    Visual productions: "Pa'ipai Folktales and Pottery Making," 1988 (with
Julie Wright), 18 min. 3/4" video. "Mirror Ritual," 1988, 23 min. 3/4" video
on women addressing issues of self image through Dianic ritual.

Manley, Roger B.
1110 Burch, Durham, NC 27701. *Phone:* (919) 490-7972. *Profession:*
Photographer, folklorist. *Affiliation:* The Jargon Society; Davenport Film
Company. *Interests:* Ethnographic photography, documentary film, folk and
primitive art, material culture artifacts, Native American studies. *Training:*
Master's program in Folklore, University of North Carolina, Chapel Hill.

Work in progress: Organizing first permanent center for Visionary Art Studies in U.S. Folktale film series for Davenport Films. NEA-funded book about St. Helena Island, South Carolina. Jargon Society book about Southern folk art, "Walks to Paradise Garden." Princeton University Press book, "The Photograph and the American Indian" (essay and photos). *Geographic focus:* Arizona (Navajo reservation), New Mexico, North Carolina, South Carolina, Virginia, Central Australia. *Technical expertise:* Archaeological photography, documentary film and still photography. *Other information:* Expedition photographer for Australian Museum of Natural History.

Visual productions: "Sullen Land," photo exhibit about central desert Aboriginals in Australia: Iris Gallery, Davidson College Gallery, Nexus Gallery, Santa Fe Gallery of Photography. "In Search of a Heritage," photo exhibit about St. Helena Island, SC, toured by SC Museum Commission to numerous galleries. "As Now Becomes Us," photo exhibit about the folklife of the Roanoke River Valley, toured to Rowe Gallery, Duke University Gallery, North Carolina Center for Creative Photography Gallery, etc. "The Navajo of Chilchinbeto," photo exhibit, toured to Princeton University, Duke University, Durham Technical Institute, Roswell Museum of Art. "Worth Keeping, Found Artists of the Carolinas," catalog and exhibit for Columbia Museum of Art. "Southern Visionary Folk Artists," catalog and exhibit, for Sawtooth Center for Visual Design, sponsored by The Jargon Society. "Australian Aboriginal Children's Art," catalog and exhibit for Durham Technical Institute, Australian Consular Service. "Cramerton, Catawba River Milltown," 28 min. b/w film. "Signs and Wonders," North Carolina Museum of Art exhibit, works by North Carolina visionary artists. "Hand and Shadow," exhibit, Institute of the Arts, Duke University, March-April 1989.

Margolies, Luise

Director, Ediciones Venezolanas de Antropología, Apartado 3305, Caracas 1010, Venezuela. *Phone:* (58-2) 979-36-49. *Profession:* Social anthropologist. *Affiliation:* Research Fellow, Universidad Central de Venezuela. *Interests:* Ethnographic filmmaking, still photography. *Training:* Ph.D. Columbia University, 1972. *Work in progress:* Translated and annotated the diary of Hiram Bingham who crossed Venezuela in 1906, including almost 1000 photographs of Venezuela at that time (an important collection for Venezuelan historiography of the early century). *Geographic focus:* Latin America and the Hispanic Caribbean, esp. Venezuela, Mexico, and Peru. *Languages:* Fluent in Spanish and reading ability in Portuguese, Italian, and French. *Other information:* "Paraguana," 1985 (with Graziano Gasparini and Carlos Gonzales). "Jose Gregorio Hernandes: Image and Symbolism," 1985, article with photographic analysis of the use of visual images in the making of a popular saint.

Visual productions: "Venezuelan Trapiche," photograph, AAA appointment calendar, 1980. "Farmstead in the Venezuelan Andes," photograph,

AAA appointment calendar, 1981. "Venezuela Otra," 1984 (with Graziano Gasparini), documentary photographs on Venezuelan change.

Marks, Daniel

Department of Anthropology, University of Southern California, Los Angeles, CA 90089-0661. *Phone:* (213) 743-7100. *Affiliations:* AAA, Royal Anthropological Institute. *Interests:* Ethnographic filmmaking, policing, juvenile delinquancy. *Training:* M.A. Visual Anthropology, University of Southern California. B.A. Economics, Manchester University. *Work in progress:* "Gang Kids," an inside look at Black gang members in Los Angeles. *Geographic focus:* Urban America, Los Angeles. *Languages:* French, German. *Technical expertise:* Cinematography, editing (film). *Other information:* Managing editor, SVA Newsletter.

Visual productions: "Gang Cops," b/w 16mm film, explores the world of Los Angeles gangs and the policing response to gang warfare.

Marshall, John Kennedy

660 Sand Hill Road, Peterborough, NH 03458. *Phone:* (603) 924-3486; work (617) 926-0491. *Training:* M.A. Anthropology, Harvard University, 1966. G.S.A.S. Anthropology, Yale University, 1960. B.A. Anthropology, Harvard University, 1957. *Geographic focus:* Africa, U.S. *Languages:* Ju/wasi.

Visual productions: Films (director, photographer): "The Hunters," 1957, about hunting among the !Kung Bushmen, Flaherty Award, 1957, Venice Festival, 1958; "Bitter Melons," 1971, about the music of a /Gwi musician, Golden Eagle American Film Festival, 1971, Festival dei Popoli, 1972; "N/um Tchai: The Ceremonial Dance of the !Kung Bushmen," about !Kung Bushmen dance and trance; "Titticut Follies," on the inmates and staff of the hospital for the criminally insane at Bridgewater, Massachusetts; "You Are Our Problem," about a conference on Black Power. "N!ai, The Story of a !Kung Woman," 1980 (co-producer, co-director, co-editor, cinematographer), 58 min. documentary incorporating !Kung footage from 1950's until 1978, showing the dramatic changes that have affected the !Kung people and their way of life, and focusing on one woman, N!ai, whom we meet at the age of three and follow for three decades, aired in Odyssey series on public television.

Martin, Mary

4719 Windsor Avenue, Philadelphia, PA 19143. Office: Middle East Center, 838 Williams Hall, University of Pennsylvania, Philadelphia, PA 19104. *Phone:* (215) 727-0656; office (215) 898-6335. *Profession:* Anthropologist, teacher, outreach coordinator. *Affiliations:* also Philadelphia College of Art (lecturer in Liberal Arts). *Interests:* Teaching with ethnographic film, ethnographic filmmaking and photography, study of art and artifacts (especially weaving in Middle East) from social, cultural, and historic points of view, analysis of visual symbolic forms. *Training:* Course in filmmaking,

Philadelphia College of Art. Ph.D. candidate Cultural Anthropology, Washington University. M.A. Cultural Anthropology, Washington University. *Work in progress:* "The Sociocultural Context of Rural Textile Production: A Case from Northeast Iran." *Geographic focus:* Iran; Middle East; worldwide (for teaching with ethnographic film and about art). *Languages:* Persian.

Matthews, Lewis Helen
Route 1, Box 270, Dungannon, VA 24245. Office: Appalshop, Whitesburg, KY 41858; and Highlander Research and Education Center, New Market, TN 37820. *Phone:* (703) 467-2240. *Profession:* Educator/filmmaker, sociologist, anthropologist. *Interests:* Film and video making, teaching with film, participatory research with video. *Training:* Ph.D. Sociology, University of Kentucky. *Work in progress:* Videos on Trammel, VA and War on Poverty in Appalachia Region, History of Appalachia Film Series. *Geographic focus:* U.S., Appalachian mountains, coal mining communities.
   Visual productions: "The Welsh Tapes," video of life in Welsh coal mining communities. "Strangers and Kin," film in History of Appalachia series (project director). "Long Journey Home," film in History of Appalachia series, (project director). "Come All You Coal Miners," slide-tape on coal mining music. "Coal Mining Women" (narration for film). Advisor for Headwaters Series, Appalshop.

Maynard, Douglas W.
Department of Sociology, University of Wisconsin, Madison, WI 53706. Home: 1141 Elizabeth Street, Madison, WI 53703. *Phone:* (608) 262-1930; department (608) 262-2921; home (608) 255-6021. *Profession:* Sociology. *Affiliation:* also Waisman Center on Mental Retardation and Human Development, University of Wisconsin. *Interests:* Analysis of naturally occurring interaction (videotape, audiotape). *Training:* Ph.D. University of California, Santa Barbara, 1979. M.A. University of California, Santa Barbara, 1975. *Work in progress:* "Asking Parents Their View of a Child's Disability." "The Delivery and Receipt of Diagnostic News Regarding Developmental Disabilities." "The Delivery and Receipt of Diagnostic News: Why Communication is Not Enough."

McConochie, Roger P.
Corporate Research International, 2222 Fuller Road, 1012A, Ann Arbor, MI 48105. *Phone:* (313) 995-3452. *Profession:* Corporate anthropologist. *Interests:* Ethnographic photography. Reflexive methodologies. *Geographic focus:* Alpine Europe. *Languages:* German.

McGee, R. Jon
Department of Sociology and Anthropology, Southwest Texas State University, San Marcos, TX 78666. *Phone:* (512) 245-2113. *Profession:* Assistant

Professor of Anthropology. *Interests:* Ethnographic filmmaking and anthropological teaching with ethnographic films. *Training:* Ph.D. Anthropology, Rice University, and studied documentary/ethnographic filmmaking at the Rice Media Center. *Work in progress:* Currently editing an ethnographic film on the ba'alche ritual of the Lacandon Maya Indians. *Geographic focus:* My principal film work has been done with the Lacandon Maya Indians who live in the rainforest of southeastern Chiapas, Mexico. *Languages:* Both read and speak Lacandon Maya, Yucatecan Maya, and Spanish. *Other information:* Writing an ethnography of the Lacadon Maya, meant to be read in conjunction with a series of films that are currently being edited, such as the film listed below on Lacandon Maya swidden.

Visual productions: "Swidden Agriculture Among the Lacandon Maya," 1986, 32 min. color 3/4" video, Maya with English subtitles. "Ghosts Along the Brazos," 1985, film on southeast Texas folklore, for Texas Committee on the Humanities.

McGilvray, Dennis B.
Department of Anthropology, University of Colorado at Boulder, Boulder, CO 80309-0233. Home: 1315 Fifth Street, Boulder, CO 80302. *Phone:* (303) 492-7198; department (303) 492-7947; home (303) 449-0501. *Profession:* Cultural anthropologist, Associate Professor. *Interests:* Ethnographic photography, ritual and trance, anthropology of architecture and artisans. *Training:* Ph.D. University of Chicago, Anthropology, 1974. B.A. Reed College, Anthropology, 1965. *Work in progress:* Continued research on ritual and family life in a matrilineal Tamil-speaking region of Sri Lanka. Plans for field research on architecture and artisan castes in Sri Lanka and south India. *Geographic focus:* South Asia, especially south India and Sri Lanka. *Languages:* French and Spanish (reading ability), Tamil (speaking, reading and writing). *Other information:* Fieldwork in Sri Lanka among both Hindus and Muslims.

Visual productions: "Symbolic Heat: Gender, Health, and Worship Among the Tamils of South India and Sri Lanka," 1986, a traveling photographic exhibit from the University of Colorado Museum, includes 71 framed color photographs and text panels, poster and illustrated brochure, and a ten minute video cassette (also available as a slide-tape) documenting a Hindu goddess festival in eastern Sri Lanka.

McKee, Lauris A.
Department of Anthropology, Franklin and Marshall College, Lancaster, PA 17604-3003. Home: 447 Stonegate Road, Millersville, PA 17551. *Phone:* (717) 291-4191; department (717) 291-4035; home (717) 872-1948. *Profession:* Anthropologist. *Interests:* Ethnographic filmmaking, use of ethnographic film in class. Proxemics—doctoral dissertation study of parents' socialization of children's expressive behaviors, particularly children's efforts to seek

security through touching parents: findings of significant sex-differentials in socialization outcomes and parents' socialization strategies (for both sex of child and sex of parent). *Training:* Ph.D. Cornell University. M.A. Cornell University. B.A. George Washington University. *Work in progress:* Inserting English subtitles and narration in video films listed below. *Geographic focus:* Highland Ecuador and the Andean Region of South America. *Languages:* Spanish (speaking and reading fluent, writing competent, but not idiomatic). *Additional expertise:* Social anthropology, psychological anthropology, medical anthropology, and demographic anthropology. *Other information:* Grants from NSF, NIH, NIMH, Cornell Center for International Studies, and Cornell International Population Program. Fulbright Fellow, 1982.

Visual productions: Film series on ethnomedicine and children (3/4" video, Spanish) for the National Museum of Ecuador: "Highland Ecuador," "Evil Air, Evil Wind," "Soul Loss," "Evil Eye," "Traditional Diagnostic Techniques," and "Traditional Beliefs and Reproduction."

Mehan, Hugh
Department of Sociology, UCSD, La Jolla, CA 92093. Home: 943 San Dieguito, Encinita, CA 92011. *Phone:* (619) 534-2957; home (619) 942-0734. *Profession:* Sociologist. *Interests:* Teach with ethnographic films, audio-visual microethnography. *Training:* Sociolinguistics—one of the first to use videomode for microethnography in sociology. *Work in progress:* Discourse analysis, concerned with nuclear war. *Geographic focus:* Southwest U.S.

Mintz, Jerome R.
Department of Anthropology, Indiana University, Bloomington, IN 47405. Home: 914 E. University Street, Bloomington, IN 47401. *Phone:* (812) 885-0216; home (812) 339-3588. *Profession:* Professor of Anthropology. *Interests:* Ethnographic filmmaking, teaching with ethnographic film. *Work in progress:* Research on Hasidim in America and Carnaval in Spain. *Languages:* Spanish (good reading and speaking).

Visual productions: 16mm films: "The Shoemaker," 1978, 30 min.; "Pepe's Family," 1978, 33 min.; "Romeria, Day of the Virgin," 1986, 57 min.; "Carnaval de Pueblo [Town Carnival]," 1986, 57 min.; "The Shepherd's Family," 1989, 20 min.; and "Perico the Bowlmaker," 1989, 34 min.

Mitchell, William E.
Anthropology Department, University of Vermont, Burlington, VT 05405. Home: Pleasant Valley Farm, Wolcott, VT 05680. *Phone:* (802) 656-3884; home (802) 888-4652. *Profession:* Cultural anthropologist, professor. *Interests:* Ethnographic filmmaking, teaching with visual/sound media. *Training:* Ph.D. Anthropology, Columbia University. *Geographic focus:* Melanesia.

Visual productions: "Magical Curing," 1989 (filming and narrating), 27 min. b/w video, with accompaning viewer's guide, distributed by Waveland Press, Prospect Heights, IL (complementary to the book Bamboo Fire).

Moerman, Michael

Department of Anthropology, UCLA, 405 Hilgard Avenue, Los Angeles, CA 90024. Home: 1105 Parkway Trail, Topanga, CA 90290. *Phone:* department (213) 825-2055; home (213) 455-3049. *Interests:* Analysis of interaction, teaching with ethnographic film, ethnographic film production, photographs as cultural records, construction of reality via film. *Work in progress:* Analysis of Thai interaction. *Geographic focus:* Thailand, USA. *Languages:* French (read), Thai (speak).

Monks, Gregory G.

Department of Anthropology, University of Manitoba, Winnipeg, Manitoba, Canada, R3T 2N2. *Phone:* (204) 474-6329; department (204) 474-9361. *Profession:* Archaeologist, professor. *Interests:* Production of videotape for public education. Analysis of sketches, scale drawings and photographs of historic period sites in conjunction with archaeological research. *Training:* Ph.D. Anthropology/Archaeology. *Work in progress:* "Upper Fort Garry As Symbolic Communication" (presented at Canadian Archaeological Association meeting, Toronto, April, 1986); "Upper Fort Garry As Symbolic Communication: Part II" (paper read at Canadian Archaeological Association meeting, Calgary, April, 1987). *Geographic focus:* Western Canadian fur trade, historical archaeology. *Languages:* French (r,w,s), German (r,w,s).

Visual productions: "Archaeology at Upper Fort Garry," 12 min. videotape for public education.

Naimark, Michael

216 Filbert, San Francisco, CA 94133. *Phone:* (415) 391-4817. *Profession:* Media artist. *Interests:* Film, videodisc, field recording, environmental display. *Training:* M.S. Visual Studies/Environmental Art, Massachusetts Institute of Technology, 1979. B.S. Cybernetic Systems (Independent major), University of Michigan, 1974. *Work in progress:* Investigating issues of "media as virtual reality"—relationship between sense-ability, effect-ability, and context; media technologies—parallels between "media" and "artificial intelligence" fields (i.e. between "is it live or is it Memorex?" and Turing Test). *Other information:* Courses taught: Future Worlds, University of Michigan, 1972-73. Creative Seeing, MIT, 1977. New Media and the Arts, San Francisco State University, 1981. Videodisc Production Workshop, Cal Arts, 1986.

Visual productions: "Michael Naimark, Media Arts, Three Recent Works," 1985, 12 min. color/sound 3/4" video, contains documentation of works that share the common theme of "media as virtual realities." "The Paris Moviemap," 1985, interactive videodisc project for the Paris Metro.

Nanda, Serena
Department of Anthropology, John Jay College, 445 West 59th Street, New York City, NY 10019. *Phone:* (212) 489-5074. *Profession:* Anthropologist (cultural). *Interests:* Teaching with ethnographic film, film reviewing. *Work in progress:* Presently working on a videotape on hijras transvestite dancers in India. *Geographic focus:* India (women, sex roles).

Narrowe, Judith
Torstenssonsgatan 4, 114 56 Stockholm, Sweden. Stockholm Jewish Community Center, Nybrog 19, S-114 39 Stockholm, Sweden. *Phone:* 08/63 95 24. *Profession:* Religious school principal, teacher, pedagogic center director. *Affiliation:* University of Stockholm, Jewish community of Stockholm. *Interests:* Ethnographic filmmaking for teaching purposes, student participatory filmmaking, video/film/photo archiving. Urban, ethnic education, Jewish education. *Geographic focus:* Sweden, Europe, Israel. *Languages:* Swedish (r,w,s), English (r,w,s), Hebrew (r,w,s), French (read).
   Visual productions: "Jonathan's Discovery," a slidetape teaching a Jewish prayer.

Nichols, Bill
Department of Film Studies, Queen's University, Kingston, Ontario K7L 3N6 Canada. *Phone:* (613) 545-2178. *Profession:* Professor. *Interests:* Problems of cultural interpretation. Ethnographic film. *Training:* Ph.D. Theatre Arts. *Work in progress:* "Questions of Magnitudes" (in documentary form). *Geographic focus:* Modes of discourse (not 'areas'). *Languages:* French, German, Italian (reading), Swahili (speaking).

Nierenberg, Judith
Documentary Educational Resources, 101 Morse Street, Watertown, MA 02172. Home: 25 Lockeland Avenue, Arlington, MA 02174. *Phone:* (617) 926-0491; home (617) 646-0325. *Profession:* Teacher, lecturer, media librarian. *Training:* M.A. Candidate, Northwestern University, 1976–79. M.A., M.Ed. Concentration in Media and Library Science, Boston State College, 1975. B.A. Anthropology, University of Connecticut, 1968.

O'Brien, Sarah
177 West 26th Street #400, New York, NY 10001. *Phone:* (212) 989-6280; business (212) 463-7889. *Profession:* Film production, anthropology, video art. *Interests:* Ethnographic film and video production, emphasis on women as subjects and producers of visual documentation, video art with anthropological underpinnings and overtones. *Training:* M.A. Visual Anthropology, Temple University, 1985. Certificate in Filmmaking, New York University, 1981. *Work in progress:* "Waiting," a color super-8 documentary on a group of waitresses in Philadelphia. Video piece on the last

of the Shakers. Video piece on Tunisian street musicians in New York. *Geographic focus:* Service workers in Western societies, separatist U.S. communities (historical and current), North African women. *Languages:* French (fluent), Russian (some reading and speaking, minimal writing). *Technical expertise:* Proficiency with super-8 and 16mm film, 3/4" and 1/2" video equipment, sound recording equipment, and 35mm still photography. *Other information:* I have worked freelance on independent documentary films as assistant editor, production coordinator, post-production supervisor, and associate producer.

Oliver-Smith, Anthony
Department of Anthropology, GPA 1350, University of Florida, Gainesville, FL 32611. Home: 708 NE 7th Avenue, Gainesville, FL 32601. *Phone:* (904) 392-2290; department (904) 392-2031; home (904) 377-8359. *Profession:* Associate Professor of Anthropology. *Interests:* Museum exhibit film scripting and design. Ethnographic filmmaking (video). *Training:* Ph.D. Anthropology. *Geographic focus:* Peru and Spain (Latin America in general). *Languages:* Spanish (fluently).
    Visual productions: "Mijas: Pueblo Blanco" (with José Lison Arcal and Hernán Vera), video. Museum film scripts, Florida State Museum: "Human Communication," "Belief Systems," "Culture Change," and "Man and the Environment."

Olsson, Stephen
Co-Director, Cultural and Educational Media, Industrial Center Building, Suite 250, Sausalito, CA 94965. Home: 1675 8th Avenue, San Francisco, CA 94122. *Phone:* (415) 331-7345; home (415) 566-1909. *Profession:* Film and video producer, cameraman, writer, editor; media consultant. *Interests:* Anthropological, ethnographic film and video production. *Training:* M.A. Visual Anthropology, Temple University, and the Anthropology Film Center, Santa Fe, NM. B.A. Anthropology, San Francisco State University. *Work in progress:* Interactive videotapes for California State Department of Education (human relations, self-esteem for high-risk youth). *Geographic focus:* South Asia, Central Asia, Middle East, U.S. *Languages:* Spanish (elementary speaking/reading), Farsi/Dari (elementary speaking). *Technical expertise:* Video, film, photography.
    Visual productions: Films distributed by DER, Watertown, MA: "To Find the Baruya Story: An Anthropologist at Work in a New Guinea Tribe," 1982; "Her Name Came on Arrows: A Kinship Interview with the Baruya of Papua New Guinea," 1982. Aired on PBS: "Afghanistan: The Fight for A Way of Life," 1987 (producer, director, cinematographer; Scott Andrews, co-producer, second camera); "And Then Came John," 1988 (co-producer; Scott Andrews producer, director, cinematographer), on a young man with Downs syndrome.

Visual productions: Films distributed by DER, Watertown, MA: "To Find the Baruya Story: An Anthropologist at Work in a New Guinea Tribe," 1982; "Her Name Came on Arrows: A Kinship Interview with the Baruya of Papua New Guinea," 1982. Aired on PBS: "Afghanistan: The Fight for A Way of Life," 1987 (producer, director, cinematographer; Scott Andrews, co-producer, second camera); "And Then Came John," 1988 (co-producer; Scott Andrews producer, director, cinematographer), on a young man with Downs syndrome.

Oppitz, Michael

Sybelstrasse 38, Berlin 12, West Germany. *Profession:* Anthropologist. *Affiliation:* Institute for Advanced Study, Berlin. *Interests:* Ethnographic film, anthropological theory. *Training:* Ph.D. Social Anthropology. *Work in progress:* "Exoticism : A Pictorial History 'Savages'." *Geographic focus:* Himalayas. *Languages:* German, French, English, Greek, Latin, Chinese, Nepali.

Visual productions: "Shamans of the Blind Country," 16mm film.

Orth, Geoffrey

P.O. Box 22, Ester, AK 99725. *Phone:* (907) 479-0014; messages (907) 474-7288. *Profession:* Marine affairs consultant, photographer. *Affiliation:* Anthropology Department, University of Alaska, Fairbanks, AK 99775. *Interests:* Ecological anthropology, maritime anthropology, documentary photography. *Training:* M.A. Anthropology, University of Alaska, 1986. B.Sc. Biology, University of the State of New York, 1979. *Work in progress:* "Bristol Bay Fisheries," photo essay. *Geographic focus:* Alaska, maritime areas. *Languages:* Spanish (poor reading and writing, good speaking). *Technical expertise:* Commercial fishing, fisheries biology, vessel operations, 35mm still photography, b/w and color processing.

Visual productions: "Fishing Strategies among Southeast Alaskan Salmon Seiners," photo essay.

Östör, Ákos

Department of Anthropology, Wesleyan University, Middleton, CT 06457. Home: 195 Maromas Road, Middletown, CT 06457. *Phone:* (203) 347-9411; (203) 347–1019. *Profession:* Professor of Anthropology; filmmaking, film studies. *Interests:* Anthropological filmmaking, teaching with film and teaching of film, research and writing about film. *Training:* Ph.D. Anthropology, University of Chicago, 1971. M.A. Ethnohistory, University of Melbourne, 1967. B.A. History, University of Melbourne, 1964. *Work in progress:* Article on interpretation of ritual in film and anthropology. Monograph length discussion with Robert Gardner concerning "Forest of Bliss." Long ethnographic essay on "Forest of Bliss." "Seed and Earth" (with Alfred Guzzetti and Lina Fruzzetti), a film on male and female in a Bengali village. *Geographic focus:* India, Central Europe, Africa. *Languages:* Bengali, German,

Hungarian (fluent); Hindi, Arabic (basic conversational); French, Latin (read).

Visual productions: 16mm color films: "Loving Krishna" (co-director with Allen Moore), 42 min. "Sons of Shiva" (co-director with Robert Gardner), 28 min. "Serpent Mother" (co-director with Allen Moore), 28 min. "Forest of Bliss" (co-produced with Robert Gardner, director), 90 min.

Ottenberg, Simon
Department of Anthropology, University of Washington, Seattle, WA 98195. Home: 2317 22nd Avenue East, Seattle, WA 98112. *Phone:* (206) 543-5240; 322-5398. *Profession:* Anthropologist. *Interests:* Ethnography of African art. *Training:* Ph.D. Anthropology, Northwestern, 1957. *Work in progress:* The aesthetics of rituals of the Limba, northern Sierra Leone: book and articles. *Geographic focus:* West Africa, esp. S.E. Nigeria, northern Sierra Leone. *Languages:* French, some Igbo, some Limba.

Pader, Ellen
Department of Anthropology, Haines Hall, UCLA, Los Angeles, CA 90024. Home: 2017 Euclid Street B, Santa Monica, CA 90405. *Phone:* (213) 825-2055; home (213) 452-1594. *Profession:* Anthropologist, lecturer, writer. *Affiliations:* also, Institute of Archaeology, UCLA. *Interests:* Social theory as applied to the interpretation of space use and material culture, in particular, semiotics and the theory of structuration. Proxemics, the roles of space-use objects and dress in power relations (e.g. gender, age, ethnicity), belief systems and prejudice, the application of these concerns to urban planning and social welfare, teaching with visual media. *Training:* Ph.D. Cambridge University, England. *Work in progress:* "Space, Objects, and the Acculturation Process." *Geographic focus:* Los Angeles, Latin Americans, cross-cultural research. *Languages:* Spanish, French (reading, some speaking).

Peek, Philip M.
Department of Anthropology, Drew University, Madison, NJ 07940. Home: 4 Lee Avenue, Madison, NJ 07940. *Phone:* (201) 377-3000 ext 383; home (201) 822-3425. *Profession:* College professor. *Interests:* Research on African visual and verbal arts; Afro-American material culture; editing of field film; teaching with ethnographic films, slides, and videotapes. Teaching topics include performance, visual arts, aesthetics, ethnographic film, proxemics, and kinesics in several cultural anthropology courses. *Work in progress:* Editing field footage on Isoko festivals and carvers. *Geographic focus:* Southern Nigeria. *Languages:* Limited research abilities in French, Spanish, and Isoko. *Additional expertise:* Consultant on several films including Gerald Davis' "The Performed Word," an NEH-funded film on African-American preachers. *Other information:* "Background Notes" for Kongi's Harvest, 1978, by Calpenny-Nigeria Films, et al., distributed with film by New Line Cinema.

Perez-Tolon, Luis
c/o Center for Visual Anthropology, University of Southern California, Los Angeles, CA 90089-0661. Home: 254 S. Vendome Street #6, Los Angeles, CA 90057. *Phone:* (213) 743-7100; home (213) 383-7104. *Profession:* Ethnographic filmmaker, producer, writer. *Affiliations:* also SVA; Film Arts Foundation. *Interests:* Ethnographic film: 10 years experience in 16mm and TV documentary production in the U.S. and abroad. Ethnicity and identity. Ethnographic film as communication of anthropological concepts to a broad audience. The "self" and film. Three years' experience with various approaches at the Center for Visual Anthropology at USC. *Training:* M.A. in Ethnographic Film and Visual Anthropology, Center for Visual Anthropology, USC, 1987. Berkeley Film Institute, 1979. B.A. in Literature and Anthropology, University of Florida, 1971. *Work in progress:* "The Bora: Natives of the Amazon," one hour feature documentary, shot in Peru. "Flamenco Gitano: A Gypsy Way of Life." California Mission Era Media Project (consultant, researcher). *Geographic focus:* Latin America, Spain, Hispanic/Latino communities in the U.S. *Languages:* Spanish (fluent), English (fluent), French (fluent), Portuguese (conversational). *Technical expertise:* Skilled in all aspects of documentary production and post-production, research, script, narration, budget and proposals, 16mm and video. *Other information:* Grants and fellowships: Western Regional Media Arts Fellowships (NEA); Emerging Film/Video Artist grant (NEA); Pioneer Fund; Zellerbach Family Fund; Del Amo Foundation; Ramon J. Sender Fellowship, Spanish Ministry of Foreign Affairs. Co-founder of CINE ACCION, Inc., San Francisco Bay Area association of Latino filmmakers.

Visual productions: "Changing Rhythms: Gitanos Today," 20 min. video with accompanying publication. "Voices of Yerba Buena," 1981 (associate producer), KQED and national PBS broadcast. "Samba in the Streets," 1982 (associate producer), KQED and national PBS broadcast. "Another View: Cuban Refugees," 1980, KPIX-TV, San Francisco.

Peters, Mary Pyle
5 Tomahawk Court, Navato, CA 94947. *Phone:* (415) 883-2588. *Profession:* Consulting ethnographer. *Interests:* Use of photographs in ethnographic interviews, particularly historic photographs in analyses of contemporary populations. *Training:* B.A., M.A. Anthropology. Seven years' experience in ethnographic studies for cultural resource management projects. *Geographic focus:* California and Great Basin. *Languages:* French and Spanish (reading).

Peterson, Nicolas
Department of Prehistory and Anthropology, Australian National University, G.P.O. Box 4, ACT 2601, Australia. *Phone:* 062-493498. *Profession:* Lecturer in Anthropology. *Interests:* Photographic images of non-western people, ethnographic filmmaking and use in teaching. *Training:* Ph.D.

Anthropology, University of Sydney, Australia. *Work in progress:* Analysis of the representation of Aborigines in popular photography, 1900-1980. *Geographic focus:* Australia and Pacific. *Languages:* French (r,w,s).

Visual productions: Anthropological adviser on ethnographic films directed by Roger Sandall for the Australian Institute of Aboriginal Studies: 7 films on men's secret ceremonies, "Camels and the Pitjanjara," 50 min., "Making a Bark Canoe," 20 min., and "A Walberigine Ceremony: Ngaljakula," 21 min.

Pierce, Dann L.
237 Buckley Center, Department of Communication Studies, University of Portland, Portland, OR. *Phone:* (503) 283-7229. *Profession:* Assistant Professor of Rhetoric and Communication Studies. *Interests:* Visual persuasion, American contemporary film, visual satire, television iconology. *Training:* Ph.D. University of Iowa. M.A. University of Portland, Oregon. *Work in progress:* Visual satire, film narrative and mundane knowledge, television iconology. *Languages:* French (reading).

Pilling, Arnold R.
Department of Anthropology, Wayne State University, Detroit, MI 48202. Home: 620 Prentis C-5, Detroit, MI 48201. *Phone:* Message center (313) 577-2935; office (313) 577-3056; museum office (313) 577-2598; home (313) 831-4679. *Profession:* Teacher/anthropologist. *Interests:* Dating early photographs. Diachronic Anthropology, Social Anthropology, Historical Archaeology. *Geographic focus:* Native Americans, Australia, Caribbean.

Pohl, John M. D.
10427 Wilshire Boulevard #6, Los Angeles, CA 90024. Institute of Archaeology, UCLA, Los Angeles, CA 90024. *Phone:* (213) 470-9517. *Profession:* Archaeologist, film special effects, animation. *Interests:* Ethnographic film, feature film, comparisons of ancient and modern visual communication systems, pictorial systems, animation.

Potterfield, Thomas G.
3627 Hamilton Street, Philadelphia, PA 19104. *Phone:* (215) 387-2813. *Profession:* College teacher. *Affiliation:* Annenberg School of Communications, University of Pennsylvania; Pennsylvania State University, Ogontz. *Interests:* Using visual media (especially film) in teaching interpersonal communication. Visual analysis of interaction settings and proxemic behavior. Visual analysis of bodily communication. *Training:* Ph.D. Annenberg School of Communications, pending. M.A. Annenberg School of Communications, 1981. *Work in progress:* Doctoral dissertation, "Second Homes, Dual Residency, and Social Communication: A Contextual Analysis." *Geographic focus:* South Jersey Shore, Trans-Allegheny Highlands of West Virginia. *Languages:* German (reading).

Pratt, Christina Carver
Dominican College, Orangeburg, NY 10962. *Phone:* (914) 359-7899, ext
267. *Profession:* Assistant Professor of Sociology and Human Services.
Affiliation: Dominican College. *Interests:* Teaching about world cultural
areas through the media of photographic slide/videotape. *Training:* Fulbright
Study/Travel Grant, Pakistan, 1983. Fulbright Study/Travel Grant, India,
1981. M.S. Sociology and Social Work, Columbia University, 1976. *Work
in progress:* "Pakistan," slide/videotape with Jerry B. Bannister, approx. 30
min. *Geographic focus:* South Asia/Asia.
    Visual productions: Two 50 min. color slide/videotapes (VHS), AV/TV
Center, Western Connecticut State University: "India: Images from the Cultural Past," 1985 (photography and narrative, with Jerry B. Bannister; Marie
O'Brien director, George Theisen producer); and "India: Images of Villages and
Cities," 1986 (photography and narrative, with Jerry B. Bannister and contri-
butions by Sal Cordaro and Linda L. Lindsey; Marie O'Brien director, George
Theisen producer).

Quiatt, Duane
Department of Anthropology, Campus Box 105, University of Colorado Denver, 1100 14th Street, Denver, CO 80202. Home: 835 7th Street, Boulder,
CO 80302. *Phone:* (303) 556-2801; home (303) 443-3398. *Profession:*
Anthropologist, primatologist. *Interests:* Primate behavior studies, biological
anthropology, paleoanthropology, analysis of households as energy exchange
centers and corporate work units. *Work in progress:* Rhesus monkeys of
L-group, Cayo Santiago, Puerto Rico (videotape). Gibbons of Khao Yai
forest, central Thailand (videotape). *Geographic focus:* Caribbean, SE Asia,
Japan (non-human primate behavior only). *Languages:* German (pretty bad
reading, speaking, writing), French and Spanish (terrible reading, speaking,
writing).
    Visual productions: "Macaque Hands," 1984, 20 min. videotape, synopsis
in International Journal of Primatology 54:400. "Gorillas Mating in the
Denver Zoo," 12 min. videotape, synopsis in American Journal of Primatology 7, 1985. "Japanese Macaque Stone Handling," 10 min. videotape.

Quimby, George I.
Burke Museum DB-10, University of Washington, Seattle, WA 98195.
Phone: (206) 543-5590. *Profession:* Anthropology Professor Emeritus,
Museum Director Emeritus. *Interests:* Ethnographic filmmaking, teaching
with ethnographic film, manifest content of photographs, culture history,
cultural reconstruction, photo essays, ethnology, archaeology, museology.
Training: B.A., M.A. Anthropology, University of Michigan, 1936, 1937.
Graduate study of Anthropology, University of Michigan 1937-38 and
University of Chicago 1938-39. *Work in progress:* Research on Edward
Curtis. *Geographic focus:* North America. *Languages:* Spanish (reading).

Visual productions: "In the Land of the War Canoes," 1973 (producer with Bill Holm), 43 min. 16mm b/w film with sound track in Kwakiutl language, restoration of Edward Curtis' 1914 documentary film of Northwest Coast Indians, University of Washington Press, Seattle. "The Image Maker and the Indians," 1979 (producer with Bill Holm), 17 min. 16mm color film with sound track, Edward Curtis and his 1914 Kwakiutl movie—Curtis made the first documentary of Native North Americans in 1914.

Quintana, Bertha B.

Montclair State College, Department of Anthropology, Upper Montclair, NJ 07043. Home: 30 Clannon Road, Livingston, NJ 07039. *Phone:* (201) 893-4119; home (201) 992-0328. *Profession:* Anthropologist; Professor and Chair, Department of Anthropology. *Interests:* Still photography: photo interviewing, descriptive ethnography, life history, culture change. Audio tapes: oral literature. *Training:* Ed.D., M.A. New York University. B.A. Upsala College. *Work in progress:* Photographic life history "Soy Gitana" (depicting 30 years' of working with the same informant). *Geographic focus:* Southern Spain. *Languages:* Spanish.

Visual productions: "Gypsies of Southern Spain: Photographic Retrospective," 1980, exhibit of 150 photographs depicting continuity and change in Andalusian Gypsy culture from 1959-1979, presented at the Annual Meeting of the Gypsy Lore Society.

Quintanales, Mirtha N.

1002 Ditmas Avenue, Apt. 6H, Brooklyn, NY 11218. *Phone:* (718) 282-6945. *Profession:* Anthropologist, writer, bilingual editor, translator. *Affiliation:* Coordinator for Latin American and Caribbean Studies, Jersey City State College. *Interests:* Role of visual arts/media in intercultural communication, the arts/media in social movement's subcultures and in revolutionary contexts, women artists, the creative process and socio-cultural contexts. *Training:* Ph.D. Anthropology, Ohio State University, 1987. *Work in progress:* "The Role of Women Filmmakers in the New Latin American Cinema" (with Sonia Rivera), CUNY, York College: interviews and conversations with Latin American women filmmakers plus historical/analytical essays by the co-authors. *Geographic focus:* Latin America and the Caribbean, Latin American and Caribbean communities in U.S. *Languages:* Bilingual English/ Spanish; full reading/some fluency Portugese and French. *Other information:* Editor, literary magazine Conditions, NYC, 1981-1983. Founder and bibliographer, The Third World Women's Archives, NYC, 1981-1985 (multilingual, multi-media materials).

Rachlin, Carol K.

1836 NW 56th Street, Oklahoma City, OK 73118. *Phone:* (405) 843-1250. *Profession:* Writer, retired university teacher. *Interests:* Applied anthropology,

Oklahoma Indian tribes, ethnology. *Training:* Graduate studies in Anthropology, Columbia University. B.S. Columbia University, 1953. New York School of Photography, 1949. *Work in progress:* Great Lakes yarn bags and mats, a photo essay with text and diagrams (expanding study done in 1958). *Geographic focus:* N.E. United States, Oklahoma. *Technical expertise:* Still photography, applied anthropology/archaeology.

Visual productions: Photo essay about Great Lakes weaving, 1958, on deposit with American Museum of Natural History. Illustrations for Kiowa Anne, 1966, by Alice Marriott. Photo illustrations for books published with Alice Marriott, 1968.

Rasson, Judith A.

Department of Anthropology, Pacific Lutheran University, Tacoma, WA 98447. Home: 815 119th Street South, Tacoma, WA 98444. *Phone:* (206) 535-7739; department (206) 535-7298; home (206) 537-0443. *Profession:* Archaeologist, teacher of anthropology. *Interests:* Teaching anthropology through ethnographic film, teaching archaeology and archaeological methods through film. *Training:* Ph.D. Anthropology, specializing in archaeology. Graduate class in filmmaking with Mark McCarty and Paul Hockings. Research assistant/aide in making film "4-Butte-1: A Lesson in Archaeology." Design and teaching of undergraduate class Anthropology Through Film. *Work in progress:* Visual record (slides and video) of archaeological field project, to be used for a record of activities and as teaching materials. *Geographic focus:* North America, Southeast Europe (esp. Yugoslavia and Hungary). *Languages:* Serbo-Croatian (fluent speaking, reading), French (fair speaking, reading), German (poor speaking, reading), Hungarian (nodding acquaintance). *Technical expertise:* Still photography (largely self-taught) as recording device for archaeological projects and ethnic manifestations in the U.S.

Remmers, Kurt W.

P.O. Box 361, Madison, NJ 07940. Office: Media Resource Center, Drew University, Madison, NJ 07940. *Phone:* (201) 377-2341. *Profession:* Director of media resource center, videographer. *Interests:* Archaeological expedition videographer. *Training:* 20 years' experience in academia directing university media center, President PHOKUS, Inc, a video consulting firm. *Work in progress:* "Caesarea Maritima: The Search for Herod's Lost City," a 58 min. video documentary—the Joint Expedition to Caesarea (Israel) headed by Dr. Bull, Drew University. Sister cities video project about Masaya in Nicaragua. *Geographic focus:* Israel, Nicaragua.

Richardson, Miles

Department of Geography and Anthropology, Louisiana State University, Baton Rouge, LA 70803. *Phone:* (504) 388-6192; department (504) 388-5942. *Profession:* Cultural anthropologist. *Interests:* How people use material culture to construct social reality. How culture is made visual. How culture comes to be in its places. *Training:* Ph.D. Anthropology, Tulane University, 1965. *Work in progress:* "In Place and Out: Christ and the Social Construction of Death in Spanish America and the American South," on the role of the material setting of the church structure in the construction of the image of Christ in the two cultures. *Geographic focus:* Spanish America, American South. *Languages:* Spanish (r,w,s), German and French (reading).

Roberts, Allen F.
Department of Anthropology, University of Iowa, Iowa City, IA 52242. *Profession:* Socio-cultural anthropologist. *Interests:* Symbolic anthropology, anthropology of art, representation, political economy, applied anthropology, museums (esp. in Africa), natural resource management. *Work in progress:* Further work through the African National Museums Program I co-founded (with art historian Mary Kujawski), follow-up of collaboration with the staffs of the national museums of Mali, Benin, and Gabon on research, conservation, and museum education. Social Change and Identity: "Reinventing" the Tabwa (book). *Geographic focus:* Zaïre (Tabwa people and others of southeastern Zaïre, northeastern Zambia, and west-central Tanzania who are culturally and historically related to them), Benin (museum research and education, iron production in precolonial Atakora), Mali (Dogon revisited, as a museum research program). *Languages:* French, excellent r,w,s (FSI 4-4+), Swahili, excellent r,w,s (FSI 3+-4). *Additional expertise:* Extensive research in applied anthropology (e.g. principal investigator for 6-year grant with NASA on solar-energy applications in developing countries, 1981–6): training, social impact assessment, technology transfer.

Roberts, John M.
122 Kent Drive, Pittsburgh, PA 15241. Department of Anthropology, University of Pittsburgh, Pittsburgh, PA 15260. *Phone:* (412) 833-7467; office (412) 648-8846; department (412) 648-7510. *Profession:* Anthropologist, Andrew W. Mellon Professor of Anthropology Emeritus, University of Pittsburgh. *Interests:* Specialist in the study of expressive culture. I am not really a specialist in visual anthropology, I am however, interested in the subject. *Training:* Ph.D. Anthropology, Yale University 1947. *Geographic focus:* North America.

Rohrl, Vivian J.
Department of Anthropology, San Diego State University, San Diego, CA 92182. Home: 5756 Tulane Street, San Diego, CA 92199. *Phone:* (619) 265-6289; department (619) 265-5527; home (619) 453-1392. *Profession:* Professor of Anthropology. *Interests:* Teaching with ethnographic film and also a course that includes teaching with feature film.

Rollwagen, Jack R.
Department of Anthropology, SUNY College at Brockport, Brockport, NY 14420. *Phone:* (716) 395-2682. *Profession:* Anthropologist. *Interests:* Anthropological filmmaking and video taping, teaching anthropological film, teaching anthropological filmmaking, teaching with anthropological and documentary film. *Training:* Ph.D. Anthropology, University of Oregon, 1968. M.A. in the Humanities (focus on documentary filmmaking), 1979. *Work in progress:* I am working on the production of a number of 3/4" videotapes on Puerto Ricans in the Northeastern United States. The first of these is "Puerto Rican Spiritism." Others should follow as time and funds allow. I am also producing a set of videos on China, the first to be titled "Elizabeth Croll: An Interview." Also working on a manuscript about the theory of anthropological film "clusters." *Geographic focus:* Latin America, Puerto Ricans in the U.S. Northeast, World system (non-geographically limited). *Languages:* Spanish (conversational). *Technical expertise:* Desktop publishing and integration with commercial publishing, film production and video production.

Rosenfeld, Gerry
SUNY, Anthropology Department, 479 Spalding, Building 4, Buffalo, NY 14261. Home: 239 Ranch Trail, Williamsville, NY 14201. *Phone:* (716) 636-2414; home (716) 688-5119. *Profession:* Professor of Anthropology. *Interests:* Regular course offering: Anthropology and Film. Planning stages: Film Studies of Person; Film Studies of Disabled Persons. *Training:* Ed.D. Anthropology and Education, 1968, Columbia University Teachers College. *Other information:* I have taught at all levels—elementary school to university—for 30 years; and I have taught in Nigeria, Botswana, China, and Malaysia.

Rubel, Paula
Department of Anthropology, Barnard College, New York, NY 10027. 560 Riverside Drive, Apt. 18P, New York, NY 10027. *Phone:* (212) 280-4316; department (212) 280-4314; home (212) 663-3694. *Profession:* Professor of Anthropology. *Interests:* Teach course on Anthropology and Film. Use ethnographic films in teaching Introduction to Cultural Anthropology. *Geographic focus:* North America, Oceania. *Languages:* French, German (reading).

Ruby, Jay
Center for Visual Communication, P.O. Box 128, Mifflintown, PA 17059. *Phone:* (717) 436-9502. *Profession:* Anthropologist. *Affiliation:* Temple University. *Interests:* The anthropology of visual communication. Ethnographic study of photography, film, television, painting, etc. Anthropological film, television, and photography. *Training:* B.A. History, UCLA, 1960. M.A. Anthropology, UCLA, 1962. Ph.D. Anthropology, UCLA, 1969.

Work in progress: A biography of Francis Cooper, Juniata County, PA photographer. A history of photography and film as viewed from a rural community. A history of death and photography in America. *Geographic focus:* United States. *Languages:* French, German. *Technical expertise:* Modest skills as photographer.

Visual productions: "A Country Auction," 1984 (executive producer, co-producer, director, writer, and researcher), 58 min. 16mm.

Rynearson, Ann
3800 Park, St. Louis, MO 63110. Home: 273 Greenbriar, St. Louis, MO 63122. *Phone:* (314) 773-9090; home (314) 965-1988. *Profession:* Cultural anthropology and ESL. *Affiliation:* International Institute, St. Louis, MO. *Interests:* Ethnographic film/video making. Use of home-made videos as research tool (many of my informants are making videos of their own). *Training:* Ph.D. Cultural Anthropology, Washington University. *Geographic focus:* Lao refugees in the United States. *Languages:* French, Spanish, Laotian.

Visual productions: "Silk Sarongs and City Streets—Traditional Music and Dance for Lao Refugees."

Safizadeh, Fereydoun
1303 Walnut Street, Berkeley, CA 94709. Office: Department of Anthropology, San Francisco State University, 1600 Holloway Avenue, San Francisco, CA 94132. *Phone:* (415) 848-3381; department (415) 469-2046. *Profession:* Assistant Professor. *Interests:* Theory and method, economic/development anthropology, peasant society, ethnographic filmmaking, teaching with ethnographic film. *Training:* Ph.D. Anthropology and Middle Eastern Studies, Harvard, 1986. One year graduate work in ethnographic filmmaking, Harvard University, 1972-73. *Geographic focus:* Peoples and cultures of the Middle East. *Languages:* Persian (r,w,s), Arabic (reading), Azeri Turkish (r,w,s), French (r,w,s). *Additional expertise:* Computers, statistical analysis: SAS, SPSS, SYSTAT.

Sair, Dana Rae
#209 – 1345 West 15th Avenue, Vancouver, British Columbia, Canada V6H 3R3. 275 South 4th Street #3R, Phiadelphia, PA 19106. *Phone:* (604) 738-8119; (215) 238-9257. *Interests:* Ethnographic and documentary film production. Popular culture, material culture, semiotics, complex societies, symbolic anthropology. *Training:* M.A. Visual Anthropology, Temple University. Anthropology Film Center, Santa Fe, New Mexico, 1986. B.A. Anthropology, University of British Columbia, 1983. *Geographic focus:* Native peoples of North America, particularly North West Coast. *Languages:* French (reading, writing, basic conversation). *Technical expertise:* 16mm film production. Strong emphasis and training on sound recording, esp. with Nagra

recording equipment. *Other information:* Related work experience: 1982-1984, British Columbia Association of Indian Friendship Centres (BCAIFC).

Saltman, Carlyn
Pixies Holt, Cherry Drive, Forty Green, Beaconsfield, Box HP9 1XP England. *Phone:* 04-946-71593. *Profession:* Producer of films, videotapes, slide-tape programs. *Interests:* Ethnographic filmmaking for teaching and research; anti-racism programs; development education programs; recording changing and disappearing metal technologies—especially iron smelting; recording dance, music, and ritual. *Training:* Anthropological Film Seminar with J. Rouch, Harvard Summer School, 1984. B.A. African History, Mt. Holyoke College, 1980. *Work in progress:* Documentary with young people in Ouagadougo, Burkina Faso. *Geographic focus:* African arts and technology, development issues in Africa. *Languages:* German and Spanish (intermediate speaking and writing), French (currently engaged in intensive training). *Technical expertise:* Ability to produce professional quality videos by shooting with a very small budget on super-8 film. I own the necessary equipment.
   Visual productions: "Danced Faiths: Bamiléké Funeral Rites," 1984 (producer). "Lost-Wax Casting in Cameroon," 1984 (producer). "We're on the Way!," Partnership for Productivity International, 1985 (producer). "Harvest of Dreams," 1986 (camera person, promotion/information), video for the Seventh Generation Fund, a non-profit Native American funding organization. "The Blooms of Banjeli: Technology and Gender in African Ironmaking," 1986 (producer, editor, camera), distributed by DER with study guide.

Sank, Diane
Department of Anthropology, CUNY, City College, Convent and West 138 Street, New York, NY 10031. Home: 173 Charlotte Place, Englewood Cliffs, NJ 07632. *Phone:* (212) 690-6609; department (212) 690–6608; home (201) 569-7297. *Profession:* Anthropology. *Interests:* Social behavior of primates (esp. Great Apes). Adaptation of primates to captivity. *Work in progress:* Preparation of videotape of primate behavior. *Geographic focus:* U.S.

Scheder, Jo
Department of Nursing, University of Hawaii, Webster Hall, Honolulu, HI 96822. P.O. Box 61215, Honolulu, HI 96822. *Phone:* (808) 948-6264. *Profession:* Independent producer, Assistant Professor. *Interests:* Human services television, ethnographic video, community programming. *Training:* Ph.D. Biocultural Anthropology, University of Wisconsin, Madison, 1981. *Work in progress:* Continued video work with Southeast Asian refugees. *Geographic focus:* Migrant farmworkers, Texas-Mexico border; Samoa; Hawaii. *Languages:* Spanish (fluent), Samoan (intermediate), Laotian (elementary). *Technical expertise:* Photography, video camera, producing, writing, directing for documentaries and community programming; theatrical

lighting design. *Other information:* Director for monthly 'live' program on cable television, "Honolulu Peace Talks." Member of steering committee for Human Services Television Network in Honolulu.

Visual productions: "No Place Like Home," a 30 min. video on Lao and Vietnamese refugees in Hawaii, with accompanying article in Humanities News, 1985. "Powwow: A Gathering in the Islands," a 50 min. video on American Indians in Hawaii, 1985.

Scheerer, Laura L.
Center for Visual Anthropology, University of Southern California, University Park, Los Angeles, CA 90089-0661. *Phone:* (213) 743-7100; home (213) 227-4872. *Profession:* Ethnographic filmmaker, cinematographer. *Interests:* Ethnographic filmmaking, teaching with ethnographic film, film and video as a research tool. *Training:* M.A. Visual Anthropology, University of Southern California, 1987. B.A. Cultural Anthropology, University of Arizona, Tucson, 1982. *Work in progress:* "Horses of Life and Death" (director; in collaboration with anthropologist Janet A. Hoskin), 16mm color film about the symbolic role of the horse in West Sumba, Indonesia. *Geographic focus:* Eastern Indonesia. *Languages:* Indonesian (speaking level). *Technical expertise:* Sound recordist and editing for film or video. *Other information:* Specialize in filming in rugged, remote field settings with lightweight equipment and small crews.

Visual productions: "No Place Like Home: A Story of Three Births," 1982 (director, camera, editor), 30 min. color 3/4" video. "Addressless," 1986, 23 min. color 16mm documentary film about a community of vehicle dwellers in Venice, CA, available through the Center for Visual Anthropology, USC. "The Heavenly Voice of China," 1987, color 3/4" video, a USC M.A. thesis film about a Peking opera club in Los Angeles. "The Feast in Dream Village," 1988 (in collaboration with Janet A. Hoskins), 27 min. color 16mm film about a ceremonial feast of exchange in West Sumba, Indonesia.

Scherer, Joanna Cohan
Handbook of North American Indians Project, Smithsonian Institution, Washington, DC 20560. Home: 13505 Collingwood Terrace, Silver Spring, MD 20904. *Phone:* office (202) 357-1861. *Profession:* Anthropologist. *Interests:* Still photographs as historical documents in analysis of culture change and stereotyping, photographic archiving. *Training:* M.A. Anthropology, Hunter College of the City University of New York, 1968. B.A. Anthropology, Syracuse University, 1963. *Work in progress:* Life Among the Indians: Camping with the Sioux and Omaha, 1881-1882, by Alice C. Fletcher (editor and author of Introduction). Compilation of repository sources of historical photographs of Great Basin Indians, with introductory article on Benedicte Wrensted, 19th century woman photographer of Northern Shoshone and Bannocks. *Geographic focus:* North American Indians and Eskimos.

Schmidt, Judith
151 Old Church Road, Greenwich, CT 06830. *Phone:* (203) 869-7862.
Profession: Visual ethnobotanist. *Affiliation:* New York Botanical Garden.
Interests: Slide shows as a means of sharing research data with the general
public. Current concentration is on the uses of wild plants for food, technology, and ceremony by the "Woodland Indians" of the Northeast. *Training:*
Ph.D. Union Graduate School, Cincinnati, 1983, (a University without walls
with an individual study program). *Work in progress:* Visually oriented chart
of plant uses by the N.E. Woodland Indians. Chapter on visual ethnobotany
for publication by Harvard University. Chapter on technology of the N.E.
Woodland Indians (with photographs) for publication of the New York
Botanical Garden. *Geographic focus:* New England through Midwest, and
Southeastern Canada. *Languages:* Spanish and French (rusty). *Technical
expertise:* Programming slide shows with 4 projectors and programmer.
 Visual productions: Slide shows: "Respect for Life," "I Was the Guest of
India," "Wild Dyes of the Outer Hebrides." Posters: "Ash Splint and Sweet-
grass Basketmaking," "Birch Bark Technology."

Schmidt, Nancy J.
African Studies Program, 221 Woodburn Hall, Indiana University, Bloomington, IN 47405. *Phone:* (812) 855-1481. *Profession:* Anthropologist. *Interests:*
Teaching with ethnographic film, ethnographic fiction film, film criticism,
film perception and communication, film narrative. *Training:* Ph.D. Anthropology, Northwestern University, 1965. *Work in progress:* African literature
on film, the cultural context of African filmmaking. *Geographic focus:*
Subsaharan Africa. *Languages:* French, Portuguese, German (reading). *Other
information:* Assisted in developing teaching materials for Faces of Change
series and co-taught a NSF Chatauqua course, Visual Evidence and Women's
Roles (with Norma Miller), 1976-77, based on this series.
 Visual productions: Developed over 20 slide sets on Africa for precol-
legiate courses and film guides for more than a dozen ethnographic and African
films.

Schwartz, Dona
1420 Raymond Avenue, St. Paul, MN 55108. Office: 111 Murphy Hall, 206
Church Street SE, Minneapolis, MN 55455. *Phone:* (612) 644-8177; office
(612) 625-9824; (612) 625-5088. *Profession:* Professor. *Interests:*
Ethnographic semiotics, media studies, ethnographic photography, analysis of
visual symbolic forms, social organization of visual media production and
reception, visual communication. *Training:* Ph.D. Annenberg School of
Communications, University of Pennsylvania. Training in photography at
Parsons School of Design, New School for Social Research, and University of
Pennsylvania. Training in filmmaking at University of Pennsylvania with
Sol Worth. *Work in progress:* The Waucoma project is an ethnography of a

rural farm community in Northeastern Iowa. Photographs were made and presented to multiple generations within five farm families in order to elicit data on sociocultural community change. The finished work will be published by Smithsonian Institution Press and will combine approximately 200 black and white photographs with analytic text.

Visual productions: "Film in the Cities," 1987, exhibition of photographs from the Waucoma ethnography project, St. Paul, MN, May 22-June 21.

Seaman, Gary

Department of Anthropology, University of Southern California, Los Angeles CA 90089-0661. *Phone:* (213) 743-7100. *Profession:* Anthropologist. *Affiliation:* Center for Visual Anthropology, USC. *Interests:* Ethnographic film, ethnographic film archives, ethnographic film and interactive video. *Work in progress:* "Pilgrimage of the Dark Emperor," a film. A companion ethnography to the film "Chinese Shamanism." *Geographic focus:* China, Japan, Asia. *Languages:* Chinese (reading), Taiwanese (speaking), Japanese (reading, speaking), German (r,w,s), Dutch (reading), French (reading).

Visual productions: Films: "Chinese Cult of the Dead," "Chinese Shamanism," "Chinese Geomancy: Feng-shui," "The Rite of Cosmic Renewal." "Journey to the West: Chinese Funeral Dramas."

See, Richard

Department of Anthropology, California State University, Fullerton, CA 92634. *Phone:* (714) 773-3626. *Profession:* Anthropologist. *Affiliation:* California State University, Fullerton. *Interests:* Ethnographic video, teaching with video and films, still photography (for research and teaching), mythological function of ethnographic films in Western culture. *Training:* Ph.D. Anthropology, UCLA, 1965. *Geographic focus:* United States, Asia, Pacific. *Languages:* French.

Seremetakis, Nadia

300 Mercer Street #14A, New York, NY 10003. Department of Anthropology, New York University, 25 Waverly Place, New York, NY 10003. *Phone:* (212) 533-2297; department (212) 998-8550. *Profession:* Anthropology teaching and research. *Interests:* Critical evaluation of visual presentation of cultures in the media and in anthropological discourse. Cognitive mapping of ritual performance. Exploration of the relation between still photography and fieldwork (i.e. the photograph as unit of ethnographic data). Visual presentation of the anthropologist's self in fieldwork process. Modes of interpretation and description. Teaching with ethnographic film. Ethnographic filmmaking. *Training:* Ph.D. Anthropology, New School for Social Research, 1987. M.A. Anthropology, New School for Social Research. M.A. Sociology, New York University. Woodrow Wilson Fellowship 1985-86. Wenner-Gren Grant-in-Aid 1986. *Work in progress:* Death rituals in Inner Mani: by com-

bining participant observation of mortuary performances and historical research, I intend to produce an ethnographic social history of Maniot mourning rituals. Among the methodologies employed for the analysis of ritual performance will be still photography and cognitive mappings of formal and informal spatial organization of the ritual based on drawings by participants. *Geographic focus:* Greece and the Mediterranean, the North Atlantic fringe. *Languages:* Greek (native speaker), Spanish and French (very good reading and writing, good speaking). *Technical expertise:* Photography.

Seubert, Emelia A.

P.O. Box 728, Times Square Station, New York, NY 10108. Office: Film and Video Center, Museum of the American Indian, Broadway at 155th Street, New York, NY 10032. *Phone:* (212) 283-2420. *Profession:* Assistant Curator. *Interests:* Archaeology and ethnohistory of pre-contact and early contact era Native people of the lower Hudson Valley. Specialization: Use of film and video by and about Native Americans of North, Central, and South America; information about Native American media production. *Training:* Master's candidate, Anthropology, Hunter College, CUNY.

Sever, Irene

The Library, Laboratory for Children's Librarianship, Haifa University, Haifa 39111, Israel. Home: Bizeum Street 3, Apt 25, Haifa 34986, Israel. *Phone:* (04) 246650. *Profession:* Library science and anthropology. *Affiliation:* SfAA, AAA. *Interests:* Use of videotape to investigate the behavior of young children in a library setting in order to learn about the needs of children and their own attitudes about reading. Use of films and other visual material in teaching social science and library subjects to graduate students. *Training:* Ph.D. Sorbonne, cross-cultural study on children's verbal arguments and argumentation. *Geographic focus:* Israel.

Sherman, Sharon R.

Folklore & Ethnic Studies, University of Oregon, Eugene, OR 97403. Home: 1442 West 11th Avenue, Eugene, OR 97402. *Phone:* office (503) 686-3966; Folklore office (503) 686-3539; English department (503) 686-3911; home (503) 343-7168. *Profession:* Professor (Folklore), independent filmmaker/videographer. *Interests:* Documentary filmmaking (especially folklore films); research on history, use and production of film for folklorists and other documentary filmmakers; teach courses on film and folklore and on fieldwork methods, emphasizing use of film and video production and documentation. Folklore and performance. Theoretical approaches manifested by filmmakers. *Training:* Ph.D. Folklore, double minor in Instructional Systems Technology, Indiana University, 1977. M.A. Folklore and Mythology, training in Ethnographic Film Program and numerous film production courses, UCLA, 1971. B.Phil. Social Science and Latin, Wayne State University,

1965. *Work in progress:* "Filming People in Action: Lessons for Documentary Filmmakers and Film Users" (book, University of Illinois Press). "Wood Magic: Oregon Sculptor Skip Armstrong" (video project). *Geographic focus:* North America, esp. United States and Canada, currently Oregon and Pacific Northwest. *Languages:* Latin (reading), German (reading, some speaking), Spanish (reading and very basic speaking). *Technical expertise:* Camera, sound, editing, negative cutting, directing, etc.

Visual productions: "Tales of the Supernatural," 1970, 29 min. b/w 16mm. "Kathleen Ware, Quiltmaker," 1979, 33 min. color 16mm. "Passover: A Celebration," 1983, 28 min. b/w 3/4" video.

Silverman, Carol

Department of Anthropology, University of Oregon, Eugene, OR 97403. Home: 3150 Portland Street, Eugene, OR 97405. *Phone:* (503) 686-5114; department (503) 686-5102; home (503) 344-4519. *Profession:* Assistant Professor of Anthropology and Folklore. *Interests:* Films on women by women. Teaching with ethnographic film. Ethnographic film criticism and theory, especially reflexivity. *Training:* Ph.D. Folklore, University of Pennsylvania, 1979. *Work in progress:* Super-8 sound footage of musical events in Bulgarian villages (shot 1980). *Geographic focus:* Balkans and Eastern Europe, Gypsies. *Languages:* Bulgarian (read, write, and speak well). *Additional expertise:* Performer of Balkan singing.

Simic, Andrei

Department of Anthropology, University of Southern California, Los Angeles CA 90089-0661. Home: 6231 Chabot Road, Oakland, CA 94618. *Phone:* (213) 743-7100; home (415) 653-0727. *Profession:* Associate Professor of Anthropology. *Interests:* Ethnographic filmmaking, teaching of social anthropology through film, participation in graduate program in ethnographic filmmaking, Center for Visual Anthropology, USC. *Training:* Ph.D. Anthropology, University of California at Berkeley, 1979. *Work in progress:* (With Joel M. Halpern, University of Washington) production of a film on 40 years of social and cultural change in the Yugoslavian village of Orasac—to be edited with Tim and Patsy Asch). *Geographic focus:* Balkans, Latin America, ethnic groups in United States. *Languages:* Serbo-Croatian (native fluency), Spanish (fluent), Russian, French, Italian (fluent reading, fair speaking).

Visual productions: 60 min. ethnographic film on the role of expressive culture among Serbian-Americans (with Les Blank) financed by NEH, NEA, and Institute for Applied Anthropology, USC.

Simon, Chris

10341 San Pablo Avenue, El Cerrito, CA 94530. *Phone:* (415) 525-0942; home (415) 644-8323. *Profession:* Filmmaker, photographer, and folklorist. *Interests:* Photography, concentrating on folkloric events in a very broad sense. Filmmaking, ethnographic in subject matter but made for a general audience. *Training:* M.A. Folklore and Mythology, University of California, Los Angeles, 1980. B.A. Anthropology, University of California, Berkeley, 1978. *Work in progress:* Photo essays: "Music and Dance in Cuba," "Portuguese Féstas in the Central Valley," "Everyday Housewife," the lives of four housewives. "Gap-Toothed Women" (associate producer, sound; director Les Blank). "Cajun Music" (2nd camera, sound, associate producer; director Les Blank, producer Chris Strachwitz), Brazos Films. *Geographic focus:* U.S. folk culture, but I am interested in working overseas. *Languages:* Spanish (intermediate), French (reading ability). *Technical expertise:* Know all aspects of 16mm filmmaking (camera, sound, lighting, production, management, editing, fundraising), still photography, including printing b/w and color. *Other information:* My personal interest is in photography. I would like to collaborate with anthropologists and folklorists to create visual documents reflecting their research interests.

Visual productions: "Carnaval in Cuba," slide presentation. "Polka Land," photo essay on Polish-American Polka dancing. "In Heaven There Is No Beer?" (interviewer and folklorist; director, producer Les Blank). "Ziveli: Medicine for the Heart" (2nd camera, folklorist; director Les Blank). "Anthropologist Andrei Simic," produced USC. "Sprout Wings and Fly" (assistant editor). "Burden of Dreams" (production manager, assistant editor, researcher; director Les Blank).

Simons, Ronald C.
Department of Psychiatry, Michigan State University, East Lansing, MI 48824. Home: 1627 Barry Road, Williamstown, MI 48895. *Phone:* (517) 355-8416; home (517) 655-2298. *Profession:* Psychiatrist, anthropologist. *Interests:* Visual approaches to ethology (human), interactional analysis, teaching with film/video. *Training:* M.D. Washington University, St. Louis, 1960. M.A. Anthropology, University of California at Berkeley, 1975. A.B. Psychology, University of Rochester, 1956. *Work in progress:* Film and video analysis of interviews. Film and video analysis of cultural elaborations of hyperstartling. *Geographic focus:* Southeast Asia. *Languages:* Malay/Indonesian (moderate fluency in reading and speaking).

Visual productions: Two 16mm color sound films, distributed by Indiana University Audio Visual Center: "Floating in the Air, Followed by the Wind: Thaipusam, A Hindu Festival," 1973 (producer, director, ethnographer; filmmaker Gunter Pfaff), 34 min., Health Sciences Communications Association and Network for Continuing Medical Education cash prize and Award of Merit for "outstanding achievement in the use of film for education in the health sciences," and "Latah: A Culture-Specific Elaboration of the Startle Reflex," 1983 (producer, director, ethnographer; filmmaker Gunter Pfaff). These films selected for the Margaret Mead Film Festival, 1983 and 1985, respectively.

Sims, Richard
Executive Director, Santa Ynez Valley Historical Society, 1624 Elverhoy, Solvang, CA 93463. *Phone:* (805) 688-7889. *Profession:* Anthropology, history, filmmaking. *Interests:* Filmmaking and videomaking related to the Southwest and its native, natural, and modern history. Exhibit design. *Training:* M.A. English, Northern Arizona University. B.A. Anthropology, University of Oregon. *Work in progress:* "Young Hopi," "Archaeology of Northern Arizona," "Paleontologists at Work," "White Mind, Native Mind: Art versus Craft" (all videotapes). *Geographic focus:* The Colorado Plateau and the general Southwest region. *Languages:* Spanish (r,w,s). *Additional expertise:* Scriptwriting, editing. *Other information:* Copy editor for several research papers, including "Navajo Weaving, Art in Its Cultural Context," by Gary Witherspoon (a semiotical study of Navajo symbols used in weaving. Flagstaff: Museum of Northern Arizona Research Paper 36.) Formerly member of a video team at the Museum of Northern Arizona, helping inaugurate a new era of museum interpretation, research, publications, and exhibits.

Visual productions: "The Children of Changing Woman," videotape, (with Peter Blystone: assisted writer, producer, director David Baxter). "Young Navajo" (co-producer, with Peter Blystone), videotape.

Singer, Philip
School of Health Sciences, Oakland University, Rochester, MI 48063. Office: Traditional Healing Films, 52370 DeQuindre, Rochester, MI 48063. *Phone:* (313) 693-9447; office (313) 731-5199; (313) 370-2456. *Profession:* Medical anthropologist. *Interests:* Ethnographic filmmaking, teaching with ethnographic film. *Training:* Ph.D. Anthropology, Syracuse. *Work in progress:* Traditional medicine in China, ethnographic medical research in Italy. *Geographic focus:* Global (including Africa, India, China, Europe, Philippines, Guiana). *Languages:* French, Italian (good r,w,s); Russian, German (some knowledge).

Skylar, Deidre
HCR 63, Box 22, Blue Hill Falls, ME 04615. *Phone:* (207) 374-5507. *Profession:* Teaching/writing in performance studies, theatre director, actors training. *Affiliation:* NYU, Department of Performance Studies. *Interests:* Ritual performance in cultural context, including dance as communication, movement analysis, experiential and symbolic approaches, issues of subjectivity, objectivity, empathy as research tool, comparative studies, and dance as alteration of consciousness and experience of religious reality. Photo and video archiving. Use of technology (computer, video) in disseminating information on cultural performance. Video documentation. Bridging anthropology and theatre, using performance as teaching tool, approaching human behavior through performance. *Training:* Ph.D. NYU, Department of Performance Studies (to be completed in 1989). Photo archiving, Museum of the American Indian, 1985–86. M.A. Dance Ethnology, University of California, Los

Angeles, 1983. Ecole de Mime d'Etienne Decroux, 1967–68. B.A. Drama, Antioch College, Ohio, 1966. *Work in progress:* Ph.D. dissertation: "Tiguas and Danzantes: Dances of the Catholic Indians of Tortugas." Slide/video documentation of Tortugas dances. *Geographic focus:* Southwest, Pueblo Indian, Hispanic/Indian syncretism. Secondary: Asia, esp. India. *Languages:* French (r,w,s), learning to speak Spanish. *Technical expertise:* Video portopak, still camera, Labanotation. *Other information:* "Tigua Dance: The Changing Meaning of Symbols," 1987, American Folklore Society meetings, Albuquerque.

Slyomovics, Susan
711 West 171st Street, Apt. 56, New York, NY 10032. Office: City Lore: The New York Center for Urban Folk Culture, 72 East First Street, New York, NY 10003. *Phone:* (212) 795-7506; (212) 529-1955. *Profession:* Folklorist-in-Residence. *Interests:* Ethnographic filmmaking, teaching with ethnographic film. *Training:* Ph.D. Department of Near Eastern Studies and Program in Folklife, University of California at Berkeley. *Work in progress:* "Mehendi," on Indian women immigrants in Queens, New York and the prenuptial ritual of decorating women's hands and feet. *Geographic focus:* New York City, Middle East, and North Africa. *Languages:* French, Arabic, and Hebrew (fluent); Spanish, Persian, and Yiddish (medium speaking and reading). *Technical expertise:* Video editing. *Other information:* Program planner for annual City Lore film and video festival. Consultant for film and video programs for festivals, museums, events, etc.

Visual productions: "City Lore Festival," 10 min. video on folk music in the NYC Central Park. "The Merchant of Art," 23 min. video on a performance of an Egyptian folk epic poet.

Spiegel, Pauline
Last available address: Mirro Productions, 335 Greenwich Street, #7B, New York, NY 10013. *Profession:* Film/video producer. *Interests:* Ethnographic filmmaking, videomaking, writing, editing. *Training:* M.A. Anthropology, Boston University. M.F.A. Film Production, New York University. *Work in progress:* "If the Shoe Fits," videotape about women's shoes. "Whose Vision Is This Anyway?," photographers vs. director in "The Plow that Broke the Plains." *Geographic focus:* U.S. *Languages:* French (read and speak excellently, write barely). *Technical expertise:* All film and video crafts.

Visual productions: 16mm film: "The Gold Pit," 23 min., on the New York Commodity Exchange. 1", 3/4", and 1/2" videotape: "The Challenge of Aging: Jewish Ethnicity in Later Life," 30 min.; and "Pen-Ruling: A Vanishing Industrial Craft," 15 min.

Staples, Amy J.
4605 Springfield Avenue #1R, Philadelphia, PA 19143. *Phone:* (215) 222-3278. *Affiliation:* AAA, SVA, Association of Independent Film and Video.

Interests: Mass media studies, ethnomusicology, popular culture studies, public access television, linguistics/semiotics. *Training:* Graduate student, Temple University M.V.A. program. Documentary Film program, Anthropological Film Center, Santa Fe, 1986. Video workshop, Albuquerque, June, 1984. B.A. Anthropology, University of New Mexico, 1980. *Work in progress:* "Tourism in Spain," paper. "The Making of a Bartender," video. *Geographic focus:* U.S. popular culture, Africa (North and West), Latin America. *Languages:* Spanish (fluent reading and writing, intermediate speaking). *Technical expertise:* Video and film skills (camera, sound, editing).

Visual productions: "Tools and Weapons," video short, Deep Dish TV, New York.

Stearns, Robert David

P.O. Box 1060, Gallup, NM 87305. *Phone:* (505) 863-9501, ext 497. *Profession:* Education specialist, Office of Indian Education Programs, Bureau of Indian Affairs. *Interests:* Ethnographic video, directed ethnography and the classroom teacher, ethnographic filmmaking. *Training:* Ph.D. Anthropology and Education, Stanford University, 1983. *Work in progress:* Interactive computer technology in Bureau of Indian Affairs Schools. *Geographic focus:* Alaskan Native villages, Southwest Reservations, Yucatan. *Languages:* Yucatec Maya, Spanish, Russian, Swedish. *Technical expertise:* Video, filmmaking, programmed multimedia, architecture, computer programming and word processing. *Other information:* Alaskan Native (Aleut).

Steele, David J.

Department of Medicine, University of Wisconsin Medical School, Milwaukee Clinical Campus, Mount Sinai Medical Center, P.O. Box 342, Milwaukee, WI 53201. Home: 2431 North 85th Street, Wauwatosa, WI 53226. *Phone:* (414) 289-8159; home (414) 453-3285. *Profession:* Medical anthropologist, Assistant Professor of Medicine and Psychiatry. *Interests:* Ethnography of communication, conversational analysis, video ethnography, medical and psychiatric anthropology, clinician-patient interaction, clinical reasoning, applied visual anthropology, communication skills training and development. *Training:* Ph.D. Sociocultural Anthropology, University of Wisconsin, Madison. Post-Doctoral Fellow, Health Psychology and Behavioral Medicine, University of Wisconsin, Madison. Faculty Development Workshop on Medical Interviewing, Brown University (SREPCIM). *Work in progress:* Research on communication in clinical settings. Also, in collaboration with a medical colleague, I am currently developing a comprehensive video-based curriculum on the medical interview, for residents in general internal medicine, sponsored by a 3 year grant from the James Picker Foundation. *Geographic focus:* Contemporary U.S. society and culture, clinical settings. *Other information:* Coordinator of the communication skills component for residency training programs in general internal medicine and psychiatry.

Stevens, Pierre Malcolm (Trap)

National Film, Television and Sound Archives, Public Archives of Canada, Ottawa, Ontario, K1A 0N3 Canada. Home: 42 Robert Street, Ottawa, Ontario, K2P 1E9 Canada. *Phone:* (613) 996-7116; home (613) 232-2016. *Profession:* Archivist, producer. *Interests:* Film, television, and sound archiving. Primitive, traditional, and urban societies. Historic past, ethnographic present, contemporary. Research and appraisal. *Other information:* Worked on or produced approximately 130 films.

Stone, Rebecca R.

1970 Palifox Drive NE, Atlanta, GA 30307. *Phone:* (404) 373-6781. *Profession:* Historian of art. *Affiliation:* Emory University. *Training:* Ph.D. Yale University. *Interests:* Visual perception, forms in works of art and artifacts, color patterning, symmetry, reconstructing cognitive patterns from design choices, textiles (Pre-Columbian, African), aesthetics. *Other information:* "Color Patterning and the Huari Artist: The 'Lima Tapestry' Revisited" (paper). Second Junius B. Bird Textile Conference Proceedings, 1985.

Stull, Donald D.

Institute for Public Policy and Business Research, 607 Blake Hall, University of Kansas, Lawrence, KS 66045. Department of Anthropology, University of Kansas, Lawrence, KS 66045. *Phone:* (913) 864-3701; department (913) 864-4103; home (913) 842-8055. *Profession:* Anthropologist. *Interests:* Ethnographic film/videomaking. Teaching with ethnographic film/video. *Training:* M.P.H., University of California at Berkeley. Ph.D. Anthropology, University of Colorado, 1973. M.A. Anthropology, University of Colorado, 1970. B.A. Anthropology, University of Kentucky, 1968. *Geographic focus:* North American Indians, esp. contemporary Indian affairs and policy.

Visual productions: Producer, script co-author, primary field interviewer for "Neshnabek: The People," 1979, 30 min. 16mm b/w, sound, 28 page discussion leader's guide; and two color 3/4" videos: "Return to Sovereignty: Self Determination and the Kansan Kickapoo," 1982, 46 min.; "Another Wind is Moving: The Off-Reservation Indian Boarding School," 1985, 59 min.

Tapp, N.C.T.

Department of Anthropology, Chinese University of Hong Kong, Shatin, New Territories, Hong Kong. *Phone:* 0 6952592. *Profession:* Anthropologist. *Interests:* Teaching with ethnographic film. Video training (courses for students). The semiotic production of ethnic minority cultural communication systems as performance in China. *Training:* Ph.D. Social Anthropology, University of London, 1985. *Geographic focus:* Southwest China, Burmese border, northern Indochina and Thailand. *Languages:* English, French, Miao (Hmong), Thai, Cantonese and Mandarin.

Visual productions: Consultant on BBC ethnographic documentaries, etc.

Tapper, Richard Lionel
Department of Anthropology, School of Oriental and African Studies, University of London, Malet Street, London WC1E 7HP, UK. Home: Reris Grange West, Milford near Goldaming, Surrey, 9U8 5EN, UK. *Phone:* 1-637-2388; home 48-682-0890. *Profession:* University teacher, anthropologist. *Interests:* I teach a course, Anthropology and Film, whose main focus is the relation between filmed and written ethnographic texts. I have shot ethnographic footage in Iran, Afghanistan, and Turkey. For many years I have been a member (and sometimes chair) of the Ethnographic Film Committee of the Royal Anthropological Institute. *Training:* Ph.D. Social Anthropology. *Geographic focus:* Middle East (esp. "northern tier"). *Languages:* French, German, Italian, Persian, Turkish (all reasonable r,w,s); some Pashto, Russian, and Arabic. *Other information:* I helped organize the 1985 International Ethnographic Film Festival in London.

Tarabulski, Michael
214 West Gilman #3, Madison, WI 53703. *Phone:* (608) 257-4306. *Affiliations:* Beloit College, Syracuse University. *Interests:* Ethnographic filmmaking, history of anthropology. *Geographic focus:* North America. *Languages:* French (fluent).
   Visual productions: "Reliving the Past: Alonzo Pond and the Logan Africa Expedition of 1930," historical documentary on a Beloit College archaeologist active in the 1920's and 1930's, teacher of Sol Tax and other anthropologists.

Tarasoff, Koozma J.
882 Walkley Road, Ottawa, Ontario, K1V 6R5 Canada. *Phone:* (613) 737-5778. *Profession:* Anthropologist, photographer, consultant, writer. *Interests:* Proxemics, neurolinguistic programming, nonverbal behavior, ethnographic filmmaking, photography, photojournalism. *Training:* M.A. Anthropology and Sociology. Communications training in neuro-linguistic programming. Photography. *Work in progress:* Opening Doors for Survival: A Handbook on Soviet-West Initiatives (book). *Geographic focus:* North America, Soviet Union. *Languages:* Russian. *Additional expertise:* Multiculturalism, interpersonal communications, and intergroup communications.
   Visual productions: "In Search of Utopia: The Doukhobors," 1979 (co-produced with Larry Ewashen and others), 60 min. documentary film.

Tefft, Stanton K.
Department of Anthropology, Box 7807, Wake Forest University, Winston-Salem, NC 27109. Home: 2451 Lyndhurst Avenue, Winston-Salem, NC 27103. *Phone:* (919) 761-5326; department (919) 761-5945; home (919) 722-7762. *Profession:* Professor of Anthropology. *Interests:* Teaching ethnographic film, sporadic courses in video documentary. *Training:* Ph.D. Anthropology, University of Minnesota. Audit courses at UNC, Greensboro

on the history of film and documentary techniques. *Geographic focus:* Southeastern United States, Africa. *Languages:* Spanish. *Visual productions:* "In Search of the Indians at Donnaha," video documentary.

Tezcan, Akile Gürsoy
Türkiye Ekonomisi Arastrima Merkezi, Marmara Universitesi, Göztepe, Kadiköy, Istanbul, Turkey. Rifki Tongsir Cad. 22/1, Idealtepe, Istanbul, Turkey. *Phone:* Istanbul 3 389655; home 366-8773. *Profession:* Social anthropologist. *Affiliation:* University of Marmara, Istanbul. *Interests:* Teaching with ethnographic film, photography. *Training:* Ph.D. Anthropology, Hacettepe University, Ankara, Turkey, 1980. B.A. Honours Anthropology, Durham University, UK, 1973. *Work in progress:* University lecturing, community health research project in Istanbul. *Geographic focus:* Middle East. *Languages:* English (r,w,s), French (r,s), Turkish (native language).

Topper, Martin D.
Box 223, Falls Church, VA 22046. Office: Mail Code A-104, US EPA/OF A, 401 M Street SW, Washington, DC. *Phone:* (202) 382-7063; home (703) 534-5409. *Professions:* Anthropologist, clinician, news/television consultant. *Affiliation:* Environmental Protection Agency. *Interests:* Public affairs, news reporting, television film, medical anthropology, mental health. *Geographic focus:* Native Americans in U.S., American Southwest, Navaho.

Trend, Mike G.
2602 Hammonds Drive, Opelika, AL 36801. *Phone:* (205) 745-4805. *Profession:* Social science research, documentary photography. *Interests:* Documentary photography, applied anthropology, econometrics. *Training:* Ph.D. Anthropology, minor in Studio Art, University of Minnesota. Ph.D. Economics (forthcoming). *Work in progress:* Study of dislocated mill workers. Study of Black farmers and their decendants. *Geographic focus:* United States, esp. Southeast. *Languages:* Spanish, Vietnamese. *Technical expertise:* Film, video. *Other information:* Guggenheim fellowship to study 19th century towns.

Trettevik, Susan K.
6050 6th Avenue, NW #2, Seattle, WA 98107. *Phone:* (206) 789-2825; work (206) 464-7165. *Profession:* Editorial Assistant. *Affiliation:* Washington State Department of Transportation. *Interests:* Teaching with ethnographic film. Ethnographic filmmaking. Study of historical photographs for insights into cultural expressions of and structurings of reality through visual symbols. Use of photography to record the use of visual symbols (multimedia and objects) to express personal identity within a given culture. *Training:* M.A. Cultural Anthropology, Washington State University, 1982. B.A. Mass

Communications (film sequence), Washington State University, 1976. *Geographic focus:* NW Coast Indians, general.

Trigger, D. S.
Department of Anthropology, University of Western Australia, Nedlands, W.A. 6009 Australia. *Phone:* (09) 380-2847. *Profession:* Lecturer. *Interests:* Use of still photographs in teaching and research. Ethnographic film. *Training:* Ph.D. Anthropology. *Geographic focus:* Australian Aboriginal studies, ethnic relations.
　　Visual productions: "Aborigines and Lawn Hill Gorge," 1984 (co-producer, with R. Robins), audiovisual display, 80 slides plus narration on tape and accompanying written text, printing and technical production by Queensland Museum (also available on videotape).

Trotter, Robert T., II
Department of Anthropology, Box 15200, Northern Arizona University, Flagstaff, AZ 86011. *Phone:* (602) 523-3180; home (602) 523-4521. *Profession:* Anthropologist. *Interests:* Ethnographic filmmaking, slide series (sync sound) production, still photography. *Training:* M.A. and Ph.D. Medical Anthropology, Southern Methodist University. B.S. Zoology and Physiology, University of Nebraska, Lincoln. *Work in progress:* "Curanderismo: Mexican American Folk Medicine" (35mm slide-tape). *Geographic focus:* United States/ Mexico border, Southwestern United States. *Languages:* Spanish (reading, some speaking).
　　Visual productions: 16mm color films: "A Trip Across Saudi Arabia," and "Los Que Curan" [Mexican American Folk Medicine]. 35mm slide-tapes: "Grandmother's Tea" [Las Yerbas de Mi Abuela], production on herbal remedies; and "Don Pedrito Jaramillo: A Mexican Folk Healer."

Trubowitz, Neal L.
Anthropology Department, Indiana University, 425 Agnes Street, Indianapolis, IN 46202. Home: 5437 Guilford, Indianapolis, IN 46220. *Phone:* (317) 257-7798; office (317) 264-8207. *Profession:* Archaeologist. *Interests:* Archaeological photography (field and lab), photo archiving, anthropological teaching with visual media, anthropological teaching with living history reenactment. *Training:* Ph.D. Anthropology, SUNY, Buffalo, 1978. M.A. Anthropology, SUNY, Buffalo, 1973. A.B. Anthropology, University of Michigan, 1971. *Geographic focus:* Eastern North America. *Technical expertise:* 15 years field and lab experience in archaeological photography. *Other information:* Eleven years experience living history reenactment, 17th to 19th century lifeways across eastern United States. Technical advisor to public television for "The Battle of Prairie Grove" [Arkansas].

Van Zile, Judy
Music Department, University of Hawaii, 2411 Dole Street, Honolulu, HI 96822. *Phone:* (808) 948-7756. *Profession:* Professor of Dance (Ethnology). *Interests:* Dance ethnology, movement analysis and notation (Labanotation), Korean dance, immigrant dance traditions. *Training:* M.A. Dance Ethnology, University of California, Los Angeles. Certified Labanotation teacher. *Work in progress:* An experiment in visual perception and movement notation. Traditional Korean dance forms, Japanese dancing in Hawaii. *Geographic focus:* Korea.

Volkman, Toby Alice
Social Sciences Research Council, 605 Third Avenue, New York, NY 10158. *Phone:* (212) 661-0280. *Profession:* Anthropologist. *Interests:* Writing about and teaching with ethnographic film. Humanities and social science research planning, conferences, and funding. *Training:* Ph.D. Anthropology, Cornell University, 1980. *Work in progress:* Restudy of Tanah Toraja, Sulawesi. Editing a guide book on Sulawesi. *Geographic focus:* Southeast Asia/Indonesia. *Languages:* Indonesian, Toraja, French.

Von Ins, Jürg E.
P.O. Box 209, CH-8803 Rüschlikon, Switzerland. Home: Hochstrasse 28, 8044 Zürich. *Phone:* 1/47 24 77. *Affiliations:* Universities of Zürich and Berne. *Interests:* Anthropology and psychology of religion. Ethnographic methods of denotation/representation of proxemics (ritual). Vision, hallucination, symbolization: how to represent the phenomena themselves? Video, film. *Training:* Habilitation, University of Berne. Field research in Senegal: curing rituals, traditional psychiatry. *Work in progress:* "The Symbolic Process," the religion of foreigners in Switzerland during the first ten years of their stay. "Ethics of Medical Technology." "Sacrifice as a Psychic Principle." *Geographic focus:* West Africa, Europe, Near East. *Languages:* German, English, French, Latin, Hebrew (Biblical), Wolof. *Additional expertise:* Editing. *Other information:* Photo essay—Etre Un Autre: Phanomenologie Der Besessenheit in Therapeutischen Ritualen (Habilitation). Berlin: Verlag D. Reimers (Unter den Eichen 57, D–1000, Berlin 45, West Germany).

Wagner, Daniel A.
Literary Research Center, A-36 Education, University of Pennsylvania, Philadelphia, PA 19104. *Phone:* (215) 898-7366, (215) 898-1025. *Profession:* Education/Anthropology/Psychology. *Interests:* Ethnographic filmmaking on child development and education. *Training:* Ph.D. Psychology. *Work in progress:* Three films on education in Morocco. *Geographic focus:* Mideast, North Africa.
    Visual productions: "Quranic Schooling in a Changing World," 23 min. color video, a comparative study of Indonesia, Yemen, Senegal, and Morocco.

Wagner, Jon C.
Coordinator, University/School Research, University/School Educational Improvement, Office of the President, University of California, Berkeley, CA 94720. Home: 1669 Capistrano, Berkeley, CA 94707. *Phone:* (415) 643-8892; home (415) 527-5199. *Profession:* University administrator. *Interests:* Visual documentation/representation of social/cultural phenomena. Teaching with visual media. *Training:* Ph.D. Sociology, University of Chicago, 1971. Teaching sociology and photography at Columbia College Chicago; Trenton State College, New Jersey; and University of California, Berkeley. *Work in progress:* Videotape studies of teachers teaching and talking about their teaching. Visual approaches to representing findings of educational research for examination by school teachers and administrators. *Geographic focus:* San Francisco Bay Area. *Additional expertise:* Field research methods, narrative verbal representation of social behavior.

Wagner, Jon G.
Knox College, Box 73, Galesburg, IL 61401. Home: RR 1 #106A, Rio, IL 61472. *Phone:* (309) 343-0112. *Profession:* Anthropology. *Interests:* Teaching with film, music, and slides. Worldview, utopianism, gender. *Training:* Ph.D. Anthropology, Indiana University. *Geographic focus:* North America, Islam.

Wallendorf, Melanie
Associate Professor of Marketing, College of Business and Public Administration, University of Arizona, Tucson, AZ 85721. *Phone:* (602) 621-7479. *Interests:* Consumer research, esp. the structure of meaning of consumption artifacts. Use still photography and video photography both as data collection and as knowledge product in research. *Training:* Ph.D. Marketing (Consumer Behavior), University of Pittsburgh, 1979. M.S. Sociology, University of Pittsburgh, 1978. *Work in progress:* Video productions (with Russell Belk): "Collectors and Collections: Glimpses of American Consumption;" and "The Automobile as Extension of Self: Expressions of Ethnicity and Social Identity." "The Sacred and the Profane in Consumer Behavior: Theodicy on the Odyssey" (with Russel Belk and John Sherry). *Geographic focus:* Contemporary U.S. culture. *Other information:* Although my training is in consumer behavior and sociology, I am finding myself drawing from and wanting to learn more about visual anthropology.

Visual productions: "Deep Meaning in Possessions: Qualitative Research Finding from the Consumer Behavior Odyssey," 1987 (with Russell Belk), 38 min. video, Marketing Science Institute, Cambridge, MA.

Walter, Nancy Peterson
17048 Sunburst, Northridge, CA 91325-2606. Office: Department of Anthropology, California State University, Northridge, CA 91330. *Phone:* (818)

349-0382; office (818) 885-3331. *Profession:* Anthropologist. *Affiliation:* also Research Associate, Los Angeles County Museum of Natural History. *Interests:* Using historic photographs to do ethnography. Teaching with ethnographic film. *Training:* Ph.D., M.A., B.A. *Geographic focus:* Great Basin, western China.

Wanner, James A.
Department of Anthropology, University of Northern Colorado, Greeley, CO 80639. *Phone:* (303) 351-1746; department (303) 351-2021. *Profession:* General anthropologist. *Interests:* Expressive culture, dance anthropology, visual arts, teaching with film. *Training:* Statistical methods, ethnographic methods, dance (ballet, jazz, and tap), sculpture, music. *Work in progress:* Psychosocial characteristics of dancers. *Other information:* Submitted for publication: "I'd Rather be Dancing: Ritual Dimensions of Western Art Dance," and "Physique and Body Image in Dancers and Aerobic Exercisers."

Watson, O. Michael
Department of Sociology and Anthropology, Stone Hall, Purdue University, West Lafayette, IN 47907. *Phone:* (317) 494-4682. *Profession:* Anthropologist. *Interests:* Proxemics, teaching visual anthropology. *Training:* Ph.D. University of Colorado, 1968. Summer Institute in Visual Anthropology (Anthropology Film Center, Santa Fe, 1972).

Weatherford, Elizabeth
115 Spring Street, New York, NY 10012. Office: Film and Video Center, Museum of American Indian, Broadway at 155th Street, New York, NY 10032. *Phone:* (212) 925-4682; office (212) 283-2420. *Profession:* College faculty, Curator of Film and Video Center (serving documentary and ethnographic filmmakers concerned particularly with Native Americans). *Affiliation:* also School of Visual Arts. *Interests:* Teaching visual anthropology (documentary and ethnographic history). Programming film series and festivals. Film archiving. Film study center. Consultations and film research with independent production. *Training:* M.A. Anthropology. Graduate faculty, The New School for Social Research. Former coordinator, New York Visual Anthropology Center (now defunct). *Geographic focus:* North, Central, and South America—Native Americans. *Languages:* French, Italian (medium speaking). *Other information:* Co-director, Native American Film and Video Festival, New York. Advisory Committee, Human Studies Film Archives (Smithsonian). Juror, American Film Festival, Arctic Film Festival.

Weibel-Orlando, Joan
Department of Anthropology, University of Southern California, University Park, Los Angeles, CA 90089-0661. P.O. Box 9949, Newport Beach, CA 92658-1949. *Phone:* (213) 743-7100; (714) 537-3123. *Profession:* Assistant

Professor of Anthropology. *Interests:* Social change, alcohol use and abuse, medical anthropology, alcohol treatment, aging, urban studies. Teaching with film. Film/video production. *Training:* Ph.D. Anthropology, UCLA, including a graduate ethnographic film course. *Work in progress:* Editing 15 hours of videotape (filmed with Toby Fleming) into approx. four 1/2 hour programs on Indian aging and return to their ancestral homeland after 25 to 30 years in urban centers. *Geographic focus:* North American Indians. *Languages:* French, Spanish, and Italian (reading). *Other information:* Graduate advisor to students in USC's master's program in Visual Anthropology. I have taught Exploring Cultures Through Film (Anthropology 263), and also have used film extensively (as well as my own slides from various field trips) in my upper division course North American Indians.

Visual productions: "Going Home: A Grandmother's Story" (with Toby Fleming), on Sioux aging.

Weil, Peter M.
Department of Anthropology, University of Delaware, Newark, DE 19716. Home: 91 Kells Avenue, Newark, DE 19711. *Phone:* (302) 451-1858; department (302) 451-2802; home (302) 737-8694. *Profession:* Anthropology professor, rural development analyst. *Interests:* Art and communication. Cultural and historical processes affecting form, style, and distribution of public art forms. Teaching with ethnographic film. Film and other media in the documentation of the visual arts in context. *Training:* Ph.D., M.A. Anthropology, University of Oregon. B.A. Anthropology and International Relations, University of Texas (Austin). *Work in progress:* "Men's Masking and Ritual in the 19th and 20th Century, Adaptive Processes of the Mandinka of Senegambia: Art History as Culture History." "Taking the Mask by the Horns: Sociocultural and Historical Processes in the Creation of Mande Regional Form and Style Analogues." *Geographic focus:* Africa, West Africa, Sahel, Senegambia. *Languages:* French (reading-good, writing-fair, speaking-fair), Mandinka (r,w,s–good).

Weiner, Annette B.
Department of Anthropology, New York University, 25 Waverly Place, New York, NY 10003. *Phone:* (212) 598-2815. *Profession:* Anthropology. *Interests:* Teaching with ethnographic film. *Geographic focus:* South Pacific. *Other information:* Member, Commission on Visual Anthropology (1984–). Actively helped in developing Certificate Progam in Ethnographic Film, Departments of Anthropology and Cinema Studies, NYU.

Wescott, Roger Williams
Anthropology Department, Drew University, Madison, NJ 07940. Home: 11 Green Hill Road, Madison, NJ 07940. *Phone:* (201) 408-3000; home (201) 377-9031. *Profession:* Professor of Anthropology and Linguistics, and

Director of Linguistics Program. *Interests:* Kinesics (body language studies). Cheiresics (sign language studies). Chromatonymics (color terminology studies). TV program directing. *Training:* M. Litt. Social Anthropology, Oxford, 1953. Ph.D. Linguistics, Princeton, 1948. *Geographic focus:* West Africa, Europe, South Asia. *Languages:* Lecture in French, read German and Italian, have taught Greek, Latin, Yoruba, Ibo. Published grammar of Bini.

Visual productions: Program director and host for "Other Views," a weekly general audience interview show on New Jersey Cable Television (from Trenton, New Jersey, and with some national satelite distribution).

Whitten, Dorothea S. and Norman E. Whitten, Jr.
Home: 507 Harding Drive, Urbana, IL 61801. *Phone:* home (217) 344-1828; office (217) 333-3616; messages (217) 333-3848. *Profession:* Sociology/ anthropology. *Affiliation:* Center for Latin American and Caribbean Studies, and Department of Anthropology, University of Illinois, Urbana-Champaign. *Interests:* Ethnographic filmmaking (television). Studio productions (television). *Training:* Not trained in filmmaking, but skilled in ethnography, ethnography writing, ethnographic visuals to complement texts. Have conducted workshops in audiovisual techniques in spite of lack of technical training. *Work in progress:* In 1984 we began serious work with television professionals, and currently we are developing an audiovisual data base on ethnographic performances in Ecuador. "Without the Wheel: Ceramics and Symbolism of the Canelos Quichua Potters of Amazonian Ecuador." *Geographic focus:* Coastal, Andean, and esp. Amazonian Ecuador. Experience in Colombia, Peru, Nicaragua. *Languages:* Spanish and Canelos Quichua, an Ecuadorian dialect of Quechua (r,w,s). *Additional expertise:* More than 25 years experience in and out of the primary field sites, so people whom we film (video) are totally relaxed and "natural" around us, regardless of camera and other apparatus.

Visual productions: "Our Knowledge, Our Beauty: The Expressive Culture of the Canelos Quichua of Ecuador," 30 min., University of Illinois Film Center, Urbana, Illinois.

Williams, Carroll Warner
Anthropology Film Center, 1626 Canyon Road, Santa Fe, NM 87501. P.O. Box 493, Santa Fe, NM 87501. *Phone:* (505) 983-4127. *Profession:* Visual anthropologist. *Interests:* Media in research, practice, methodology. The teaching of visual anthropology, observation-perception and cultural difference. Art, design, craft, music, generalist. *Training:* Purdue University, Indiana University, Black Mountain College. Worked on and/or produced about 285 motion pictures. Union journeyman cards as cameraman, soundman, and editor. Credits also as writer, director, and producer. Have traveled extensively, lectured at many universities. *Work in progress:* Book or books. *Geographic focus:* Western Hemisphere with some exceptions. *Additional expertise:* A

founder of Professional Motion Picture and Video Equipment Manufacturers Association. Designed and manufactured professional equipment. Designed and built 5 production studios, CBS, WBAI Ultra Electronics, HI FI HQ. *Other information:* Founder of Visual Anthropology Film Center.

Visual productions: A few films.

Williams, Drid

Music Department, University of Sydney, Sydney, New South Wales 2006, Australia. Friend's address in U.S.: Lynn Martin, 307 East 44th Street #418, New York, NY 10017. Sister: Doris Irvine, 2060 154th Lane NW, Andover, MN 55304. *Phones:* (02) 692-2923; Martin (212) 490-1934; Irvine (612) 421-5073. *Profession:* Social anthropologist. *Affiliation:* also Australian Institute of Aboriginal Studies, G.P.O. Box 553, Acton House, Canberra, ACT 2601. *Interests:* The dance, martial arts, sign languages, etc.: i.e. "the anthropology of human movement." Theoretical orientation is semasiology. Senior editor, Journal for the Anthropological Study of Human Movement (JASHM). At University of Sydney: teach and direct an M.A. degree in The Dance and The Arts of Human Movement Studies. *Training:* Diploma, B.Litt., D.Phil. Social Anthropology, St. Hugh's College, Oxford University. *Work in progress:* Book (with Brenda Farnell) entitled The Laban Script: An Ordinary Approach to Movement Writing. *Geographic focus:* Currently, Cape York Peninsula, Australia. Major work done in England and North America. I have done most of my anthropology on my own or a parallel culture. *Languages:* French (reading only); Labanotation (writing, teaching). *Technical expertise:* I am a theoretician and methodologist, not a technician. *Other information:* I work extensively with linguists, ethnomusicologists, and other anthropologists; am currently interested in problems of human action and behavior.

Williams, Joan S.

Anthropology Film Center, P.O. Box 493, Santa Fe, NM 87504. Home: 1626 Canyon Road, Santa Fe, NM 87501. *Phone:* (505) 983-4127. *Profession:* Executive Director of non-profit foundation, lecturer, visual anthropologist. *Affiliation:* also Anthropology Film Center Foundation. *Interests:* Teaching and practice of production and grants management, ethnographic film projects. Visual and oral ethnohistory and community history. Film archival consultation. Ethnographic film projects consultant. *Training:* University of New Mexico Graduate Institute courses. 23 years joint owner of professional motion picture production company. M.A. Educational Foundations, Teachers College, Columbia University (emphasis on Education and Anthropology). B.A. Anthropology, Harvard, 1954. *Work in progress:* Survey of community-based visual archive projects in the Southwest U.S. Curriculum development for applied work in visual and oral history documentation. Study of community land use in northern New Mexico. *Geographic focus:* Southwest U.S. *Languages:* French (reading).

Technical expertise: Professional motion picture editor (NABET). *Other information:* Annual Festival Organizer, SVA/AAA Film and Video Festival. AAA Film Screenings Sessions Organizer.

Visual productions: Experimental education films: writer, producer, director. "For Those Who Stay," 1962, island of Grenada. "First Impressions: An Ixil Setting Film," 1966.

Wilson, James W.
Route 2, Box 51N, Bridgewater, VA 22812. Office: Manager, Microcomputing Services, James Madison University, Harrisonburg, VA 22807. *Phone:* work (703) 568-7062. *Profession:* Archaeology; photography; microcomputer programming, training, and consulting. *Interests:* I use images (still photography, stereo photography, film, video, computer graphics) to record events, places, people, and things. I plan to use computers as a central medium to archive these images, to process them in different ways and then produce educational materials. Most of my work over the last few years has been in relation to archaeology and historic preservation. I hope to broaden my scope to include current events and issues relating to Virginia (Shenandoah Valley in particular) and their relationship to world events and issues. *Training:* B.S. Anthropology and Geography, Southern Methodist University, 1982. *Work in progress:* Currently planning and developing skills for implementing a computer based information retrieval system. *Geographic focus:* Virginia, archaeology, historic preservation. *Languages:* Elementary German, several computer languages and lingo. *Other information:* In the future I want to stay on top of emerging technologies (CD-I: Compact Disk Interactive, DVI: Digital Video Interactive, CD-ROM: Compact Disk-Read Only Memory) that will allow the merging of vast quantities of visual information with text, sound, and software to produce an interactive system that will revolutionize the way information is used around the world.

Winner, Irene Portis
19 Garden Street, Cambridge, MA 02138. *Phone:* (617) 868-2387. *Profession:* Associate Professor, Anthropology. *Affiliations:* Department of Critical Studies, Massachusetts College of Art; also Center for the Philosophy of Education, School of Education, Harvard University; and Program in Semiotic Studies, Center for the Philosophy and History of Science, Boston University. *Interests:* Cultural anthropology: peasantry, comparative, and specialization in Eastern Europe. Ethnicity: Slovenes in urban and rural U.S. Semiotics of culture: The Moscow-Tartu School, The Prague School and Western European and American semiotics. Semiotic theory and particularly aesthetics and the relation of the visual and verbal. Also theories of narration, montage, texts and metatexts in semiotics of culture. Semiotics of anthropology. *Training:* Ph.D. Anthropology, University of North Carolina. M.A. Anthropology, Columbia University. *Work in progress:* "Semiotics of

Culture: The State of the Art" (new and revised edition of 1982 bibliographic reference, Bochum Publications in Evolutionary Semiotics, Bochum, Germany). "The Human Sign as an Integrative Concept," proceedings of the Anthropology and Semiotics conference, Bochum Publications in Evolutionary Semiotics, Semiotics and the Individual Sciences. *Geographic focus:* Fieldwork in Eastern Europe and U.S. (Ohio and Michigan). Research in Semiotics—U.S.S.R., Poland, Hungary, Germany and U.S. *Languages:* Serbo-Croatian, Slovene, French.

Wizelman, Raul

Canning 180, 1414 Buenos Aires, Argentina. Office: Campichuelo 888, 1405 Buenos Aires, Argentina. *Phone:* 854-6620; 982-9701. *Professions:* M.D. and anthropologist. *Affiliation:* AAA (U.S.), IUAES, and AAMA (Argentina). *Interests:* Ethnographic filmmaking, teaching with ethnographic film. *Work in progress:* Fieldwork in northern state of Argentina, covering ethno-medical aspects (filmmaking, slides, tapes). *Languages:* Spanish, English, French, Jewish, Italian, Portuguese. *Other information:* Interested in visual anthropology of medical anthropology.

Visual productions: Auca Indians (slide-tapes), India (slide-tapes).

Wood, William W.

160 Columbia Avenue, Athens, OH 45701. Office: Department of Sociology and Anthropology, Lindley Hall, Ohio University, Athens, OH 45701. *Phone:* (614) 593-3214, 593–1350. *Profession:* Anthropology. *Interests:* Cultural ecology, interparadigm analysis—symbols in human adaptation, medical anthropology, film for representing cultural process, ethnographic film (super-8) as research support. *Training:* Ph.D. Anthropology, University of North Carolina. *Geographic focus:* Southeast Asia, Bali.

Worth, Tobia L.

4620 Osage Avenue, Philadelphia, PA 19143. International Encyclopedia of Communications, University of Pennsylvania, Blockley Hall, Philadelphia, PA 19104-6021. *Phone:* (215) 476-5199; (215) 898-1600. *Profession:* Editor. *Interests:* Editing in the areas of art, drama, and visual communication. I am essentially an encyclopedist, but I have done books and scholarly journals as well. *Training:* B.A. English. ABD English and Aesthetics. Twenty-five years in book publishing (McGraw-Hill, nineteen years; University of Pennsylvania, nine years). *Languages:* French (r,w,s).

Wright, Julie

2635 Monmouth Avenue, Los Angeles, CA 90007. *Phone:* (213) 749-4965. *Profession:* Visual anthropologist, videographer. *Interests:* Tourism in Latin America and the Caribbean. *Training:* M.A. Visual Anthropology, University of Southern California, 1989. *Work in progress:* "The Toured," 45 min.

3/4" video concerning tourism in Barbados. *Languages:* Spanish. *Technical expertise:* Cinematography, editing.

Visual productions: "Pa'ipai Folktales and Pottery Making," 1988, 18 min. 3/4" video.

Wylie, Laurence
1010 Memorial Drive #5-F, Cambridge, MA 02138. Office: 1540 William James Hall, Harvard University, Cambridge, MA 02138. *Phone:* (617) 876-3227; office (617) 495-3834. *Profession:* C. Douglas Dillon Professor of the Civilization of France (Emeritus). *Interests:* Life in small French communities. Nonverbal communication in France. Body behavior on films and video as basis for learning French. *Training:* Jacques Lecoq School—Mime, Mouvement, Theatre, 1972–73. Postdoctoral training, Anthropology, University of Pennsylvania 1945–50. Ph.D. Brown University, 1940. A.M. Indiana University, 1933. A.B. Indiana University, 1931. *Work in progress:* Development of language (French) learning series based on twenty dialogues filmed for the purpose. *Geographic focus:* France. *Languages:* French (all top levels). *Additional expertise:* Frame-by-frame analysis of movies for study of nonverbal communication. Still photography of day-to-day behavior. *Other information:* Publication in many books and articles of photographs from collection of stills on French rural life and nonverbal communication.

Visual productions: "French Gestures," 1973 (with Alfred Guzzetti), film. "Un Américain découvre la France," 1973, film, French First Chain. "Quand les gestes prennent la parole," 1978, film, French First Chain, Psychology Series. Participation in making Georges Rouquier's film "Biquefarre," 1983.

Yoder, P. Stanley
Development and Communications Unit, Annenberg School of Communications, University of Pennsylvania, 3620 Walnut Street, Philadelphia, PA 19104-6220. Home: 826 Fitzwater Street, Philadelphia, PA 19147. *Phone:* (215) 898-9727 or 898-9032; home (215) 925-1557. *Profession:* Medical anthropologist. *Interests:* Ethnographic film production. Ethnomedicine. Patient choice of practitioners. Photographic documentation of ritual therapies. *Training:* M.A. African Studies, M.P.H. International Health, and Ph.D. Anthropology: UCLA. *Work in progress:* Video/filmography on African health and illness (please send titles and information). Film on the social context of Cokwe [Zaïre] healing and divining. Two 10–12 min. films for anthropology classes on Cokwe divination and on Cokwe use of medicinal plants. *Geographic focus:* Central and West Africa. *Languages:* French, Portuguese, German, Cokwe, Kiswahili.

Young, Colin
National Film and Television School, Beaconsfield, Bucks HP9 ILG, England. Home: 11 King Henry's Road, London, NW3 JQP, England. *Phone:* 44-4-

946-71234; 44-1-722-2802. *Affiliations:* Fellows of RAI, member of AAA, SVA, Sound and Television Society. *Training:* St. Andrews: Philosophy, Moral Philosophy. UCLA: Film. *Work in progress:* The training of professional anthropologists in filmmaking, in cooperation with the RAI and CNRS. Recent work in Mali, Venezuela, Pakistan, and Northern England. Also the training of filmmakers to work collaboratively with ethnographers e.g. such as recently in North India, Alaska, Alabama, and British Columbia. *Languages:* French (almost fluent), Spanish (poor), Swedish (feeble). *Technical expertise:* All filmmaking skills. *Other information:* President of CILELY (International Film and Television Schools Association), Chairman of Edinburgh International Film Festival.

Visual productions: Produced: "The Village," UCLA (filmmaker, Mark McCarty; anthropologist, Paul Hockings); "The Warao," UCLA (filmmaker, Jorge Preloran); and "La Tirana," UCLA, (director, Richard C. Hawkins).

Young, John A.
Department of Anthropology, Oregon State University, Corvallis, OR 97331. Home: 7805 NW Siskin Drive, Corvallis, OR 97330. *Phone:* (503) 754-4515; home (503) 753-2087. *Profession:* Cultural anthropologist. *Interests:* Ethnographic filmmaking. Teaching with ethnographic film. Applied anthropology. *Training:* Ph.D. Anthropology, Stanford University. Short course on ethnographic film with Karl Heider. *Geographic focus:* China, South Pacific, Fiji, U.S. *Languages:* Mandarin and Cantonese (basic speaking), some familiarity with Fijian. *Additional expertise:* Specialize in applied anthropology and rural development. *Other information:* Have taught course on ethnographic film.

Visual productions: "Carasala Ki Lovoni: Opening the Way to Lovoni," 49 min., from 8mm film, post-production on videotape, shows Fijian village ceremonies for visiting urban clan members.

Young, Katharine
526 Greystone Road, Merion, PA 19066. *Phone:* (215) 667-8757. *Profession:* Folklorist, anthropologist, literary theorist. *Interests:* Phenomenology of the body, aesthetics of the ordinary, emotion, the self, the body, the mind/body problem, frame analysis. *Training:* B.A. Philosophy, U.C. Berkeley; post-graduate research in aesthetics, University of Edinburgh. M.A., Ph.D. Folklore and Folklife, University of Pennsylvania. *Work in progress:* Book on the phenomenology of the body in medicine. Study of expressive properties of the body in Italian masks. *Geographic area:* Europe and U.S., Western culture.

Zantzinger, Gei
P.O. Box 2, Devault, PA 19432. *Phone:* (215) 933-0662. *Profession:* Ethnographic/documentary filmmaker. *Affiliation:* Constant Spring Produc-

tions, Devault, PA. Also Research Associate with the Department of Radio–Television–Film, Temple University and with African Section, University Museum, University of Pennsylvania. *Interests:* Making ethnographic/documentary film. *Training:* Ph.D. candidate, University of Pennsylvania. M.A. candidate, Annenberg School of Communication. B.A./M.A. Cultural Anthropology/Folklore and Folklife, University of Pennsylvania. *Work in progress:* Follow up study to "Songs of the Adventurers" (with David Coplan), migrant labor poetry of the Basotho, who work in the mines of South Africa. Communicative value of textiles among Highland Maya in Guatemala. *Geographic focus:* Southern Africa, Central Africa, Latin America. *Languages:* Spanish (reading, speaking), Portuguese (reading), assorted smattering of other Romance languages, German. *Additional expertise:* Ethnomusicology, folklore, oral literatures in non-Western languages.

Visual productions: "Ola Belle Reed: Memories," 1975, 14 min. 16mm color experimental film about pre-1934 dance movement in Appalachia, with balladic texts. "Songs of the Badius" (Cape Verde). "Dances of Southern Africa," 1968, 90 min. 16mm color film, available from 111 Amsterdam Avenue, New York, NY [55 min version, 1973, 16 mm or 3/4 Umatic, distributed by Pennsylvania State Audio-Visual Services.] Six films in series on Zimbabwe: "Mbira dza Vadzimu: Dambatsoko, an Old Cult Centre with Muchatera and Ephrat Mujuru" (1978, 51 min.), "Mbira dza Vadzimu: Religion at the Family Level with Gwanzura Gwenzi" (1978, 66 min.), "Mbira dza Vadzimu: Urban and Rural Ceremonies with Hakurotwi Mudhe" (1978, 45 min.), "Mbira: Matepe dza Mhondoro—A Healing Party" (1978, 20 min.), "Mbira: Njari, Karanga Songs in Christian Ceremonies with Simon Mashoko" (1977, 24 min.), "Mbira: The Technique of the Mbira dza Vadzimu" (1976, 19 min.). [All films in series available in 16 mm and 3/4" Umatic, distributed by Pennsylvania State Audio-Visual Services.] "Songs of the Adventurers" (Lesotho), Constant Spring Productions. "Susumu," 1989, 16mm [also tranferred to video], color 1/2 hr documentary about the internment of three generations of people of Japanese descent.

Zeller, Anne

Department of Anthropology, University of Waterloo, Waterloo, Ontario, Canada N2L 3G1. Home: 25 Severn Street, Kitchener, Ontario, Canada N2M 2V3. Summer: General Delivery Fulford Harbour, B.C. Canada V0S 1C0. *Phone:* (519) 885-1211, ext 3050; home (519) 745-4644; summer (604) 653-4257. *Interests:* Use of film to study fine details of facial communication in primates, particularly macaques. Making films of primates to use in teaching primate behavior courses. Semiotic aspects of primate gestural communication. *Training:* Ph.D. University of Toronto, 1978. M.A. University of Toronto, 1971. B.Sc. Trent University, 1970. *Work in progress:* Comparison of facial gesture film in Macaca sylvanus with Macaca fuscata and

Macaca fascicularis. Film of male/infant interaction in free-ranging Macaca facicularis. *Geographic focus:* Gibraltar, Indonesia, primate research centers. *Languages:* French (reading). *Technical expertise:* Still photography.

Visual productions: "Primate Patterns II," teaching film on behavior of 6,200 living primate species.

BIBLIOGRAPHY

Adra, Najwa
   1983 Qabyala: The Tribal Concept in the Central Highlands of the Yemen Arab Republic. (Tribal dancing as representation of tribal values.) Ph.D. dissertation, University of Michigan. (University Microfilms International.)
   1985 The Tribal Concept in the Central Highlands of the Yemen Arab Republic. *In* Arab Society, Social Science Perspectives. Nicholas S. Hopkins and Saad E. Ibrahim, eds. Pp. 275–285. Cairo: The American University of Cairo Press,
   1988a Dance Scholarship in the Middle East. Paper presented at the Conference on Dance Scholarship Today; Beyond Performance, Essen, West Germany, June 10–15.
   1988b Film review: About the Jews of Yemen: A Vanishing Culture, by Joanna Spector. American Anthropologist 90(2):492–493.
   1988c Sections on Middle East, Yemen, Zar. International Encyclopedia of Dance. Selma Jeanne Cohen, ed. New York: Charles Scribner's Sons.

Aibel, Robert
   1987 Ethnographic Fiction as 'Data of' and 'Data about' Culture: Georzel Rouquier's Farrebique. *In* Visual Explorations of the World: Selected Papers from the International Conference on Visual Communication. Jay Ruby and Martin Taureg, eds. Pp. 205–216. Aachen, Federal Republic of Germany: Edition Herodot.
   1988 Documentary Film Ethics: A Case Study. *In* Image Ethics: The Moral Rights of Subjects in Photography, Film, and Television. Larry Gross, John Katz, and Jay Ruby, eds. New York: Oxford University Press.

Allen, Peter S.
   1983 (with Carole Lazio) Archaeology on Film. Boston: Archaeological Institute of America.

Albers, Patricia C. and William R. James
   1983 Tourism and the Changing Photographic Image of the Great Lakes Indian. Annals of Tourism Research 10:123–148.
   1984a Utah's Indians and Popular Photography in the American West: A View From the Picture Postcard. Utah's Historical Quarterly 52: 72–91.

1984b   The Dominance of Plains Indian Imagery on the Picture Postcard. *In* Fifth Annual 1981 Plains Indian Seminar in Honor of Dr. John Ewers. G. Horsecapture and G. Ball, eds. Cody, Wyoming: Museum of the Plains Indian.

1985a   Images and Reality: Postcards of Minnesota's Ojibway Peoples, 1900–80. Minnesota History 49:229–240.

1985b   Postcard Encounters of Another Kind. The Postcard Collector 3: 26–28.

1987   Illusion and Illumination: Visual Images of American Indian Women in the West. *In* The Women's West. S. Armitage and B. Jamison, eds. Pp. 51–72. Norman: University of Oklahoma Press.

1988   Travel Photography: A Methodological Approach. Annals of Tourism Research 15(1):134-158.

Forthcoming   Private and Public Images: A Study of Photographic Contrasts in Postcard Pictures of Great Basin Indians, 1893-1919. Visual Anthropology.

Aron, William S.

1979   A Disappearing Community. *In* Images of Information: Still Photography in Social Sciences Today. Jon Wagner, ed. Pp. 59–67. Beverly Hills, California: Sage Publications.

1982   Soviet Jews Today. Movement Magazine 8(1):29–36.

1984   Two Views of Venice, California. *In* Exploring Society Photographically. Howard Becker, ed. Pp. 46–53. Chicago: University of Chicago Press.

1985   From the Corners of the Earth. Philidelphia: The Jewish Publication Society.

Asch, Timothy and Patsy Asch

1986   (with Linda Connor) Jero Tapakan: Balinese Healer. New York: Cambridge University Press.

Aschenbrennen, Joyce

1983   (with K. Skinner)   Family Art Traditions in Contemporary Society. *In* Town Talk: The Dynamics of Urban Anthropology. G. Ansari and P.J.M. Nas, eds. Pp. 112–121. Leiden: E.J. Brill.

Ascher, Robert

1975a   How To Build A Time Capsule. Journal of Popular Culture 8:242–253.

1975b   (with Marcia Ascher)   The Quipu as a Visible Language. Journal of Visible Language 9:329–356.

1981   (with Marcia Ascher)   Code of the Quipu: A Study in Media, Mathematics and Culture. Ann Arbor: University of Michigan Press.

1983 The Space Between People. *In* Perspectives in Adaptation, Environment, and Population. J.B. Calhoun, ed. Pp. 158–60. New York: Praeger.

1985a Sculpting Americans. Anthropology and Humanism Quarterly 10:16–17.

1985b Myth Onto Film. Anthropolgia Visualis 1:37–40.

Balikci, Asen

1966 (with Quentin Brown) Ethnographic Filming and the Netsilik Eskimos. Educational Services Inc. Quarterly Report (Spring): 19–33.

1975 Reconstructing Cultures on Film. *In* Principles of Visual Anthropology. Paul Hockings, ed. Pp. 191–200. World Anthropology series. The Hague: Mouton.

1985 Ethnographic Film in the Museum setting. MUSEUM-UNESCO: 16–24.

Bán, András

1983– . (co-editor with Peter Forgács) Research papers in Visual Anthropology (Vizuális antropológiai kutatás, munkafüzetek). Five issues, Budapest: Müvelódéskutató Intézet.

1983– . (co-editor with Peter Forgács) Newsletter, Research in Visual Anthropology. Two issues, Budapest: Müvelódéskutató Intézet.

1983 (with László Beke) The World of Video (A videó világa). Budapest.

1984a About Photography (Fotográfozásról). (An anthology of Hungarian Photoculture.) Budapest: Muzsák.

1984b Self-Image and Design (Onkép és design). (Lecture.) First National Industrial Design Conference, Budapest.

Banta, Melissa

1980 Photographic Archives Computerization Project, Peabody Museum, Harvard University. Society for the Anthropology of Visual Communication 8(3).

1982 Hidden Treasures: Peabody Museum Photographic Archives. Views, The Journal of Photography in New England 3(4).

1985 A Timely Encounter: 19th-Century Photographs of Japan. Symbols (Winter).

1986 (with Curtris M. Hinsley) From Site to Sight: Anthropology, Photography, and the Power of Imagery. Peabody Museum, Cambridge, Massachusetts: Peabody Museum Press.

Barrow, Anita M.

1987 Film review: Rastafari: Conversations Concerning Women. American Anthropologist 89:262–63.

Baskauskas, Liucija

1986   Unmasking Culture: Cross Cultural Perspectives in the Sound and Behavioral Sciences. Novato, California: Chandler and Sharp.

Becker, Karin E. (also Karen B. Ohrn)

1977   What You See Is What You Get: Dorothea Lange and Ansel Adams at Manzanar. Journalism History 4(1):14–22.

1980   Dorothea Lange and the Documentary Tradition. Baton Rouge: Louisiana State University Press.

1981a (with Richard P. Horwitz) Mac's and Mil's. *In* Exploring Society Photographically. Howard S. Becker, ed. Evanston, Illinois: Mary and Leigh Block Gallery. (Published in conjunction with exhibit of the same title, Block Gallery, October 15–November 29.)

1981b (with Hanno Hardt) The Eyes of the Proletariat: The Worker-Photography Movement in Weimar Germany. Studies in Visual Communication 7(3):46–57.

1981c (with Steven Ohrn) Point of View: Using Photography to Document a Region. Center for Southern Folklore 3(3):5.

1985a Forming a Profession: Ethical Implications of Photojournalistic Practice on German Picture Magazines, 1926–1933. Studies in Visual Communication 11(2):44–60.

1985b Photographs for: The Strip: An American Place, by Richard P. Horwitz. Lincoln: University of Nebraska Press.

1986   The Corlville Strip. *In* Einblick, Ausblick: Der persönliche Standpunkt. Bilder und Texte vom 1. Münchner Fotosymposion. Hella Neubert and Joachim W. Schiwy, eds. Pp. 16–26. Munich: ZANGO ev. Fotoforum.

1989   Photojournalism History. *In* International Encyclopedia of Communications. Erik Barnouw, ed. New York: Oxford University Press.

Behar, Ruth

1986   Santa María del Monte: The Presence of the Past in a Spanish Village. (Historical ethnography with closely-linked photographs forming a separate text.) Princeton: Princeton University Press.

Belk, Russell W.

1986   Art Versus Science as Ways of Generating Knowledge About Materialism. *In* Perspectives on Methodology in Consumer Research. David Brinberg and Richard J. Lutz, eds. Pp. 3–36. New York: Springer-Verlag.

1987a Symbolic Consumption of Art and Culture. *In* Artists and Cultural Consumers. Douglas V. Shaw, William S. Hendon and C. Richard Waits, eds. Pp. 168–178. Akron, Ohio: Association for Cultural Economics.

1987b The Role of the Odyssey in Consumer Behavior and Consumer Research. Advances in Consumer Research 14:357–361.

1987c A Child's Christmas in America: Santa Claus as Deity, Consumption as Religion. Journal of American Culture 10(1):87–100.

1988a Qualitative Analysis of Data From the Consumer Behavior Odyssey: The Role of the Computer and the Role of the Researcher. *In* American Psychological Association Proceedings, Washington, D.C.

1988b A Naturalistic Inquiry into Buyer and Seller Behavior at a Swap Meet. (Includes photos.) Journal of Consumer Research (March).

1988c Collectors and Collections. Advances in Consumer Research 15.

Benthall, Jonathan

1975 A Prospectus as Published in Studio International, July 1972. *In* The Body as a Medium of Expression. Jonathan Benthall and Ted Polhemus, eds. New York: E.P. Dutton.

Bertocci, Peter J.

1984 Bengali Cultural Themes in Ray's "World of Apu." Journal of South Asian Literature 19(1):15–34.

1985 Satyajit Ray's War on Want: "Distant Thunder" and the Spectre of World Hunger. *In* Bengal Vaishnavism, Orientalism and the Arts. Joseph T. O'Connell, ed. Pp. 183–187. Asian Studies Center, South Asia Series, Occasional Paper No. 35. East Lansing: Michigan State University.

Biella, Peter

1984 Theory and Practice in Ethnographic Film: Implications of the Maasai Film Project. Ph.D. dissertation, Temple University.

1985 A Visual Anthropologist's Survival Guide. (In-country production advice; funding tips.) Paper presented at the American Anthropological Association meetings, Washington D.C., December 4–8.

1988 Against Reductionism and Idealist 'Self-Reflexivity': The Ilparakuyo Film Project. *In* Anthropological Filmmaking. J.R. Rollwagen, ed. New York: Harwood Academic Publishers.

Birdwhistell, Ray L.

1952a Introduction to Kinesics: An Annotation System for Analysis of Body Motion and Gesture. Louisville, Kentucky: University of Louisville Press (and) Washington, D.C.: U.S. Department of State, Foreign Service Institute. (Also available from University Microfilms, Ann Arbor, Michigan.)

1952b Field Methods and Techniques: Body Motion Research and Interviewing. Human Organization 11(1):37–38.

1961   Paralanguage: 25 Years After Sapir. *In* Lectures on Experimental Psychiatry. Henry W. Brosin, ed. Pittsburgh: University of Pittsburgh Press.

1966   Some Relations Between American Kinesics and Spoken American English. *In* Communication and Culture. Alfred G. Smith, ed. New York: Holt, Rinehart, and Winston.

1968   Communication. (and) Kinesics. *In* International Encyclopedia of the Social Sciences 3:24 (and) 8:379. David L. Sills, ed. New York: Crowell, Collier, and Macmillan.

1969   Nonverbal Communication in the Courtroom: What Message is the Jury Getting? *In* Persuasion: The Key to Damages. Grace W. Holmes, ed. Pp. 189–204. Ann Arbor, Michigan: The Institute of Continuing Legal Education.

1970a Kinesics and Context: Essays on Body Motion Communication. Philadelphia: University of Pennsylvania Press.

1970b Kinesics: Inter- and Intra-Channel Communication Research. Social Science Information 7:9–26. (Reprinted 1972. Studies in Semiotics. Thomas A. Sebeok, ed. The Hague: Mouton.)

1971   (with Gregory Bateson, Henry W. Brosin, Charles F. Hockett, Henry L. Smith, Jr., George L. Trager, and Norman A. McQuown, ed.) The Natural History of an Interview. Microfilm Collection of Manuscripts on Cultural Anthropology, series 15 (95–98). Chicago: University of Chicago Library.

Bishop, John

1978   An Ever-changing Place. (Field work on langur monkeys in a Sherpa village). New York: Simon and Schuster.

1980   Making Home Video. New York: Wideview Books.

1985   Home Video Production. New York: McGraw-Hill.

Blackman, Margaret B.

1973   The Application of Photogrammetry to Photographic Ethnohistory. Society for the Anthropology of Visual Communication Newsletter 5(1):9–15.

1976   Blankets, Bracelets, and Boas: The Potlatch in Photographs. Anthropological Papers of the University of Alaska 18:43–67.

1980a Posing the American Indian. Natural History 89(10):68–75.

1980b Believing is Seeing: Anthropology in Pictures. Odyssey (Published in coordination with the Odyssey television series).

1981   Window on the Past: The Photographic Ethnohistory of the Northern and Kaigani Haida. National Museum of Man, Mercury Series, Paper No. 74.

1982a Copying People: Northwest Coast Native Response to Early Photography. B.C. Studies 52:86–112.

1982b (with Edwin S. Hall, Jr) The Afterimage and Image After: Visual Documents and the Renaissance in Northwest Coast Art. American Indian Art 7(2):30–39.

1984 Tradition and Innovation: The Visual Ethnohistory of the Kasaan Haida. *In* The Tsimshian and Their Neighbors of the North Pacific Coast. Jay Miller and Caro Eastman, eds. Pp. 151–189. Seattle: University of Washington Press.

1986 Introduction. *In* From Site to Sight: Anthropology, Photography, and the Power of Imagery. Melissa Banta and Curtis M. Hinsley. Cambridge, Massachusetts: Peabody Museum Press.

Blakely, Pamela A. R.

1978 Material Culture in a Hemba Village. 2 volumes. M.A. thesis, Folklore Institute, Indiana University. [Includes 489 field photographs: 286 black and white prints in Volume 2, and 203 slides in the African Art Slide Archive, Fine Arts Department, Indiana University, Bloomington. Slide captions are at the end of Volume 1.]

1987 Dances of Death: Women's Mourning Performances in Hêmbá Funerals. *In* Semiotics 1983. Pp. 477–486. Jonathan Evans and John Deely, eds. Lanham, Maryland: University Press of America.

Blakely, Thomas D.

1981 To Gaze or Not to Gaze: Visual Communication in Eastern Zaïre. Working Papers in Sociolinguistics, nos. 82–87. Reprinted in Case Studies in the Ethnography of Speaking. Richard Bauman and Joel Sherzer, eds. Pp. 234–248. Austin, Texas: Southwest Educational Development Laboratory.

1986 (with Adam Kendon, eds.) Approaches to Gesture. Semiotica, Special Issue 62(1–2).

1989 Hêmbá Visual Communication and Space. (Sources in Semiotics Monograph Series.) Lanham, Maryland: University Press of America. [Including 529 research photographs, and 45 diagrams and maps.]

Blakely, Thomas D. and Pamela A. R. Blakely

1987 *Só'ó* Masks and Hêmbá Funerary Festival. African Arts 21(1): 30–37, 84–86.

Forthcoming Visual Signs and Verbal Art in Central African Funerary Observances. *In* Religion in Africa: Experience and Expression. Thomas D. Blakely, Spencer Palmer, and Dennis Thompson, eds. London: James Currey.

Blaustein, Richard

1983a Using Video in the Field. *In* Handbook of American Folklore. R. Dorson, ed. Pp. 397–401. Bloomington: Indiana University Press.

1983b Video in the Classroom and Community Outreach Projects. *In* Handbook of American Folklore. Richard Dorson, ed. Pp. 513–517. Bloomington: Indiana University Press.

Borchert, Jim
1973 Alley Life in Washington: An Analysis of 600 Photographs. Columbia Historical Society Records 48:276–88.
1980 Alley Life in Washington: Family, Community, Religion and Folklife in the City, 1850–1970. Urbana: University of Illinois Press.
1981a Analysis of Historical Photographs: A Method and a Case Study. Studies in Visual Communication 7:30–63.
1981b Alley Life in Washington. (Photo essay.) Society 18:96–99.
1982 Historical Photo-Analysis: A Research Method. Historical Methods 15:35–44.

Bruner, Edward M.
1986 (with Victor Turner, eds.) The Anthropology of Experience. Urbana: University of Illinois Press.

Burns, Allan F.
1984 Film review: The Living Maya, by Hubert Smith. American Anthropologist 86(1):233.
Forthcoming Video Production as Dialogue: The Story of Lynch Hammock. *In* Toward a Dialogic Anthropology. Dennis Tedlock and Bruce Mannheim, eds. Philadelphia: University of Pennsylvania Press.

Byrne, William G.
1970 Audiovisual Aids for African Studies. *In* The African Experience. Vol. IIIb. John N. Paden and Edward W. Soja, eds. Evanston, llinois: Northwestern University Press.
1979 Attitude and Attitude Change About Africa. (Using film.) Ph.D. dissertation, Northwestern University.

Cabezas, Sue Marshall
1974 Teachers' Guide to the Structure of Human Society. (Teacher's accompaniment to Philip Hammond's Introductory Sociology Textbook of the same name.) Lexington, Massachusetts: Heath.
1978a D.E.R. Update. Society for the Anthropology of Visual Communication Newsletter 7(1).
1978b Perception and Film. National Women's Anthropological Newsletter 3(3).
1986 (with Judith Nierenberg and Mary Anne Wolff) Ethnographic Film in the Classroom. Practicing Anthropology 8(3–4).

Cabezas, Sue Marshall and Judith Nierenberg
1988   D.E.R. A New Generation of Film. Second edition. Watertown,
       Massachusetts: Documentary Educational Resources. (First edition
       1986, with Judith Nierenberg and Mary Anne Wolff.)

Cabezas, Sue Marshall and Toby Alice Volkman
1982   Films From D.E.R. (Original conception with John Marshall.)
       Watertown, Massachusetts: Documentary Educational Resources.

Caldarola, Victor J.
1985   Visual Contexts: A Photographic Research Method in Anthro-
       pology. Studies in Visual Communication 11(3):33–53.
1987   The Generation of Primary Photographic Data in Ethnographic
       Fieldwork: Context and Objectivity. *In* Visual Explorations of the
       World: Selected Papers from the International Conference on Visual
       Communication. Jay Ruby and Martin Taureg, eds. Pp. 217–227.
       Aachen, Federal Republic of Germany: Edition Herodot.

Campos, Yezid
1986   The Tutu: Symbolic Underpinnings of the Arhuaco's Cosmolog-
       ical System. Paper presented at the American Anthropological
       Association meetings, Philadelphia, December 3–7.

Cancian, Frank
1974   Another Place: Photographs of a Maya Community. Centerville,
       Massachusetts: Scrimshaw Press.

Carucci, Laurence M.
1980   The Renewal of Life: A Ritual Encounter in the Marshall Islands.
       Ph.D. dissertation, Department of Anthropology, University of
       Chicago. ("Chapter 7. Spatial and Social Logistics." "Chapter 8. The
       Symbolics of the Senses in Kurijmoj.")
1981   Sly Moves: A Semiotic Analysis of Movement in Marshallese
       Culture. *In* Semiotics. J.N. Deely and M.D. Lenhart, eds. New York:
       Plenum. (Revised version published 1986, Semiotica 62(1–2):
       165–177.)
In Press (with Michael Brown and Lynne Pettler) Shared Spaces: Contexts
       of Interaction in Chicago's Ethnic Communities. New York: AMS
       Press.

Cedrini, Rita
1983   Per una presenza dinamica dell'Immagine nella didattica. Sicilia
       2:164–167. (Palermo: Assessorato Regionale dei Beni Culturali,
       Ambientali e Publica Istrucione.)

1985a Antropologia visuale: problemi metodologici e tecnici. *In* Teorie e Techniche dell'Antropologia Visuale. Rita Cedrini, ed. Pp. 73–88. Palermo: Stass.

1985b Bibliografia. *In* I colori del sole. Antonino Buttitta, ed. Pp. 273–300. Palermo: Flaccovio.

1986 Immagine e culture. Palermo: Flaccovio.

1987 La Memoria Raccontata. *In* Donna e Societa. Janne Vibaek, ed. Pp. 138–144. Palermo: Quaderni del Circolo Semiologico Siciliano.

1988a Le Vie dell'Acqua. *In* Saline di Sicilia. Gesualdo Bufalino, ed. Pp. 101–106. Palermo: Sellerio.

1988b I Salinari. Le Forme dell Lavoro. Antonino Buttita, ed. Pp. 202–211. Palermo: Flaccovio.

1988c I Calderai. Le Forme dell Lavoro. Antonino Buttita, ed. Pp. 333–342. Palermo: Flaccovio.

1988d Jean Rouch: Vedere l'Uomo. Nuove Effemeridi 2:25–31. (Palermo: Guida.)

1988e (with Vipalba Valenti) Bambi in Caribu. (Interview with Asen Balikci.) Nuove Effemeridi 4:20–24.

Chalfen, Richard

1971 (with Jay Haley) Reaction to Socio-Documentary Film Research in a Mental Health Clinic. American Journal of Orthopsychiatry 41(1):91–100.

1977 Human Images: Teaching the Communication of Ethnography. Anthropology and Education Quarterly 8(1):8–11.

1978 Which Way Media Anthropology? Journal of Communication 28(3):208–214.

1979 Photography's Role in Tourism: Some Unexpected Relationships. Annals of Tourism Research 6(4):435–47.

1981 A Sociovidistic Approach to Children's Filmmaking: The Philadelphia Project. Studies in Visual Communication 7(1):2–33.

1984 The Sociovidistic Wisdom of Abby and Ann: Toward an Etiquette of Home Mode Photography. Journal of American Culture 7(1–2): 22–31.

1986 Home Movies in a World of Reports: An Anthropological Appreciation. Journal of the University Film and Video Association 38(3–4):58–62.

1987 Snapshot Versions of Life. Bowling Green, Ohio: Popular Press.

In Press Turning Leaves: The Photograph Collections of Two Japanese American Families. Albuquerque: University of New Mexico Press.

Chin, Daryl

1978– . Annual Catalogues for the Asian-American Film Festival. (Contributing essays.) New York: Asian Cinevision.

1985   Introduction. *In* The Asian-American Media Reference Guide. Amy Chen and Berenice Chu, eds. New York: Asian Cinevision.
1986–87   Art & Cinema (New Series). (Editor) 1(1); 1(2); 1(3). Imperial Beach, California: B.R.I.

Chiozzi, Paolo

1984a   Visuelle Anthropologie: Funktionen und Strategien der ethnographiscer Films. *In* Ethnologie als Sozialwissenschaft. Special issue, E.W. Muller, R. Koenig, K.P. Koepping, and P. Drechsel, eds. Koelner Zeitschrift für Ethnologieund Sozialpsychologie (26):448–512.
1984b   Antropologia visuale. Florence: La Casa Usher.
1985   La ricostruzione nel film etnografico (and) Per un archivio video-sonoro delle societa complesse. *In* Teorie e tecniche de Antropologia visuale. M. Canevacci, M. Catani, R. Cedrini, and P. Chiozzi, eds. Pp. 21–28 (and) 29–40. Palermo: Laboratorio Antropologico Universitario.
1987   On Some of the Effects 'Induced' by the Development of New Technologies in Visual Anthropology. CVA Newsletter (October): 23–28.
1988a   Stephen Sommier: etnologia ed etno-fotografia. AFT 4(7):13–61.
1988b   Rethinking Ethnographic Film: Visual Anthropology and the Dynamics of Change. *In* Issues in Visual Anthropology. Pp. 11–22. P. Chiozzi and F. Haller, eds. Aachen: Alano-Edition Herodot.
1988c   For a Critique of the Ethnographic Film Festivals in Italy. *In* Catalogo del XIX Festival dei Popoli. Pp. 147–162. Florence.
1989   Reflections on Ethnographic Film with a General Bibliography. (Translated by Denise Dresner.) Visual Anthropology 2(1):1–84.
Forthcoming   Teaching Visual Anthropology. Florence: Edizioni Scientifiche Fiorentine.

Coggeshall, John M.

1988   (with Jo Anne Nast) Vernacular Architecture in Southern Illinois: The Ethnic Heritage. Carbondale: Southern Illinois University Press.

Collier, John Jr.

1949   (with Anibal Buitron) The Awakening Valley. (A visual ethnography of the textile culture of Otovalo, Ecuador.) Chicago: University of Chicago Press.
1967   Visual Anthropology: Photography as a Research Method. New York: Holt Rinehart and Winston.
1973   Alaskan Eskimo Education. (Film analysis of cultural confrontation in the schools.) New York: Holt, Rinehart, and Winston.

1987   Visual Anthropology's Contribution to the Field of Anthropology. Visual Anthropology 1(1):37–46.

Collier, John Jr. and Malcolm Collier
1986   Visual Anthropology: Photography as a Research Method. Second edition. Albuquerque: University of New Mexico Press.

Collier, Malcolm
1979   A Film Study of Classrooms in Western Alaska. Fairbanks: University of Alaska, Center for Cross Cultural Studies.

1983   Nonverbal Factors in the Education of Chinese American Children: A Film Study. San Francisco: San Francisco State University, Asian American Studies.

Cone, Cynthia A.
1978   (with Keith Kendall) Space, Time, and Family Interaction: Visitor Behavior at the Science Museum of Minnesota. Curator 21:245–258.

1986   (with Berta E. Perez) Peer Groups and the Organization of Classroom Space. Human Organization 45(1):80–88.

Conklin, Harold C.
1955   Hanunóo Color Categories. Southwestern Journal of Anthropology. 11(4):339–44.

1973   Color Categorization. American Anthropologist 75(4):931–42.

1976a Ethnographic Semantic Analysis of Ifugao Landform Categories. *In* Environmental Knowing. G.T. Moore and R.G. Gollege, eds. Pp. 235–246. Stroudsburg, Pennsylvania: Dowden, Hutchingson and Ross.

1976b (with Miklos Pinther) Pseudoscopic Illusion. Science 194(4263): 374.

1980a Folk Classification: A Topically Arranged Bibliography of Contemporary and Background References Through 1971. (Revised reprinting with author index. Sections on color, orientation, and sensation.) New Haven: Yale University, Department of Anthropology.

1980b Ethnographic Atlas of Ifugao: A Study of Environment, Culture and Society in Northern Luzon. New Haven: Yale University Press. (Also printed in London.)

Damon, George H. Jr.
1983   A Survey of Political Cartoons dealing with the Middle East. *In* Split Vision. Edmund Ghareeb, ed. Pp. 143–153. Washington, D.C.: American-Arab Affairs Council.

d'Azevedo, Warren L.
1958   A Structural Approach to Esthetics: Toward a Definition of Art in Anthropology. American Anthropologist 60:702–14.
1973a The Traditional Artist in African Societies. (Editor.) Bloomington: Indiana University Press.
1973b Mask Makers and Myth in Western Liberia. *In* Primitive Art and Society. Anthony Forge, ed. London: Oxford University Press.
1975a The Artist Archetype in Gola Culture. Dover: Liberian Studies Program, University of Delaware.
1975b (with Catherine S. Fowler) Nevada Indian Historical Map. Detroit: Hearne Brothers.
1986   Washoe. *In* Handbook of North American Indians, Volume 11, Warren L. d'Azevedo, ed. Washington D.C.: Smithsonian Institution.

de Brigard, Emilie
1972   The History of Ethnographic Film. Master's thesis, University of California, Los Angeles.
1973   Anthropological Cinema. New York: Museum of Modern Art, Department of Film.
1975   The History of Ethnographic Film. *In* Principles of Visual Anthropology. Paul Hockings, ed. Pp. 13–43. World Anthropology series. The Hague: Mouton.
1987   Review of From Site to Sight: Anthropology, Photography, and the Power of Imagery. A photographic exhibition from the collections of the Peabody Museum of Archaeology and Ethnology and the Department of Anthropology, Harvard University (September, 1986 to October, 1987). Visual Anthropology 1(1):75–79.

de Brigard, Emilie and John Kennedy Marshall
1975   Idea and Event in Urban Film. *In* Principles of Visual Anthropology. Paul Hockings, ed. Pp. 133–145. The Hague: Mouton.

De Friedmann, Nina S.
1976   Cine documento: Una herramienta para investigación y comunicación social. Revista Colombiana de Antropología 10. (Bogotá.)
1979   (with Richard Cross) Ma Ngombe: Guerreros y Ganaderos en Palenque. Bogotá: Carlos Valencia Editores.
1985   Carnaval en Barranquilla. Bogotá: Editorial La Rosa.

Desmond, Lawrence G.
1985   Waiting for the Dawn: Mircea Eliade in Perspective. David Carrasco and Jane Swanberg, eds.; photographs by Lawrence G. Desmond. Boulder, Colorado: Westview Press.

1988   (with Phyllis M. Messenger) A Dream of Maya. (Life and work of Augustus Le Plongeon who took photographs with wet collodion glass-plate negatives to document ruins in northern Yucatan in the 1870's.) Albuquerque: University of New Mexico Press.

Dewey, Alice G.

1985   Boundary and Batik: A Study in Ambiguous Categories. *In* Cultural Values and Human Ecology. Karl L. Hutterer, George Lovelace, and A. Terry Rambo, eds. Michigan Papers on South and Southeast Asia, No. 27.

Diaz-Granados, Carol

1966   Massive Lightweights (3-Dimensional Design). (Photo essay.) Arts and Activities, June. Pp. 29–31.

1980   Three-Dimensional Design. Arts and Activities 88(1):32–33.

1983   Rocky Hollow Revisited. (Recommendations on the preservation of Woodland petroglyph site in Missouri, and possible interpretations of the design symbolism.) Jefferson City: Anthropology Through the Arts.

Di Sparti, Antonio

1975a Linguaggio pubblicitario.   Analisi linguistica di un copus. pubblicitario di sigarette americane. Palermo: Circolo Semiologica.

1975b Il computer, creativo pubblicitario? SIPRA 5:109–116.

1977   Condizione femminile e linguaggio. Palermo: Clemenza.

1979   Le figure del discorso tra linguistica e intelligenza artificiale. Osservazioni preliminari ad una elaborazione automatica del discorso figurato. *In* Linguaggi e formalizzazioni. A cura di D. Gambarara, F. Lo Piparo, G. Ruggiero. Pp. 631–641. Roma: Bulzoni editore.

1982   Diaspora nel televisivo: lingue minoritarie e mass media. A proposito del plurilinguismo arbëresh di Piana degli Albanesi (Palermo). *In* Etnia albanese e minoranze linguistiche in Italia. A cura di A. Guzzetta. Pp. 177–258. Palermo: 1st. Lingua e Lett. Albanese.

1983   Pronome personale come performativo: osservazioni sul sistema pronominale karok. La Memoria 2:121–151. (Annali Fac. Lett. Filos. Palermo.)

1984   Verbale vs non-verbale, emisfero destro vs emisfero sinistro,... *In* Proceedings of the 3rd Congress of IASS. The Hague: Mouton.

1985   Semantica del noi. Media, mitopoiesi e aggregazione linguistica nel caso Moro. La memoria 3. (Annali Fac. Lett. Filos. Palermo.)

Dornfeld, Barry

Forthcoming   Analysis of Certain Structural Aspects of "Chronicle of a Summer". Visual Anthropology.

Drewal, Henry John

1977 Traditional Art of the Nigerian Peoples: The Ratner Collection. Washington, D.C.: Museum of African Art.

1978 The Arts of Egungun among Yoruba Peoples. (Guest Editor with Introduction.) African Arts, Special Issue 11(3).

1980 African Artistry: Technique and Aesthetics in Yoruba Sculpture. Atlanta, Georgia: The High Museum of Art.

1983 (with Margaret Thompson Drewal) Gelede: Art and Female Power Among the Yoruba. Bloomington: Indiana University Press.

Forthcoming (with Margaret Thompson Drewal) Composing Time and Space in Yoruba Art in Studies. *In* Yoruba Verbal and Visual Arts. R. Abiodun, ed. Ile-Ife: University of Ife Press.

Dumont, Jean-Paul

1970 (with Jean Monod) Le Foetus Astral: Essai d'Analyse Structurale d'un Mythe Cinematographique. Paris: Bourgouis.

Durrans, Brian

1982 (with Robert Knox) India: Past into Present. London: British Museum Publications, Ltd.

Edson, Paul

1983 Design in America: The Cranbrook Vision, 1925–1950. New Art Examiner 11(5):21.

1984 Masterpieces of African Art. New Art Examiner 12(9):61.

1985 Automobile and Culture—Detroit Style. New Art Examiner 13 (2):67–68.

El Guindi, Fadwa

1986 The Myth of Ritual: A Native's Ethnography of Zapotec Life-Crisis Rituals. (Essay on ethnographic methodology and fieldwork as they relate to anthropological theory.) Tucson: University of Arizona Press.

Erdman, Joan L.

1978 The Maharaja's Musicians: The Organization of Cultural Performance at Jaipur in the 19th Century. *In* American Studies in the Anthropology of India. Sylvia Vatuk, ed. New Delhi: Manohar.

1979 Research Potential in the Archival Materials of Rajasthan. American Institute of Indian Studies Newsletter. New Delhi.

1980 The Changing Patronage of Musicians in Twentieth Century Jaipur: A Semiotic Approach. *In* The Communication of Ideas. (ICAES Series 3.) V. Gautam, and J.S. Yadava, eds. Pp. 111–23. New Delhi: Concept.

1982 The Empty Beat: Khali as a Sign of Time. American Journal of Semiotics 1(4).

1984 Who Should Speak for the Performing Arts? The Case of the Delhi Dancers. *In* Cultural Policy in India. Lloyd I. Rudolph, ed. New Delhi: Chanakya Publications. (Also in Public Affairs, 1983.)

1985a Patrons and Performers in Rajasthan: The Subtle Tradition. New Delhi: Chanakya Publications.

1985b Today and the Good Old Days: South Asian Music and Dance Performances in Chicago. Selected Reports in Ethnomusicology VI: Asian Music in North America. Berkeley: University of California, Program in Ethnomusicology Monographs.

1987 Performance as Translation: Uday Shankar in the West. Drama Review 31(1):64-88.

In press Arts Patronage in India: Methods, Motives, and Markets. (A volume of papers from a 1983 conference at the University of Chicago.) New Dehli: Chanakya Publications.

Forthcoming The Idea of Rajasthan: Explorations in Regional Identity. 2 volumes. (Co-editor.) New Dehli and Riverdale, Maryland: Manohar Book Service and Riverdale Press.

Erickson, Frederick

1982a (with Jeffrey J. Shultz) The Counselor as Gatekeeper: Social Interactions in Interviews. New York: Academic Press.

1982b Audiovisual Records as a Primary Data Source. (Special Issue, Sound-Image Records in Social Interaction Research, A. Grimshaw, ed.) Sociological Methods and Research 11(2):213–232.

1986 Listening and Speaking. *In* Language and Linguistics: The Interdependence of Theory, Data, and Application. (Georgetown University Round Table on Languages and Linguistics, 1985.) Washington, D.C.: Georgetown University Press.

Eyde, David B.

1981 Orozco as Myth: A Structural Analysis. *In* Proceedings of the Rocky Mountain Council on Latin American Studies Conference. John J. Brasch and Susan R. Rouch, eds. Lincoln: University of Nebraska.

1983 Review of Christian Images in Hispanic New Mexico, by William Wroth. American Ethnologist 10:821.

1984 Three Modes in Traditional Korean Culture. Korean Cultural Anthropology 125–142.

Faris, James C.

1972 Nuba Personal Arts. London: Duckworth.

1978 The Productive Basis of Aesthetic Traditions. *In* Art in Society. Michael Greenhalgh and Vincent Megaw, eds. Pp. 317–339. London:

Duckworth.
1980   Polluted Vision. Sudanow 5(5):38.
1983   From Form to Content in the Structural Study of Aesthetic Tradition. *In* Structure and Cognition in Art. Dorothy K. Washburn, ed. Pp. 90–112. New York: Cambridge University Press.
1986   Visual Rhetoric: Navajo Art and Curing. Medical Heritage 2(2): 136–147.
1988a   The Significance of Differences in the Male and Female Personal Art of the Southeast Nuba. *In* Marks of Civilization: Artistic Transformations of the Human Body. A. Rubin, ed. Los Angeles: Museum of Culture History, UCLA.
1988b   Southeast Nuba: A Biographical Statement. *In* Anthropological Filmmaking. J. R. Rollwagen, ed. Pp. 111–121. New York: Harwood Academic Publishers.
1988c   ART/artifact: On the Museum in Anthropology. *In* Current Anthropology 29(5):775–779.
In press   Photography of the Southeast Nuba: Colonial Considerations. *In* Photography and the Colonial Encounter. (Sponsored by the Royal Anthropological Institute, London.) New Haven: Yale University Press.

Farnell, Brenda M.
1985   The Hands of Time: An Exploration into Some Features of Deixis in American Sign Language. Journal for the Anthropological Study of Human Movement 3(3):100–116.
1988   Some Problems With Spoken Language Models in the Analysis of Sign Languages. Journal for the Anthropological Study of Human Movement 5(1):19–32.
1989   Movement Notation. *In* International Encyclopedia of Communications. Erik Barnouw, ed. New York: Oxford University Press.

Feest, Christian F.
1967   The Virginia Indian in Pictures, 1612–1624. The Smithsonian Journal of History 2(1):1–30.
1980   Native Arts of North America. London: Thames and Hudson.
1986   Northeastern North America. Iconography of Religion 10(7).

Fernea, Robert A.
1973   (with George Gerster) Nubians in Egypt: Peaceful People. (Written and photographic essay.) Austin: University of Texas Press.

Finnegan, Gregory A.
1974   Film review: Africa: Continent in Change, by The National Geographic Society. American Anthropologist 76(1):214.

1977   Film review: A Namprusi Village.   (British Ministry of Information.) American Anthropologist 79(3):748.

1974–81   Eleven various film reviews in American Anthropologist.

1980   Memories of Underexposure: Reflections of Women in Film. (Review article.) Choice 18(1):34–53.

Fleischhauer, Carl

1981   (with Lyntha S. Eiler and Terry Eiler)   Blue Ridge Harvest. (Photographic book.) Washington, D.C.: Library of Congress.

Flowers, Nancy M.

1965   Majestic Workboats of a Portuguese Lagoon.   Natural History 74(2):20–25.

1969   The Royal Fleece of the Andes.   Natural History 78(4):36–42.

1969   Pottery of Barcelos: Folk Art that is a Link with Roman Past. Natural History 75(6):44–51.

Ford, Thomas M.

n.d.   Infantile Sensuality.   (One hundred eight-photo sequence plates and descriptive data.   A social anthropological study of the form, use, meaning and function of the erotic experiences associated with physical intimacy and stimulation, hunger in the self, and parent-child relationships of infancy and childhood. Unpublished, but available to qualified scholars for research purposes through the Kinsey Institute for Research in Sex, Gender and Reproduction, 416 Morrison Hall, Indiana University, Bloomington, Indiana 47405.)

Gardner, Robert G.

1957   Anthropology and Film.   Daedalus 86:344–352.

1960   A Human Document.   Daedalus 89:144–149.

1969   (with Karl G. Heider.)   Gardens of War. Life and Death in the New Guinea Stone Age.   (Photo book.) New York: Random House.

Gatewood, John B.

1981   (with Robert Rosenwein) Interactional Synchrony: Genuine or Spurious?   Critique of Recent Research.   Journal of Nonverbal Behavior 6(1):12–29.

Gearing, Frederick O.

1979   (with Lucinda Sangree, eds.) Toward a Cultural Theory of Education and Schooling. World Anthropology Series. The Hague: Mouton.

Geary, Christraud M.

1983   Bamum Two-Figure Thrones: Additional Evidence. African Arts

16(4):46–53.

1985a (with Adamou Ndam Njoya) Mandou Yenou. Photographies du pays Bamoum, royaume ouest-africain, 1902–1915. Munich: Trickster Verlag. (Also in German.)

1985b (with Paul Jenkins) Photographs from Africa in the Basel Mission Archive. African Arts 18(4):56–63.

1986 Photographs as Materials for African History: Some Methodological Considerations. History In Africa 13:89–116.

1987 Basketry In the Aghem-Fungom Area of the Cameroon Grassfields. African Arts 20(3):42–53,89–90.

1988a Images From Bamum: German Colonial Photography at the Court of King Njoya, Cameroon, West Africa, 1902–1915. Washington, D.C.: Smithsonian Press.

1988b Art and Political Process In the Kingdom of Bali-Nyonga and Bamum (Cameroon Grassfields). Canadian Journal of African Studies 22(1):11–41.

1988c Messages and Meaning of African Court Arts: Warrior Figures from the Bamum Kingdom. Art Journal 47(2):103–113.

Gidley, Mick

1979 With One Sky Above Us: Life on an Indian Reservation at the Turn of the Century. (Photographs by E.H. Latham, U.S. Indian Agency Physician.) New York: Putnam.

1982 Edward S. Curtis as Filmmaker. Studies In Visual Communication 8(3):70–79.

1983 American Photography. British Association for American Studies Pamphlet Series No. 12.

Ginsburg, Faye

1987a Local Knowledge In the Global Village. Society of Visual Anthropology Newsletter 2.

1987b Ethnographies on the Airwaves. Osaka, Japan: Senri Ethnological Studies, National Museum of Ethnology.

Gmelch, George

1980 J. M. Synge In Wicklow, West Kerry and Connemara. (Photo essay.) New York: Rowman and Littlefield.

1980 Photographs for: Tinkers and Travellers, by Sharon Gmelch. Dublin: The O'Brien Press.

Graburn, Nelson H. H.

1976 Ethnic and Tourist Arts: Cultural Expressions from the Fourth World. (Editor.) Berkeley: University of California Press.

1982   Television and the Canadian Inuit. (Editor.) Etudes/Inuit/Studies 6:7–17
1983a The Anthropolgy of Tourism. (Editor.)   Annals of Tourism Research, Special Issue 10:1.
1983b To Pray, Pay, and Play: The Cultural Structure of Japanese Domestic Tourism. Aix-en-Provence: Centre des Hautes Etudes Touristiques.
1986   L'Evolution d'Art Touristique. Aix-en-Provence: Centre des Hautes Etudes Touristiques.

Graves, Thomas E.

1979   Photographs for: A Tree Smells Like Peanut Butter, Folk Artists In a City School. Trenton, New Jersey: State Council on the Arts.
1983a Liebsen Kinder Und Verwandten: Death and Ethnicity. Keystone Folklore NS-1(2):1–2, 6–14.
1983b Ethnic Artists, Artifacts, and Authenticity: Pennsylvania German and Ukrainian Folk Crafts Today. Pioneer America 15(1):21–34.
1984   The Pennsylvania German Hex Sign: A Study In Folk Process. Ph.D. dissertation, Department of Folklore and Folklife, University of Pennsylvania. (University Microfilms 8422908.)
1985   Photographs for: Buddy, A Luzerne County Powwower. *In* The Art of Spiritual Healing, by Julian Richter. Focus Magazine (Feb. 10): 4–5 and cover.
1986   You Will See Results Friday: A Performance Model of the 'Fortune-Telling' Event. *In* Papers From the 6th and 7th Annual Meetings of the Gypsy Lore Society, North American Chapter. Joanne Grumet, ed. Pp. 17–28. New York: GLSNAC.
1988a Pennsylvania German Gravestones: An Introduction. (Also ethnographic photography for this volume.) *In* The Annual Markers (The Journal for the Association of Gravestone Studies) 5:60–95.
1988b Robert Moore: Native American Craftsman (and) The Selling of Pennsylvania German Folk Art. (Also photographs.) *In* Craft and Community: Traditional Craft In Contemporary Society. Shalom Staub, ed. Nashville, Tennessee: American Association for State and Local History (and Balch Institute for Ethnic Studies).
1989   (with Don Yoder) The Pennsylvania German Hex Sign. New York: E.P. Dutton.

Griffin, Michael S.

1983   (with Frank Eadie and Brian Sutton-Smith) Filmmaking by 'Young Filmmakers.' Studies In Visual Communication 9(4).
1985   What Young Filmmakers Learn from Television: A Study of Structure In Films Made By Children. Journal of Broadcasting and Electronic Media 29(1).

1987   History and Ethnographic Method In Visual Communication Research. *In* Visual Explorations of the World: Selected Papers from the International Conference on Visual Communication. Jay Ruby and MartIn Taureg, eds. Pp. 240–254. Aachen, Federal Republic of Germany: Edition Herodot.

Griffin, Michael S. and Dona Schwartz

1986   Amateur Photography: The Organizational Maintenance of an Aesthetic Code. *In* Natural Audiences: Qualitative Research of Media Uses and Effects. Thomas Lindlof, ed. Longwood, New Jersey: Ablex Publishing Co.

Grimshaw, Allen D.

1982a   Sound-Image Records In Social Interaction Research. (Editor.) Sociological Methods and Research 11(2):115–255.

1982b   Introduction. (and) Some Questions and Answers about Sound-Image Data Records for Research on Social Interaction. (and) Whose privacy? What harm? Sociological Methods and Research 11(2):115–119, 121–144, 233–247.

1988.   Collegial Discourse: Professional Conversation Among Peers. (On the collaborative study of the MAP sound-image record.) Norwood, New Jersey: Ablex.

Forthcoming   What's Going on Here? Complementary Studies of Professional Talk. (Editor.) (Studies of the MAP sound-image record authored by several of the project's researchers). Norwood, New Jersey: Ablex.

Forthcoming   (with Steven Feld and David Jenness) The Multiple Analysis Project: Background, History, Problems, Data. *In* What's Going On Here? Allen D. Grimshaw, ed. Norwood, New Jersey: Ablex.

Gross, Larry

1973a   Modes of Communication and the Acquisition of Symbolic Competence. *In* Communication Technology and Social Policy. George Gerbner, Larry Gross, and William Melody, eds. New York: Wiley. (Also Chapter 3. Media and Symbols: The Forms of Expression, Communication, and Education, 74th Yearbook of the Society for the Study of Education. Dr. R. Olson, ed. Chicago: University of Chicago Press, 1974.)

1973b   Art As the Communication of Competence. Social Science Information 12:115–141.

1981   Studying Visual Communication: Papers by Sol Worth. Edited and introduced by Larry Gross. Philadelphia: University of Pennsylvania Press.

1983   Why Johnny Can't Draw. (Special issue: Art and the Mind.) Art Education 36(2):74–77.

1985 Life vs. Art: The Interpretation of Visual Narratives. Studies In Visual Communication 11(4):2–11.

1986 (with George Gerbner, etal.) Living With Television: The Dynamics of the Cultivation Process. *In* Perspectives On Media Effects. Jennings Bryant and Dolf Zillman, eds. Pp. 17–40. Hillsdale, New Jersey: Lawrence Erlbaum.

1988 (with John Katz and Jay Ruby, eds.) Image Ethics: The Moral Rights of Subjects in Photography, Film, and Television. New York: Oxford University Press.

1989a International Encyclopedia of Communications. Associate Editor (Erik Barnouw, Editor In Chief). New York: Oxford University Press.

1989b Art. *In* International Encyclopedia of Communications. Volume 1. Erik Barnouw, ed. Pp. 111–120. New York: Oxford University Press.

1989c Mode. *In* International Encyclopedia of Communications. Volume 3. Erik Barnouw, ed. Pp. 111–120. New York: Oxford University Press.

Hall, Edward T.

1966 The Hidden Dimension. Garden City, New York: Doubleday.

1974 Handbook for Proxemic Research. Washington, D.C.: Society for the Anthropology of Visual Communication. [Eds. note: available from SVA, American Anthropological Association, 1703 New Hampshire Avenue NW, Washington, D.C. 20009.]

1976 Beyond Culture. Garden City, New York: Doubleday.

1979 Let's Heat People Instead of Houses. Human Nature (January).

1986 Foreword. *In* Visual Anthropology: Photography as a Research Method. Second edition. John Collier, Jr. and Malcolm Collier. Albuquerque: University of New Mexico Press.

1987 (with Mildred Reed Hall) Hidden Differences: Doing Business with the Japanese. Garden City, New York: Doubleday. [6 other books on Hidden Differences (Hamburg: Gruner + Jahr) treat German–Japanese, German–French, German–American intercultural communication.]

Hall, Stephanie A.

1984 Train Gone Sorry. (Conversational etiquette in a deaf social club.) Sign Language Studies 4:291–309.

Forthcoming Reality is a Crutch for People Who Can't Deal with Science Fiction. (Slogan buttons among science fiction fans.) Keystone Folklore Quarterly.

Halpern, Joel M.

1967a The Changing Village Community. Modernization of Traditional Societies Series. Englewood Cliffs, New Jersey: Prentice-Hall.

1967b A Serbian Village. Revised edition. New York: Harper and Row.

1971   Yugoslavian Villagers. (Photos and primary resource scientist for Unit 4; based on A Serbian Village.) Teacher's Guide. (Materials from A Serbian Village and Peasant Culture and Urbanization [1965]). *In* Inquiring About Technology, Studies in Economics and Anthropology. M. Schultz and W. Fiedler, eds. Pp. 112–121 and 139–152. New York: Holt, Rinehart, and Winston.

1972   (with Barbara Kerewsky) The People of Serbia. *In* People in States. Mary Durkin, ed. Pp. 130–199. Menlo Park, California: The Taba Program in Social Science, Addison-Wesley.

1980   Photographs, in Southeast Asian Studies: Emerging Nations of Indochina. New York: Educational Enrichment Materials Co., The New York Times, Inc.

1983   (with James Hafner and Barbara Kerewsky Halpern, eds.) River Road Through Laos: Reflections of the Mekong. Occasional Papers Series No. 10. Luang Prabang to Pak Tha: A Field Trip. Pp. 12–15. Amherst: International Area Studies Programs, University of Massachusetts.

1986   (with Barbara Kerewsky Halpern) Serbian Village in Historical Perspective. New York: Holt, Rinehart, and Winston.

Hammond, Joyce D.

1980   Tifaifai of Eastern Polynesia. Field Museum of Natural History Bulletin 51(7):4–9.

1986   Tifaifai and Quilts of Polynesia. Honolulu: University of Hawaii Press.

Haratonik, Peter L.

1974   Video Kids. New York: Gordon and Breach.

Hardin, Kris

1987a Rock-A-Bye Baby. *In* Generations: A Universal Family Album. Anna Cohn and Lucinda Leach, eds. New York: Pantheon.

1987b Aesthetics and the Cultural Whole: A Study of Kono Dance Occasions. Empirical Studies of the Arts, 1987/88.

1988   Ghosts in the Wall. *In* The Vietnam Veterans Memorial. Michael Katakis, author. (Includes 50 photographs [chosen from 16,000] by Michael Katakis.) New York: Crown Publishers.

Harper, Douglas

1978   Toward the Use of Photographs as Data: Self Definition on Skid Row. Washington D.C.: American Sociological Association.

1979   Life on the Road. *In* Images of Information: Still Photographs in Social Sciences Today. Wagner, Jon, ed. Pp. 86–93. Beverly Hills, California: Sage Publications.

1982   Good Company. (Visual ethnography of the railroad tramp.) Chicago: University of Chicago Press.

1986   Portraying Bricolage. Knowledge and Society 6:209–232.

1987a Working Knowledge: Skill and Community in a Small Shop. (Visual ethnography of a rural mechanic's life and work.) Chicago: University of Chicago Press.

1987b The Visual Ethnographic Narrative. Visual Anthropology 1(1):1–19.

1988   Visual Sociology: Expanding Sociological Vision. American Sociologist (Fall).

Hart, Lynn M.

1988   (with T. O. Eisemon and E. Ong'esa) Schooling and Self Employment in Kenya: The Acquisition of Craft Skills In and Outside Schools. International Journal of Educational Development 8(4): 271-278.

1989   (with T. O. Eisemon and E. Ong'esa) Stories in Stone: Soapstone Sculpture in Northern Quebec and Kenya. Ottawa: National Musuem of Civilization, Canada, and the Federation of Cooperatives of Northern Quebec.

In press (with B. White, eds.) Living Traditions in Art. Montréal: Canadian Assocation for the Study of Living Traditions in Art.

In press South Asian Women's Ritual Art. *In* Living Traditions in Art. L. M. Hart and B. White, eds. Montréal: Canadian Association for the Study of Living Traditions in Art.

Hauck, Shirley A.

1984   Ethnicity and the Kirch Weih Ritual: Symbolism for German-Romanians of Banat. *In* Papers for the Fifth Congress of Southeast European Studies. Shangri Ladze and Townsend, eds. Pp. 217–226. Columbus, Ohio: Slavica Publishers, for U.S. National Committee of the AIESEE.

1986   Extinction and Reconstruction of Aleut Music and Dance. Ph.D. dissertation, University of Pittsburgh. (University Microfilms.)

Heidenreich, C. Adrian

1969   Photography in America during the 1930's: A Collective Portrait. Rocky Mountain Review 6(1):88–106.

1971   Ethno-Documentary of the Crow Indians of Montana, 1824–1862. Ph.D. dissertation, University of Oregon, Eugene.

1983   Comment on: The Problem of the Ethnographic Real, by I.C. Jarvie. Current Anthropology 24(3):322.

1984 The Content and Context of Crow Indian Ledger Art. *In* Proceedings of the 5th Annual Plains Indian Seminar. George P. Horse Capture and Gene Ball, eds. Cody, Wyoming: Buffalo Bill Historical Center.

1985 Background and Interpretation of Crow and Gros Ventre Ledger Art Done at Crow Agency, Montana Between 1879 and 1897; Recovery and Preservation of the Barstow Collection; and Catalog of the Charles H. Barstow Collection. Billings, Montana: Yellowstone Art Center.

In press Warfare in the Pictographic Art of the Northwestern Plains. *In* Proceedings of a symposium on Plains Pictographic Art: An Evolving Tradition. Oklahoma City: Oklahoma Historical Society Series in Anthropology.

Heidenreich, C. Adrian and Virginia L. Heidenreich

1982 Montana Landscape, One Hundred Years: 1830's to 1930's. (Exhibition catalog.) Exhibit May–July 1982. Billings, Montana: Yellowstone Art Center.

Heidenreich, Virginia L.

1976 Farmers in the Tropical Mountains (Igorots of Mountain Philippines). Highlights for Children 31(7):40–41.

1977 Bearcreek, Montana: An Interdisciplinary Photographic and Historical Study of a Coal Mining Community, with Evaluations of Research Methods. (With major photo essay.) M.A. thesis, George Washington University.

1979 Sheep Shearing...Rangeland Ritual. Magazine of the National Cowboy Hall of Fame 9(2):22–29.

1980 Perspectives on Art: Philosophy, Sociology, Anthropology, and Physics. (Editor.) Billings, Montana: Yellowstone Art Center.

Heider, Karl G.

1969 (with Robert Gardner) Gardens of War. (Photo book.) New York: Random House.

1970 The Dugum Dani: A Papuan Culture in the Highlands of West New Guinea. Chicago: Aldine.

1972 The Dani of West Irian: Ethnographic Companion to the Film Dead Birds. New York: Warner Modular Publications.

1976 Ethnographic Film. Austin: University of Texas Press.

1979 Grand Valley Dani: Peaceful Warriors. New York: Holt, Rinehart, and Winston.

1979–1982 Anthropologist's Appointment Calendar. (Editor.) Washington, D.C.: American Anthropological Association.

1966–1983 Films for Anthropological Teaching (7 editions). (Editor.) Washington, D.C.: American Anthropological Association.

Henley, Paul
   1985   British Ethnographic Film. Anthropology Today 1(1):5–17.

Hockings, Paul
   1975   Educational Uses of Videotape. (and) Conclusion. *In* Principles of
   Visual Anthropology. Paul Hockings, ed. Pp. 383–384; 377–380.
   The Hague: Mouton.
   1988   (with Yasuhiro Omori, eds.) Cinematographic Theory and New
   Dimensions of Ethnographic Film. Senri Ethnological Series no. 24.
   Osaka, Japan: National Musuem of Ethnology.

Holaday, Duncan Alan
   1977   Review of: Principles of Visual Anthropology, Paul Hockings, ed.
   Studies in the Anthropology of Visual Communication 4(1): 59–62.
   1981   The Cultural Importance of Film Communication. *In* Komunikasi
   Massa. Faculty of Social Science, University of Indonesia, eds. Pp.
   44–55. Jakarta: University of Indonesia.
   1984a Making Media Fit: The Introduction of a New Communications
   Technology to a West Javanese Village. Ph.D. dissertation, Annenberg School of Communications, University of Pennsylvania.
   1984b Review of: Concept in Film Theory, by Dudley Andrew. Malay-
   sian Journalism Review (Autumn).

Homiak, John P.
   1987   The Mystic Revelation of Rasta-Far-Eye: Visionary Communication in a Prophetic Movement. *In* Dreaming: Anthropological and
   Psychological Interpretations. Barbara Tedlock, ed. Cambridge: Cambridge University Press.

Hoskins, Janet Alison
   1985   A Life History From Both Sides: The Changing Poetics of Personal Experience. Journal of Anthropological Research 41(2): 147–169.
   1986   So My Name Shall Live: Stone-Dragging and Grave Building in
   Kodi, West Sumba. Bijdragen tot de Taal, Land, en Volkenkunde
   142:31–51.
   1988a Arts and Cultures of Sumba. *In* Islands and Ancestors. Douglas
   Newton and J-P Barbier, eds. New York and Geneva: Metropolitan
   Museum and Musée Barbier-Mueller.
   1988b Why Do Ladies Sing the Blues? Indigo, Cloth Production, and
   Gender Symbolism in Kodi. *In* Cloth and Human Experience. T.
   Weiner and J. Schneider, eds. Washington, D.C.: Smithsonian.

Husmann, Rolf
   1978   Ethnographic Filming: The Scientific Approach. Reviews in

Anthropology 5(4):487–501.
1983 Film and Fieldwork: Some Problems Reconsidered. *In* Methodology in Anthropological Filmmaking. N. Bogaast and H. Vetelaar, eds. Pp. 93–111. Göttingen, Federal Republic of Germany.
1985 The Training of Anthropology Students in Filmmaking: A Curriculum. International Journal of Visual Sociology 1:30–34.
1987 Mit der Kamera in Fremden Kulturen. (Editor.) [2nd AIW Symposium on Visual Anthropology, Göttingen.] Emsdetten: A. Gehling.

Hymes, Dell
1964 Introduction. *In* The Ethnography of Communication. American Anthropologist 66(6, pt.2):1–34. J.J. Gumperz and D.H. Hymes, eds. Washington, D.C.: American Anthropological Association.
1967 The Anthropology of Communication. *In* Human Communication Theory: Original Essays. Frank E.X. Dance, ed. Pp.1–39. New York: Holt, Rinehart, and Winston.
1972 (with John Gumperz) Directions in Sociolinguistics: The Ethnography of Communication. New York: Holt, Rinehart, and Winston.
1974 Foundations in Sociolinguistics: An Ethnographic Approach. Philadelphia: University of Pennsylvania Press.
1981 In Vain I Tried to Tell You. (Essays in Native American ethnopoetics.) Philadelphia: University of Pennsylvania Press.

Irvine, Dominique
1987 Resource Management by the Runa Indians of the Ecuadorian Amazon. Ph.D. dissertation, Anthropology Department, Stanford University. (Ann Arbor: University Microfilms DA8720400).
1989 Succession Management and Resource Distribution in an Amazonian Rain Forest. Advances in Economic Botany 7:223-237.

Jablonko, Allison
1968 Dance and Daily Activities among the Maring People of New Guinea: A Cinematographic Analysis of Body Movement Style. Ph.D. dissertation, Department of Anthropology, Columbia University. (Microfilm 69-3077, Ann Arbor, University Microfilms).
1975 (with E.R. Sorenson) Research Filming of Naturally Occurring Phenomena: Basic Strategies. *In* Principles of Visual Anthropology. Paul Hockings, ed. Pp. 151–163. The Hague: Mouton.
1988a New Guinea in Italy: An Analysis of the Making of an Italian Television Series from Research Footage of the Maring People of Papua, New Guinea. *In* Anthropological Filmmaking: Anthropological Perspectives on the Production of Ethnographic Film and Video for General Public Audiences. Jack R. Rollwagen, ed. Pp. 169–196. New York: Harwood Academic Publishers.

1988b (with Elizabeth Kagan) An Experiment in Looking: Reexamining the Process of Observation. The Drama Review 32(4):148–163.

Jablonko, Allison and Marek Jablonko
1988 Review of Anthropologia Visuale: Riflessioni sul film etnografico con bibliografia generale, by Paolo Chiozzi. (Florence, Italy: La Casa Usher.) Visual Anthropology 1(1):71–79.

Jablonko, Marek
1964 Problems of Field Filming. Paper presented at the Seventh International Congress of Anthropological and Ethnographic Sciences, Moscow.

Jacknis, Ira
1976 Savage Icons: Victorian views of primitive art. M.A. thesis, University of Chicago.

1978 (with Jane Swanson) Anthropology on Film. Field Museum Bulletin 49(7):16–21.

1984 Franz Boas and Photography. Studies in Visual Communication 10(1): 2–60.

1985 Franz Boas and Exhibits: On the Limitations of the Museum Method of Anthropology. *In* Objects and Others: Essays on Museums and Material Culture. History of Anthropology, No. 3. George W. Stocking, Jr., ed. Pp. 75–111. Madison: University of Wisconsin Press.

1987 The "Picturesque" and the "Scientific": Franz Boas' Plan for Anthropological Filmmaking. Visual Anthropology 1(1):59–64.

1988 Margaret Mead and Gregory Bateson in Bali: Their Use of Photography and Film. Cultural Anthropology 3(2):160-177.

1989 The Storage Box of Tradition: Museums, Anthropologists, and Kwakiutl Art, 1881-1981. Ph.D. dissertation, Department of Anthropology, University of Chicago. (Accepted for publication by Smithsonian Institution).

Forthcoming James Mooney as an Ethnographic Photographer. Visual Anthropology.

James, William R. [see: Albers and James]

Jell-Bahlsen, Sabine
1985 From Divine Earth-Divine Water to Mami Wata. Anthropologia Visualis 1(1).

Forthcoming Book review: Die Fremden sehen: Ethnologie und Film, by M. Friedrich, A. Hagemann-Doumbia, R. Kapfer, W. Petermann, R. Thomas, M.–J. van de Loo, eds. [Seeing Foreigners: Ethnology and Film.] Visual Anthropology.

Johnson, David M.

1976   An Overview of Nonverbal Behavior Research Among Humans. Paper presented at the Annual Meeting of Southern Anthropological Society, Atlanta, Georgia. (Organizer and chair of symposium.)

1981   Disney World as Structure and Symbol: Re-creation of the American Experience. Journal of Popular Culture 15(1).

Johnson-Dean, Lynn

1979   The Use of Portable Video Systems in El Salvador. Proceedings of CREDEM. Ahmedabad, India.

1986   The Effectiveness of Videotape Programs as a Communication Tool in the Small-Scale Livestock for Rural Farming Women Project, Honduras. Las Cruses: New Mexico State University, Department of Sociology and Anthropology.

1987   The Efficacy of the Use of a Portable Video System in a Development Project in Northern Honduras. Paper presented at the Society for Applied Anthropology Meeting, Oaxaca, Mexico.

Jones, Michael Owen

1975   The Hand Made Object and Its Maker. Berkeley: University of California Press.

1980   (with Robert A. Georges) People Studying People: The Human Element in Fieldwork. Berkeley: University of California Press.

1988   (with Michael D. Moore and Richard C. Snyder) Inside Organizations: Understanding the Human Dimension. Newbury Park: Sage Publications.

Kaplan, Flora S.

1980   Una Tradicion Alfarera: Conocimiento y Estilo. Mexico City: Instituto Nacional Indigenista.

1981a Images of Power: Art of the Royal Court of Benin. (Editor and contributor.) New York: New York University, The Grey Art Gallery.

1981b (with David M. Levine) Cognitive Mapping of a Folk Taxonomy of Mexican Pottery: A Multivariate Approach. American Anthropologist 83(4):868–884.

1981c Privies, Privacy, and Political Process: Some Thoughts on Bathroom Graffiti and Group Identity. *In* Group Cohesion: Theoretical and Clinical Perspectives. Henry Kellerman, ed. Pp. 392–410. New York: Grune & Stratton.

1985   Measuring, Mapping, and Meaning of Pots. Review of The Folk Classificiation of Ceramics: A Study of Cognitive Prototypes, by Willett Kempton. American Anthropologist 87(2):357–364.

1987 Nigeria. *In* Art Museums of the World. (James L. Connelly, Virginia Jackson, Marlene A. Palmer, Eric J. Zafran, eds.) Austin, Texas: Greenwood Press. [Reference work.]

In press Potter for the Dead: Role and Function of Blackware in Puebla, Mexico. *In* Ceramics and Civilizations: Roles and Functions of Ceramincs in Society (volume 5 in series), W. David Kingery, ed.

Forthcoming Some Uses of Photographs in Recovering Cultural History at the Royal Court of Benin, Nigeria. *In* International Studies on Ethnophotography. Joanna C. Scherer, ed. Special issue of the journal Visual Anthropology.

Forthcoming The Queen Mother of Benin "Iye Oba": Sexual Ambiguity and Gender in the Royal Court Art of Benin, Nigeria. *In* Studies in Benin History. Ekpo Eyo, ed. London: Ethnografica Press.

Kealiinohomoku, Joann W.

1974 Field Guides. *In* New Dimensions in Dance Research: Anthropology and Dance—The American Indian. CORD Research Annual 6. Tamara Comsteek, ed. Pp. 245–260.

1976 A Comparative Study of Dance as a Constellation of Motor Behaviors Among African and United States Negroes. (From M.A. thesis, 1965.) *In* CORD Dance Research Annual 7. Adrienne L. Kaeppler, ed. Pp. 1–179.

1985 Hula Space and its Transmutations. *In* Dance as Cultural Heritage, Vol. 2. CORD Research Annual 15. Betty True Jones, ed. Pp. 11–21.

Kirkpatrick, Joanna

1984 The Painted Ricksha As Culture Theater. Studies in Visual Communication 10(3):73–85.

Kolodny, Rochelle

1975 Photography: The Metamorphosis of Reality. *In* Saying Cheese: Studies in Folklore and Visual Communication. Folklore Forum 13:51–58.

1978 Towards an Anthropology of Photography: Frameworks of Analysis. M.A. thesis, McGill University.

1985–86 Photographs as Artifacts: The Work of Rosalind Solomon. Photo Communique 7(4):10–17.

Kreamer, Christine Mullen

1986 Art of Sub–Saharan Africa: The Fred and Rita Richman Collection. Atlanta: The High Museum of Art.

1987 Moba Shrine Figures of Northern Togo. African Arts 10(2): 52–55, 82–83.

1988 Space and Liminality in Moba Initiation Rites (Northern Togo).

Drama Review.

Krouse, Susan Applegate
1981 Capturing the Vanishing Race: The Photographs of Dr. Joseph K. Dixon. M.A. thesis, Indiana University.
1987 Filming the Vanishing Race. *In* Visual Explorations of the World: Selected Papers from the International Conference on Visual Communication. Jay Ruby and Martin Taureg, eds. Pp. 255–266. Aachen, Federal Republic of Germany: Edition Herodot.

Kugelmass, Jack
1983 The Miracle of Intervale Avenue. (Photographs and text.) New York: Schocken Books.

Laban/Bartenieff Institute of Movement Studies, Inc.
1987– . Movement Studies (journal: issue 1 on Sports and Fitness; issue 2 on Reliability in Movement Research). New York: LIMS, Inc.

Lacy, Christabel
1976 Greek Views of the Barbarians in the Hellenistic Age (from artistic evidence). Ph.D. dissertation, Department of Anthropology, University of Colorado.
1985 (with Robert White) Rural Schools and Communities in Cape Girardeau County. Cape Girardeau: Center for Regional History and Cultural Heritage, Southeast Missouri State University.

Lansing, J. Stephen
1983 The Three Worlds of Bali. New York: Praeger.
1987 Balinese Water Temples and the Management of Irrigation. American Anthropologist 89(2). [Relates to the film "The Goddess and the Computer."]

Lass, Andrew
1986a Presencing, Historicity, and the Shifting Voice of Written Relics in Eighteenth Century Bohemia. Paper presented at the Faculty Seminar, Department of Anthropology, University of Chicago, April 25.
1986b Romantic Documents and Political Monuments: The Meaning-Fulfillment of History in Nineteenth Century Czech Nationalism. Paper presented at the American Anthropological Association meetings, Philadelphia, December 3–7.

Linklater, Liza
1981 Anthropology and Photography: Approaches and Issues. M.A. thesis, York University, Toronto, Canada.

Lobo, Susan

1978– . Photographic community resource archives, Intertribal Friendship House, American Indian Center, Oakland, California. Ongoing collection and circulation of urban Indian community in San Francisco Bay Area. [Research coordinator since founding in 1978.]

1982 A House of My Own: Social Organization in the Squatter Settlements of Peru. Tucson: University of Arizona Press.

Lomax, Alan

1960 Folk Songs of North America. New York: Doubleday.

1968 Folk Song Style and Culture. [3 chapters on Choreometrics.] Washington, D.C.: American Association for the Advancement of Science. (Reprinted by Transaction Books, New Brunswick, New Jersey.)

1971 Toward An Ethnographic Film Archive. Filmmakers Newsletter 4(4):31–38.

1972 An Appeal for Cultural Equity. The World of Music 14(2). [Quarterly journal of the International Music Council, UNESCO] (Reprinted in 1977, Journal of Communication 27(2).)

1972 (with Norman Berkowitz) The Evolutionary Taxonomy of Culture. Science 117:228–239.

1975 Audiovisual Tools for the Analysis of Culture Style. *In* Principles of Visual Anthropology. Paul Hockings, ed. Pp. 303–322. World Anthropology series. The Hague: Mouton.

1976 Cantometrics: An Approach to the Anthropology of Music. (Accompanied by 7 cassettes.) Berkeley: University of California Extension Media Center.

1977 A Stylistic Analysis of Speaking. Language and Society 6.

1978 Cross-cultural Factors in Phonological Change. Language and Society 2:161–175.

1981 Culture-Style Factors in Face-to-Face Interaction. *In* Organization of Behavior in Face-to-Face Interaction. Adam Kendon, R.M. Harris, and M.R. Key, eds. The Hague: Mouton 1981.

Long, Joseph K.

1967 Anthropology Films. Green Bay: University of Wisconsin.

1968 Kodachrome Slides as Programmed Instructional Media. Transactions, Conference on Social Issues II. Pp. 35–40. Green Bay: University of Wisconsin.

Longo, Donna A. [directory listing: DiMichele, Donna Longo]

1980 Photographing the Hopi. Pacific Discovery 33(3):11–19.

1987 Toward Understanding Historical Photographs. *In* Anthropology at American: Essays in Honor of George L. Harris. Pp. 28–43.

Occasional Papers Series, Vol. 2. Washington, D.C.: The American University, Department of Anthropology.

Lüem, Barbara

1987 (with Michele Galizia) Versuch einer Typologisierung des Ethno-Film. *In* Mit der Kamera in fremden Kulturen. Rolf Husmann, ed. Pp. 23–36. Emsdetten: Verlag Andreas Gehling.

Luskey, Judith

1980 (with James R. Glenn) Two-Level Control of Photographic Collections of the NAA [National Anthropological Archives]. Studies in Visual Communication 8(3):2–6.

1985a (with Sylvia H. Williams) Go Well, My Child. (Photographs by Constance Stuart Larrabee in collaboration with Alan Paton.) Washington, D.C.: Smithsonian Press. [Photographic exhibition of South African tribal peoples, 1947–1949, coordinated with quotations from the novel Cry, the Beloved Country, 1949.]

1985b Profile of the Eliot Elisofon Archives. International Bulletin for the Photographic Documentation of the Visual Arts 12(3):1–6.

1986a (with Paula Richardson Fleming) The North American Indians in Early Photographs. New York: Harper and Row. [Other editions published in 1988, London: Oxford University Press, and Munich: C. H. Beck (Die Indianer Nordamerikas in Fruhen Photographien).]

1986b The Art of West African Kingdoms. Washington, D.C.: Smithsonian Press.

1986c The Eliot Elisofon Archives. (Brochure/guide to the photographic collections, Smithsonian Institution, National Museum of African Art.) Washington, D.C.: Smithsonian Press.

1988a Early Anthropologists as Photographers. Visual Resources: An International Journal of Documentation 4:359–372.

1988b Why Things Are Considered Money. Faces 4(10):16–22. [Faces: The Magazine About People; A Young Reader's Social Anthropology (ages 8–14). Peterborough, New Hampshire: Cobblestone Publishing Co., in cooperation with the American Museum of Natural History.]

Lutkehaus, Nancy C.

1985 The Flutes of the Tanepoa: The Dynamics of Hierarchy and Equivalence in Manam, Papua New Guinea. Ph.D. dissertation, Anthropology Department, Columbia University.

MacDougall, David

1975 Beyond Observational Cinema. *In* Principles of Visual Anthropology. Paul Hockings, ed. Pp. 109–124. The Hague: Mouton.

1978   Ethnographic Film: Failure and Promise. Annual Review of
Anthropology 7.
1987   Media Friend or Media Foe. Visual Anthropology 1(1):54–58.

Manley, Roger B.
1987   (with Tom Patterson, Jonathan Williams, and Guy Mendes) St.
EOM, In the Land of Pasaquan. Winston-Salem, North Carolina: The
Jargon Society.
1988   A Blessing from the Source. Raleigh, North Carolina: North
Carolina State University.
1989   (with Howard Fenster and Tom Patterson)   Howard Fenster:
Stranger from Another World. Man of Visions Now on this Earth.
New York, New York: Abbeville Press.

Marshall, John Kennedy [also see: de Brigard and Marshall]
1958   Man As a Hunter. Natural History Magazine 67(6):291–309.

Martin, Mary
1978   Turkmen Women, Weaving, and Cultural Change.   Heresies,
(Winter):114–115.
1980a Making a Living in Turan: Animals, Land, and Wages. Expedition
22(4):29–35.
1980b Pastoral Production: Milk and Firewood in the Ecology of Turan.
Expedition 22(4):24–28.

Maynard, Douglas W.
1984a Inside Plea Bargaining. New York: Plenum Press.
1984b (with Don H.Z. Zimmerman)   Topical Talk, Ritual, and the
Social Organization of Relationships. Social Psychology Quarterly
47:301–316.
1985a How Children Start Arguments. Language in Society 14:1–29.
1985b On the Functions of Social Conflict Among Children. American
Sociological Review 50:207–223.
1986   Offering and Soliciting Collaboration in Multi-Party Disputes
Among Children (and other humans). Human Studies 9(2–3):261–85.
1989   Notes on the Delivery and Reception of Diagnostic News Regarding Mental Disabilities. *In* New Directions in Sociology. Tim
Anderson, David Helm, Albert J. Meeham, and Ann Rards, eds. New
York: Irvington Press.

McConochie, Roger P.
1983   Alpine Images: A Photographic Essay on Anthropological Fieldwork in the Alps. Ann Arbor, Michigan: Cultural Studies Press.
[P.O. Box 8438, Ann Arbor, Michigan 48107].

1987 Europe: Up and Down the Alps. Faces 3(5):18–23. [Peterborough, New Hampshire: Cobblestone Publishing Co., in cooperation with the American Museum of Natural History.]

Mehan, Hugh
1975 The Reality of Ethnomethodology. New York: Wiley Interscience.
1979 Learning Lessons. Cambridge, Mass.: Harvard University Press.
1986 Handicapping the Handicapped. Palo Alto: Stanford University Press.

Mitchell, William E.
1987 Bamboo Fire: Field Work with the New Guinea Wape, Second edition. Prospect Heights, Illinois: Waveland Press.

Monks, Gregory G.
1986 (with B. Loewen) A History of Structures at Upper Fort Garry, Winnepeg, 1835–1887. (247 pages.) Microfiche Report Series, #330. Ottawa: Parks Canada.
1988 (with B. Loewen) A Note on Visual Depictions of Upper Fort Garry. Prairie Forum 13(1):1–24.

Nanda, Serena
1977a (with Joan Gregg) Audiovisual notes on films about India: Devi [The Goddess], Mahangar [The Big City], and Two Daughters, by Satyajit Ray. American Anthropologist 79:213.
1977b (with Joan Gregg) Audiovisual notes on films about women and ethnicity: Yudie, Mamma, Ama L'uomo Tuo, Women of the Northside Fight Back, and Rent Strike. American Anthropologist 79:213–214.
1980a Cultural Anthropology. New York: Van Nostrand.
1980b Freedom and Culture: Women in the Films of Satyajit Ray. Community Review (Spring).
1985 Using Films in the Classroom. Anthropology and Education Quarterly, Special Issue: Teaching Anthropology 16(4):274–275.
1987 Film review: Modern Brides. American Anthropologist 89:259.
1988 Film review: India Cabaret. American Anthropologist 90:492–93.

Nichols, Bill
1981 Ideology and the Image. (Three chapters on documentary and ethnography) Bloomington: Indiana University Press.

Nierenberg, Judith [see also: Cabezas and Nierenberg]
1986 (with Sue Marshall Cabezas and Mary Anne Wolff) Ethnographic Film in the Classroom. Practicing Anthropology 8(3–4).

Oppitz, Michael

    1981   Schamanen im Blinden Land. (Picture book.) Syndikat Press.

Östör, Ákos

    1987   Cinema and Society in India and Senegal: The Films of Satyajit Ray and Ousmane Sembene, Part 1. Splice 3:6–31. [Calcutta]

    In Press   Cinema and Society in India and Senegal: The Films of Satyajit Ray and Ousmane Sembene, Part 2. Splice 5. [Calcutta]

Ottenberg, Simon

    1975a   The Masked Rituals of Afikpo: The Context of an African Art. Seattle: University of Washington Press.

    1975b   Afikpo Masqueraders: Audience and Performers. African Arts 6(4):32–35, 94–95.

    1982   Illusion, Communication, and Psychology in West African Masquerades. Ethos 10(2):149–85.

    1983   Igbo and Yoruba Art Contrasted. African Arts 16(2):48–55, 97–98.

    1985   (with Linda Knudsen) Leopard Society Masquerades: Symbolism and Diffusion. African Arts 18(2):37–44, 93–95, 103–104.

    1988   Psychological Aspects of Igbo Art. African Arts 21(2).

Pader, Ellen

    1982   Symbolism, Social Relations, and the Interpretation of Mortuary Remains. (A theoretical and methodological study of the viability of applying interpretive schema developed for, and from, not-material forms of behavior to material forms of behavior.) Oxford: B.A.R.

Peek, Philip M.

    1976   Isoko Sacred Mud Sculpture. African Arts 9(4):34–39, 91.

    1978   Afro-American Material Culture and the Afro-American Craftsman. Southern Folklore Quarterly 42(2/3):109–34.

    1980   Isoko Artists and Their Audiences. African Arts 13(3):58–61, 91.

    1983   The Celebration of Oworu Among the Isoko. African Arts 16(2):2, 34–41, 98.

    1984   Film review: To Live With Herds, by D. and J. MacDougall. Journal of American Folklore 97(383):69–71.

    1985   Ovia Idah and Eture Egvedi: Traditional Nigerian Artists. African Arts 18(2):54–59,102.

    1986   The Isoko Ethos of Ivri and Its Visual Forms. African Arts 20(1): 42–47.

Peters, Mary Pyle
1984 Through the Lens of the Past: A Case Study in Visual Anthropology Among the Western Mono. M.A. thesis, California State University, Sacramento.

Peterson, Nicolas
1985 The Popular Image. *In* Seeing the First Australians. Ian Donaldson and Tamsin Donaldson, eds. Pp. 164–180. Sydney and Boston: G. Allen and Unwin.

Pilling, Arnold R.
1974 Dating Early Photographs by Card Mounts and Other External Evidence: Tentative Suggestions. Image 17(1):11–16.

Potterfield, Thomas G.
1981 An Ethnographic Approach to Independent Filmmaking: Political Documentary and Experimental Art Film Production and Exhibition Activities. M.A. thesis, Annenberg School of Communications, University of Pennsylvania.
1983 The Family Living Room as Seen by the Communications Researcher. Paper presented at the Fifth International Conference on Culture and Communication, Philadelphia.
1985a Riverine Camps in the Trans-Allegheny Highlands: Folk Dwellings in the Status System of a Modern Community. Paper presented at the American Folklore Society annual meetings, Cincinnati.
1985b Housing Aesthetics and Social Status in a Seaside Resort Community: Contextual Analysis of Photographic Data. Paper presented at the International Visual Communications Conference, Philadelphia, Spring.

Quimby, George I.
1980 (with Bill Holm) Edward Curtis in the Land of the War Canoes: A Pioneer Cinematographer in the Pacific Northwest. Seattle: University of Washington Press.

Quintana, Bertha B.
1986 Que Gitano: Gypsies of Southern Spain, Second Issue. Prospect Heights, Illinois: Waveland Press.

Rachlin, Carol K.
1970 (with Alice Marriott) Peyote. New York: Harcourt Brace.

1972   (with Alice Marriott) American Indian Mythology. New York: NAL.

Richardson, Miles

1982   Being-in-the-Market vs. Being-in-the-Plaza: Material Culture and the Construction of Social Reality in Spanish America. American Ethnology 9(2):421–436.

1984   Place: Experience and Symbol. (Editor.) Baton Rouge, Louisianna: Geoscience Publication.

Roberts, Allen F.

1983   "Perfect" Lions, "Perfect" Leaders: A Metaphor for Tabwa Chiefship. Journal de la Société des Africanistes 53(1–2):93–105.

1984   "Fishers of Men": Religion and Political Economy Among Colonized Tabwa. Africa 54(2):49–70.

1986a Social and Historical Contexts of Tabwa Art. *In* The Rising of a New Moon: A Century of Tabwa Art. A. Roberts and E. Maurer, eds. Ann Arbor: University of Michigan Museum of Art.

1986b Duality in Tabwa Art. African Arts 19(4):26–35, 86–8.

1986c Les arts du corps chez les Tabwa. Arts d'Afrique noire 59:15–20.

1988a Tabwa Tegumentary Inscription. *In* Marks of Civilization: Artistic Transformations of the Human Body. Arnold Rubin, ed. Los Angeles: Museum of Cultural History, UCLA.

1988b Of Dogon Crooks and Thieves. African Arts 21(4):70–75,90–91.

1988c Through the Bamboo Thicket: The Social Process of Tabwa Ritual Performance. The Drama Review.

Rohrl, Vivian J.

1981   Effective Teaching of Anthropology: The Feature Film as an Alternative to the Standard Lecture Format. Paper presented at American Anthropological Association meetings, Los Angeles, December 2–6.

Rollwagen, Jack R.

1983   Two examples of the Use of Ethnographic Film for Teaching Introductory Undergraduate Anthropology Courses. SAVICOM Newsletter 10(3):205–210.

1980–84 SAVICOM Newsletter. (Editor.) (Including ten topic-oriented issues between August 1980 and December 1984. Example: Museum and Archival Cataloging of Ethnographic and Ethnohistorical Photographs: An Introductory Survey of the Arts.) Brockport, New York: Society for the Anthropology of Visual Communication.

1988a Anthropological Filmmaking: Anthropological Perspectives on the Production of Ethnographic Film and Video for General Public Audiences. (Editor.) New York: Harwood Academic Publishers.

1988b Anthropological Theory and 'Ethnographic' Filmmaking. *In* Anthropological Filmmaking. Jack R. Rollwagen, ed. New York: Harwood Academic Publishers.

Ruby, Jay

1975 Is an Ethnographic Film a Filmic Ethnography? Studies in the Anthropology of Visual Communication 2(2).

1980 Exposing Yourself: Reflexivity, Anthropology and Film. Semiotica 3(1–2):153–179.

1981 Seeing Through Pictures: The Anthropology of Photography. Camera Lucida 3:20–33.

1982 A Crack in the Mirror: Reflexive Perspectives in Anthropology. (Editor.) Philadelphia: University of Pennsylvania Press.

1984a Post-Mortem Portraiture in America. History of Photography 8(3): 201–222.

1984b Robert J. Flaherty, A Biography. Paul Rotha, author. (Editor.) Philadelphia: University of Pennsylvania Press.

1985 Images of the USA, 1920–1940: Three European Photographers: Emil O. Hoppe, Harald Lechenperg, Bernd Lohse. (Exhibition catalog.) (Editor.) Philadelphia: University of Pennsylvania.

1987 (with Martin Taureg, eds.) Visual Explorations of the World: Selected Papers from the International Conference on Visual Communication. Aachen, Federal Republic of Germany: Edition Herodot/ Herodot Literatur Verlag.

1988 (with Larry Gross and John Katz) Image Ethics: The Moral Rights of Subjects in Photography, Film, and Television. New York: Oxford University Press.

Saltman, Carlyn

1984 Color photographs for: Red Gold of Africa. Copper in Precolonial History and Culture, by Eugenia W. Herbert. Madison: University of Wisconsin Press.

Scherer, Joanna Cohan

1973 (with Jean B. Walker) Indians: The Great Photographs that Reveal North American Indian Life, 1847–1929. (From the unique collection of the Smithsonian Institution.) New York: Crown Ridge Press. (German edition, Albert Mueller Verlag, 1975 with corrections. Reprinted by Bonanza Books, Crown distributors, 1982 with corrections.)

1975 You Can't Believe Your Eyes: Inaccuracies in Photographs of North American Indians. Studies in the Anthropology of Visual Communication 2(2). (Reprinted 1979: Exposure 16(4). [The Journal of the Society for Photographic Education, Columbia College, Chicago].

Reprinted 1980: Working Papers on Photography, Science Museum of Victoria, Australia.)

1981   Historical Photographs of the Subarctic: A Resource for Future Research, and Repository Sources of Subarctic Photographs. Arctic Anthropology 18(2).

1985   Review: The Vanishing Race and Other Illusions: Photographs of Edward S. Curtis, by C.M. Lyman. Studies in the Anthropology of Visual Communication 11(2).

1988   The Public Faces of Sarah Winnemucca. Cultural Anthropology 3(2):178–204.

Forthcoming   International Studies on Ethnophotography. (Editor.) Special issue of the journal Visual Anthropology.

Forthcoming   International Studies on the Visual Anthropology of Amateur or Family Photography. (Editor.) Special issue of the journal Visual Anthropology.

Schmidt, Nancy J.

1975   Ethnographic Films about American Indians. Council on Anthropology and Education Quarterly 6(1):34–35.

1982a   African Literature on Film. Research in African Literatures 13(4): 518–531.

1982b   Photographic Narratives. Reviews in Anthropology 9(2):201–204.

1985a   Teaching Anthropology with Film. Society of Visual Anthropology Newsletter 1(2):1, 10–14.

1985b   African Filmmaking, Country by Country. African Studies Review 28(1):111–114.

1986   Subsaharan African Films and Filmmakers: A Preliminary Bibliography. Bloomington, Indiana: African Studies Program.

1988   Subsaharan African Films and Filmmakers: An Annotated Bibliography. New York: Oxford Hans Zell/Sauer.

1989   Culture and Nationalism in Sub-Saharan African Filmmaking. Visual Anthropology 2(1):85–91.

Schwartz, Dona   [also see: Griffin and Schwartz]

1986a   Camera Clubs and Fine Art Photography: The Social Construction of an Elite Code. Urban Life 15(2):165–195.

1987a   Doing the Ethnography of Visual Communication: The Rhetoric of Fine Art Photography. Reasearch in Language and Social Interaction 21.

1987b   Camera Club Photo-Competitions: An Ethnographic Approach to the Analysis of a Visual Event. Research in Language and Social Interaction 21.

1987c   Fine Arts Photography: Constructing an Exclusive Pictorial Code. *In* Visual Explorations of the World. Jay Ruby and Martin Taureg, eds. Pp. 299–314. Aachen, West Germany: Edition Herodot.

Seremetakis, Constantina-Nadia
1983 Structuralism, Universalism, and Peasant Particularities. The Greek Review of Social Research 51. (Also in Greek.)

1984 The Eye of the Other: Watching Death in Rural Greece. Journal of Modern Hellenism 1(1).

Seubert, Emelia A. [also see: Weatherford and Seubert]
1987 An Overview of Native American Media in the United States. Film and Politics in the Third World. New York: Praeger.

Sherman, Sharon R.
1974 Folkloristic Filmmaking: A Preliminary Report. Folklore Forum, Bibliographic and Special Series 12:107–116.

1981 Film and Folklore: An Inductive Teaching Method. Southwest Folklore 5:11–20.

1983a Studying American Folkloric Films. *In* Handbook of American Folklore. Richard Dorson, ed. Pp. 441–46. Bloomington: Indiana University Press.

1984 Bombing, Breakin', and Gettin' Down: The Folk and Popular Culture of Hip-Hop. Western Folklore 43:287–293.

1986a "That's How the Seder Looks": A Fieldwork Account of Videotaping Family Folklore. Journal of Folklore Research.

1986b Human Documents: Folklore and the Films of Jorge Preloran. Southwest Folklore 6:17–61.

Skylar, Deidre
1985 Etienne Decroux's Promethean Mime. Drama Review 29(4):108.

1987 Making Belief: The Museum of the American Indian as a Cultural Performance. MUSE 5(2):26–31. (Pp. 31–36 in French.)

Spiegel, Pauline
1984 The Care of the Well-Mannered Guest. The Ethnographic Filmmaker as Insider and Outsider. The Independent 7(3):15–17.

Stearns, Robert David
1983 Linking Classroom and Community: Directed Ethnography in Rural Yucatan. Ph.D. dissertation, School of Education, Stanford University.

1984 Culture, Cooperation, Community, and the Classroom. *In* Alaskan Native News (February). [Anchorage, Alaska. Rosita Worl, ed.]

1986 Using Ethnography to Link School and Community in Rural Yucatan. Anthropology and Education Quarterly 17(1).

Steele, David J.
> 1981   (with Henry P. Lundsgaarde and Pam Fischer) Human Problems in Computerized Medicine. Lawrence, Kansas: University of Kansas Publications in Anthropology 13.

Stone, Rebecca R.
> 1983   Possible Uses, Roles, and Meanings of Chavin-Related Painted Textiles from the South Coast of Peru. *In* Investigations of the Andean Past: Proceedings of the First Annual Northeast Conference on Andean Archaeology and Ethnohistory. D. Sandweiss, ed. Ithaca, New York: Cornell University Press.
> 1986   Color, Culture, and Cosmos in a Selected Group of Huari Tapestry Tunics from Ancient Peru. Bogota, Columbia: International Congress of Americanists, Memorias.

Tarasoff, Koozma J.
> 1969   Pictorial History of the Doukhobors. Saskatoon: Modern Press.
> 1977   Traditional Doukhobor Folkways: An Ethnographic and Biographic Record of Prescibed Behavior. Ottawa: National Museum of Man.
> 1980   Persistent Ceremonialism: The Plains Creek and Saulteaux. Ottawa: National Museum of the Man.
> 1982   Plakun Trava: The Doukhobors. Grand Forks, B.C.: MIR Publications.

Trettevik, Susan K.
> 1981   Toward An Analytical Anthropological Film. Studies in the Anthropology of Visual Communication, Newsletter 9(1):2–5.

Trubowitz, Neal L.
> 1978   Slides of Iroquois Archaeology. *In* Prehistoric Iroquois Indians Field Archaeology Set, by Robert Dean and Marian White. Fort Atchinson, Wisconsin: NASCO.

Van Zile, Judy
> 1977   Film, A Research Tool in Dance Ethnology. *In* Dance and Film. Selma Landen Odom, ed. Pp. 35–36. Ontario: Art Gallery of Ontario.
> 1982   The Musician as Dancer. Journal of Korean Dance 1(1):37–44.
> 1983   Balasaraswati's "Tis Ram Alarippu": A Choreographic Analysis. *In* Performing Arts in India. Essays of Music, Dance, and Drama. Bonnie Wade, ed. Pp. 47–104. Lanham, Maryland: University Press of America.
> 1984   (with Irmgard Bartenieff, Peggy Hackney, Betty True Jones, and Carl Wolz). The Potential of Movement Analysis as a Research Tool: A Preliminary Analysis. Dance Research Journal 16(1):3–26.

1986   What is the Dance?   Implications for Dance Notation.   Dance Research Journal.

Volkman, Toby Alice [see also: Cabezas and Volkman]

1982a The San in Transition: A Guide to N!ai, The Story of a !Kung Woman. Occasional Paper No. 9.   Cambridge and Watertown, Massachusetts: Cultural Survival and Documentary Educational Resources.

1982b Kiepja and Truganini: The Last Voices.   Dialectical Anthropology 7.

1985a Feasts of Honor: Ritual and Change in the Toraja Highlands. Urbana and Chicago: University of Illinois Press.

1985b Film on Indonesia.   New Haven: Yale University Southeast Asian Studies.

1986   Expressive Culture in Papua New Guinea: A Guide to Three Films.   Watertown, Massachusetts and Boroko, Papua New Guinea: Documentary Educational Resources and the Institute for PNG Studies.

1987   Film review: The Lure of Asian Music: Colin McPhee, by Michael Blackwood.   American Anthropologist 89(3).

1988   Out of South Africa: 'The Gods Must Be Crazy.'   *In* Image Ethics: The Moral Rights of Subjects in Photography, Film, and Television. Larry Gross, John Katz, and Jay Ruby, eds.   Pp. 236–247.   New York: Oxford University Press.

Wagner, Jon C.

1977   Environmental Assessment: Photographic Monitoring.   *In* Twin Rivers: Study of a Planned Community.   Suzanne Keller, author.   Pp. 425–504.   Washington, D.C.:   National Technical Information Services.

1979   Images of Information: Still Photography in the Social Sciences. (Editor of volume and author of chapters 1, 6, 10, 13 and 20.)   Beverly Hills, California: Sage Publications.

Wallendorf, Melanie

1988a (with Russell Belk and John Sherry)   A Naturalistic Inquiry into Buyer-Seller Interactions at a Swap Meet.   (Discusses use of video and still photography in field work at a swap meet.)   Journal of Consumer Research 14 (March).

1988b (with Eric Arnould)   My Favorite Things: A Cross-Cultural Analysis of Possessiveness, Attachment, and Social Linkage.   (Uses photographs of informants with their favorite objects as one source of data on the meaning of favorite objects for informants in the U.S. and Niger.)   Journal of Consumer Research 14 (March).

Walter, Nancy Peterson
1982 Photographs and Their Uses in Contract Archaeology. Contract Abstracts and CRM Archaeology 3(1).

Watson, O. Michael
1970 Proxemic Behavior: A Cross-Cultural Study. The Hague: Mouton.
1972a Proxemics and Semiotics. Program in Ethnographic Film (PIEF) Newsletter 3(2):11–13.
1972b Proxemics and Proxetics. Program in Ethnographic Film (PIEF) Newsletter 3(3):13–14.

Weatherford, Elizabeth
1983 Native American Media Makers at Work. The Independent 6(3): 17–19.

Weatherford, Elizabeth and Emelia Seubert
1981 Native Americans on Film and Video. (Editors.) New York: Museum of the American Indian/Heye Foundation.
1988 Native Americans on Film and Video. Second edition. (Editors.) New York: Museum of the American Indian/Heye Foundation.

Weil, Peter M.
1971 The Masked Figure and Social Control: The Mandinka Case. Africa 41(4):279–93.
1987 Fighting Fire with Fire: The Mandinka Sengko Mask. *In* Tricksters, Transvestites, and Warriors. Sydney L. Kasfir, ed. Tervuren: Musée Royal de l'Afrique Centrale.

Weiner, Annette B.
1978 Epistemology and Ethnographic Reality: A Trobriand Island Case Study. American Anthropologist 80(3):752–57.

Wescott, Roger Williams
1970 Bini Color Terms. Anthropological Linguistics 12(9):349–360.
1975 Proto-Indo-Hittite Color Terms. *In* Linguistics and Anthropology. K.L. Hale, M.D. Kinkade, and O. Werner, eds. Pp. 691–699. Lisse, Netherlands: Peter de Ridder Press.
1978 Visualizing Vision. *In* Visual Learning, Thinking, and Communication. Bikkar S. Randhawa and William E. Coffman, eds. Pp. 21–38. New York: Academic Press.
1982 Views of Imaging. Journal of Mental Imagery 6(1):99–100.
1983 Color Metaphors in Three Language Phyla. *In* The First Delaware Conference on Language Studies. Robert J. Di Pietro, William Frawley, Alfred Wedel, eds. Pp. 87–98. London: Associated

University Press.

1984   Archaic Images. Journal of Visual/Verbal Languaging (Spring): 73–76. (Journal of the International Visual Literacy Association.)

Williams, Drid

1977   The Arms and Hands, With Special Reference to an Anglo-Saxon Sign System. Semiotica 21 (1–2):23–73.

1979   The Human Action Sign and Semasiology. Research Annual (CORD) 10:39–64.

1980   Taxonomies of the Body. Journal for the Anthropological Study of Human Movement 1(1):1–19, 1(2):98–122.

1982   Semasiology: A Semantic Anthropological View of Human Actions and Movement. *In* Semantic Anthropology (ASA Monographs 22). David Parkin, ed. London: Academic Press.

1986a (Non)Anthropologists, The Dance, and Human Movement. *In* Theatrical Movement: A Bibliographical Anthology. B. Fleshman, ed. Metuchen, New Jersey: Scarecrow Press.

1986b Prefigurements of Art: A Reply to Sebeok. Journal for the Anthropological Study of Human Movement 4(2):68–80.

1987   A Survey of Australian Literature on Dancing. Journal for the Anthropological Study of Human Movement 4(4):189–246.

In press   Ten Lectures on Theories of the Dance. Metuchen, New Jersey: Scarecrow Press.

Forthcoming   On Relations Between Music and Dancing. (Editor.) Sydney and London: Sydney University Press/Oxford University Press.

Winner, Irene Portis

1971   A Slovenian Village: Zerovnica. Providence, Rhode Island: Brown University Press.

1976   (with T.G. Winner) The Semiotics of Cultural Texts. Semiotica 18:101–156.

1977   The Semiotic Character of the Aesthetic Function as Defined by the Prague Linguistic Circle. *In* Language and Thought. William C. McCormack and Stephen A. Wurm, eds. Pp. 407–440. The Hague: Mouton.

1978   Cultural Semiotics and Anthropology. *In* The Sign. Semiotics Around the World. R.W. Bailey, L. Matejka and P. Steiner, eds. Pp. 335–63. Ann Arbor: Michigan Slavic Publications.

1979   (with J. Umiker-Sebeok, eds.) Semiotics of Culture. The Hague: Mouton.

1982   Semiotics of Culture: The State of the Art. Toronto Semiotic Circle. Monographs, Working Papers and Prepublications. Toronto: Victoria University.

1984a   (with T.G. Winner, eds.)   The Peasant and the City in Eastern Europe. Cambridge, Massachusetts: Schenkman.
1984a   Lotman and Semiotics of Culture. *In* Semiosis. In Honorem Georgi Lotman. Morris Halle, et al., eds. Pp. 28–36. Ann Arbor, Michigan Studies in the Humanities.
1984b   Theories of Narration and Ethnic Culture Texts. *In* Sign, System, and Function. Proceedings of the First and Second Polish American Semiotics Colloquia. J. Pelc, T.A. Sebeok, E. Stankiewics, and T.G. Winner, eds. Pp. 439–455. Berlin: Mouton de Gruyter.
1986   Semiotics of Culture. *In* Frontiers of Semiotics. John Deely, Brooke Williams, and Felicia E. Kruse, eds. Pp. 181–184. Bloomington: Indiana University Press.
1987   The Decoding of Visual and Verbal Ethnic Culture Texts of the Slovenes in Cleveland. *In* Festschrift for Rado Lencek. H.R. Cooper, Jr., O. Nedeljkovic, and T. Priestly, eds. Columbus, Ohio: Slavica.
1988   Ethnic Culture as Narration. *In* Literary Anthropology: A New Interdisciplinary Approach to People, Signs, and Literature Fernando Poyatos, ed. Amsterdam and Philadelphia: J. Benjamins.

Worth, Tobia L.
1977–85   Studies in Visual Communication. (Associate Editor.)
1989   International Encyclopedia of Communications. (Managing Editor.) (Erik Barnouw, Editor in Chief). New York: Oxford University Press.

Wylie, Laurence
1974   Village in the Vaucluse. Third Edition. Cambridge, Massachusetts: Harvard University Press.
1977   Beaux Gestes. New York: E.P. Dutton.
1985   Language Learning and Communication. French Review 58(6).

Yoder, P. Stanley
1982   Issues in the Study of Ethnomedical Systems in Africa. *In* African Health and Healing Systems. P. Stanley Yoder, ed. Los Angeles: Crossroads Press.

Young, Colin
1975   Observational Cinema. *In* Principles of Visual Anthropology. Paul Hockings, ed. Pp. 65–80. The Hague: Mouton.
1982   MacDougall Conversations. Royal Anthropological Institute Newsletter 50.

Young, Katharine
1989   Disembodiment: The Phenomenology of the Body in Medical Examinations. Semiotica 73(1–2).

Zantzinger, Gei

1975 (with Andrew Tracey) A Companion to the Films "1973 Mgodo wa Mbanguzi" and "1973 Mgodo wa Mkandeni." (Study guide.) Roodepoort, South Africa: International Library of African Music.

Zeller, Anne

1984 Social Aspects of Facial Expressions in Primates. The Code of Macaca sylvanus. Paper presented at the Symposium on the Semiotics of the Human Face. Fifth International Summer Institute of Semiotic and Structural Studies, Victoria College, University of Toronto, June.

1985 Component Patterns in Gesture Formation in Macaca sylvanus of Gibraltar. Canadian Review of Physical Anthropology 4(2):35–42.

1986a Comparison of Component Patterns in Threatening and Friendly Gestures in Macaca sylvanus of Gibraltar. *In* Current Perspectives in Primate Social Dynamics. D.M. Taub and F.A. King, eds. Pp. 487–504. New York: Van Nostrand Reinhold Press.

1986b Methodologial Factors in Primate Film Analysis. Paper presented at SVA Conference on Visual Research, American Anthropological Association meetings, Philadelphia, December 2–3.

1986c Coding Primate Facial Gestures. Paper presented at the American Anthropological Association meetings, Philadelphia, December 2–7.

INDEX OF CONTRIBUTORS' WORLD AREA INTERESTS
(including Scholarly and Fieldwork Languages)

Afganistan T. Asch, Balikci, Olsson, Tapper

Africa Adra, Andrews, T. Asch, Barrow, Biella, Bishop, P. Blakely, T. Blakely, Bosko, Bruner, Byrne, Cabezas, Coplan, Damon, d'Azevedo, de Brigard, Dornfeld, Drewal, Edson, El Guindi, Faris, E. Fernea, R. Fernea, Finnegan, Gardner, Geary, Gonçalves, Hardin, Hart, Husmann, M. Jablonko, Jell-Bahlsen, Kaplan, Kealiinohomoku, Koons, Kreamer, Luskey, D. MacDougall, J. MacDougall, Malcolm, Marshall, O'Brien, Östör, Ottenberg, Peek, A. Roberts, Rosenfeld, Saltman, N. Schmidt, Singer, Slyomovics, Staples, Stone, Tefft, Volkman, Von Ins, D. Wagner, Wallendorf, Weil, Wescott, Yoder, C. Young, Zantzinger

Africa, Central P. Blakely, T. Blakely, Geary, A. Roberts, Yoder, Zantzinger

Africa, East [and **Horn of Africa**] T. Asch, Biella, Bishop, P. Blakely, T. Blakely, Bruner, Gardner, D. MacDougall, J. MacDougall, Malcolm, A. Roberts

Africa, North Adra, Andrews, Biella, Bruner, Damon, El Guindi, Faris, E. Fernea, R. Fernea, O'Brien, Slyomovics, Staples, Tarabulski, D. Wagner

Africa, Southern T. Asch, Bosko, Cabezas, Coplan, Gardner, Luskey, Marshall, Rosenfeld, Volkman, Zantzinger

Africa, West T. Blakely, Coplan, d'Azevedo, de Brigard, Dornfeld, Drewal, Finnegan, Gardner, Geary, Hardin, Jell-Bahlsen, Kaplan, Koons, Kreamer, Luskey, Östör, Ottenberg, Peek, A. Roberts, Rosenfeld, Saltman, Staples, Von Ins, Wallendorf, Weil, Wescott, Yoder, C. Young, Zantzinger

African Americans [see also **Caribbean** and **Latin America**] Brown, Burns, Chalfen, Chin, De Friedmann, Drewal, Elder, Erickson, Fabian, Gonçalves, E. Hall, Homiak, Kealiinohomoku, Lane, Lomax, Marks, Peek, Trend

Alaska Brooks, J. Collier, M. Collier, Dekin, Gmelch, Graburn, Halpern, Hauck, Magdanz, Orth, Stearns, C. Young

American Sign Language S. Hall

Andes Campos, J. Collier, M. Collier, Doughty, Flowers, Margolies, McKee, Oliver-Smith, Stone, D. Whitten, N. Whitten

Apache Brandt, Farrer

Arabic Adra, Andrews, Dallalfar, Damon, El Guindi, Faris, E. Fernea, R. Fernea, Geertz, Husmann, Johnson-Dean, Kellers, Östör, Safizadeh, Slyomovics, Tapper

Arctic Balikci, Brooks, J. Collier, M. Collier, Dekin, de Peña, Gmelch, Graburn, Halpern, Hart, Hauck, Koolage, Magdanz, Orth, Scherer, Stearns

Argentina Wizelman

Asia Abrams, Andrews, P. Asch, T. Asch, Balikci, Bannister, Beatty, Bertocci, Bishop, Blanc-Szanton, Bogue, Brown, Bruner, Caldarola, Chin, Cho, Conklin, Dewey, Dumont, Durrans, Erdman, Eyde, Ford, Gardner, Geddes, Geertz, Grimshaw, Gropper, E. Hall, Halpern, Hart, Heider, Hockings, Holaday, Holleman, Hoskins, Iqbal, T. Johnson, Kirkpatrick, Lansing, Lerner, Lewis, Linklater, Lüem, Luskey, Martin, McGilvray, Moerman, Nanda, Olsson, Oppitz, Östör, Pratt, Quiatt, Rollwagen, Rosenfeld, Safizadeh, Scheder, Scheerer, Seaman, See, Simons, Singer, Skylar, Tapp, Tapper, Van Zile, Van Zile, Volkman, Walter, Wescott, Wood, C. Young, J. Young, Zeller

Asia, East Beatty, Bogue, Chin, Cho, Geddes, E. Hall, T. Johnson, Quiatt, Rollwagen, Rosenfeld, Seaman, Singer, Tapp, Van Zile, Walter, J. Young

Asia, South Bannister, Bertocci, Bishop, Chin, Durrans, Erdman, Gardner, Grimshaw, Gropper, Hart, Hockings, Iqbal, Kirkpatrick, Lerner, McGilvray, Nanda, Oppitz, Östör, Pratt, Singer, Skylar, Wescott

Asia, Southeast Abrams, Andrews, P. Asch, T. Asch, Bannister, Bishop, Blanc-Szanton,

Brown, Bruner, Caldarola, Conklin, Dewey, Dumont, Durrans, Geddes, Geertz, Halpern, Heider, Holaday, Holleman, Hoskins, Lansing, Lewis, Linklater, Lüem, Moerman, Quiatt, Rosenfeld, Scheder, Scheerer, Simons, Tapp, Volkman, D. Wagner, Wood, Zeller
Asia, Southwest T. Asch, Balikci, Martin, Olsson, Oppitz, Safizadeh, Tapper
Asian Americans Andrews, Beatty, Bogue, Brown, Chalfen, Chin, M. Collier, Dornfeld, Erdman, Ginsburg, Kealiinohomoku, Linklater, Rynearson, Scheder, Slyomovics, Stull, Van Zile
Assiniboine Farnell
Australia P. Asch, Ascher, Lewis, Geddes, D. MacDougall, J. MacDougall, Manley, Peterson, Pilling, Trigger, D. Williams
Badaga Hockings
Bali Abrams, P. Asch, T. Asch, Belk, Bruner, Geertz, Lansing, Wood
Balinese Geertz, Lansing
Bangladesh Durrans, Kirkpatrick
Bengali Bertocci, Erdman, Kirkpatrick, Östör
Benin A. Roberts
Bidayuh [Dayak] Geddes
Bini Wescott
Bolivia Bugos, Heath
Botswana Rosenfeld
Borneo Caldarola [Kalimantan], Durrans, Geddes
Brazil Barrow, Belk, Bick, Drewal, Field, Flowers, Gonçalves, Leeds
Bulgaria Silverman
Bulgarian Balikci, Silverman
Burkina Faso Saltman
Burma Kirkpatrick, Tapp
Cameroon Geary, Saltman
Canada [see also **North America (Native Americans)**] Balikci, Blackman, J. Collier, Dekin, de Peña, Graburn, Hart, Jacknis, Kolodny, Koolage, Linklater, Monks, J. Schmidt, Sherman, Stevens, Tarasoff, C. Young
Caribbean Alegria, Barrow, Biella, De Friedmann, Elder, Fabian, Finnegan, Gmelch, Gonçalves, Henley, Homiak, Lomax, Long, Margolies, Quiatt, Quintanales, Pilling, Simon, J. Williams, Wright
Cebuano Dumont
Central America Benedict, Biella, Brown, Clements, Fabian, Field, Howe, Johnson-Dean, Lee, Lobo, Remmers, Seubert, Weatherford, D. Whitten, N. Whitten, C. Williams, J. Williams, Zantzinger
Chile Field
China Bogue, Button, Geddes, Luehrsen, Rollwagen, Rosenfeld, Seaman, Singer, Tapp, Walter
Chinese Blaustein, Bogue, Oppitz, Seaman; *Cantonese, Mandarin:* Tapp, Y. Young
Cokwe Yoder
Colombia Campos, J. Collier, De Friedmann, D. Whitten, N. Whitten, Diaz-Granados
Costa Rica Biella, Doughty
Czech Bosko, Lass
Czechoslavakia Lass
Dani (Papuan) Heider
Danish P. Blakely
Dutch Conklin, Dewey, Geertz, Heider, Hoskins, Lansing, Lewis, Lüem, Seaman
Ecuador J. Collier, Irvine, McKee, D. Whitten, N. Whitten
Egypt Andrews, Biella, Bruner, R. Fernea, El Guindi, Fagan, Slyomovics
El Salvador Doughty, Johnson-Dean
English All directory contributors

Eskimo Graburn, Magdanz (*St. Lawrence Island Yupik*)
Ethiopia Gardner
Europe Allen, Bán, Bass, Beatty, Becker, Behar, P. Blakely, Burns, Cedrini, Chin, Chiozzi, Di Sparti, Edson, Eisenbeis, Gearing, Gmelch, Hagebölling, E. Hall, Halpern, Hauck, Hockings, A. Jablonko, M. Jablonko, Lacy, Lass, Leeds, Leininger, Lerch, Lockwood, Lomax, Luehrsen, Lüem, McConochie, Mintz, Naimark, Narrowe, Östör, Perez-Tolon, Quintana, Rasson, Seremetakis, Silverman, Simic, Singer, Von Ins, Wescott, D. Williams, Winner, Wylie, C. Young, K. Young, Zeller
Europe, Alpine A. Jablonko, Lüem, McConochie, Von Ins
Europe (Balkans) Gearing, Halpern, Hauck, Lockwood, Rasson, Silverman, Simic
Europe, Central Bán, A. Jablonko, Lass, Östör, Rasson
Europe, Eastern Bán, Edson, Halpern, Hauck, Lass, Lockwood, Östör, Rasson, Silverman, Simic, Winner
Europe (Mediterranean) Allen, Bass, Buxbaum, Gearing, Lacy, Serematakis
Europe (Scandinavia) Baskauskas, Becker, P. Blakely, Narrowe
Europe, Western Beatty, Becker, Behar, Burns, P. Blakely, Cedrini, Chin, Chiozzi, Di Sparti, Edson, Gmelch, E. Hall, Hockings, A. Jablonko, M. Jablonko, Leeds, Lockwood, Lomax, Lüem, McConochie, Mintz, Naimark, Narrowe, Oliver-Smith, Perez-Tolon, Quintana, Singer, Von Ins, D. Williams, Winner, Wylie, C. Young, K. Young, Zeller
Fiji Geddes, J. Young
Fijian J. Young
Flores P. Asch, T. Asch, Lewis
France Chin, E. Hall, Lerch, Naimark, Wylie
French Adra, Alegria, Albers, Allen, Andrews, T. Asch, Balikci, Bán, Banta, Bass, Behar, Belk, Bertocci, Bick, Biella, Birdwhistell, Bishop, P. Blakely, T. Blakely, Blaustein, Brooks, Buxbaum, Byrne, Carucci, Chalfen, Chiozzi, Clements, Coggeshall, Conklin, Coplan, Dakowski, Dallalfar, Damon, d'Azevedo, de Brigard, De Friedmann, Dekin, Dewey, Di Sparti, Dornfeld, Drewal, Dumont, Duncan, Durrans, Edson, Eisenbeis, El Guindi, Erdman, Eyde, Fabian, Faris, Farnell, Feest, E. Fernea, R. Fernea, Field, Finnegan, Flowers, Gardner, Gatewood, Geary, Geddes, Geertz, Gidley, Ginsburg, Gonçalves, Graburn, Graves, Griffin, Gropper, Hagebölling, S. Hall, Halpern, Hammond, Haratonik, Hardin, Hart, C. Heidenreich, Heider, Henley, Hockings, Holleman, Hoskins, Husmann, Hymes, Irvine, A. Jablonko, Jacknis, James, Jell-Bahlsen, Jones, Kaplan, Kealiinohomoku, Kellers, Kirkpatrick, Kolodny, Koons, Kreamer, Krouse, Kugelmass, Lacy, Lane, Lansing, Leeds, Lerch, Lewis, Lockwood, Lomax, Lüem, Luskey, Lutkehaus, D. MacDougall, Magdanz, Malcolm, Margolies, Marks, McGilvray, Moerman, Monks, Narrowe, Nichols, O'Brien, Oppitz, Östör, Ottenberg, Pader, Peek, Peters, Peterson, Pierce, Quiatt, Quintanales, Rasson, Richardson, A. Roberts, Rubel, Ruby, Rynearson, Safizadeh, Sair, Saltman, J. Schmidt, N. Schmidt, Seaman, See, Seremetakis, Simic, Simon, Singer, Skylar, Slyomovics, Spiegel, Tapp, Tapper, Tezcan, Volkman, Von Ins, Weatherford, Weibel-Orlando, Weil, Wescott, D. Williams, J. Williams, Winner, Wizelman, Worth, Wylie, Yoder, C. Young, Zeller
German Aschenbrennen, Bass, Beatty, Becker, Birdwhistell, Brandt, Buxbaum, Coggeshall, Conklin, d'Azevedo, de Brigard, de Peña, Durrans, Eisenbeis, Eyde, Faris, Farnell, Feest, Finnegan, Gatewood, Geary, Geertz, Graburn, Graves, Gropper, Hagebölling, Hauck, V. Heidenreich, Heider, Henley, Hockings, Hoskins, Husmann, Hymes, A. Jablonko, Jell-Bahlsen, D. Johnson, Jones, Kaplan, Kellers, Kreamer, Kugelmass, Lacy, Lane, Lass, Leeds, Lerch, Lewis, Long, Luehrsen, Lüem, Lutkehaus, Marks, McConochie, Monks, Nichols, Oppitz, Östör, Potterfield, Quiatt, Rasson, Richardson, Rubel, Ruby, Saltman, N. Schmidt, Seaman, Sherman, Singer, Slyomovics, Tapper, Von Ins, Wescott, Wilson, Yoder, Zantzinger
Germany Becker, Eisenbeis, Geary, Hagebölling, E. Hall, Lass, Luehrsen, Winner

Gibraltar Zeller
Great Britain [see **United Kingdom**]
Greece Allen, Buxbaum, Gearing, Lacy, Seremetakis
Greek Allen, Bass, Gearing, Hymes, Kellers, Lacy, Lane, Oppitz, Seremetakis, Wescott
Guatemala Burns, Doughty, C. Williams, J. Williams, Zantzinger
Gypsies Graves, Gropper, Lockwood, Perez-Tolon, Quintana, Silverman
Hanunóo Conklin
Hawaii Brooks, Kealiinohomoku, Scheder, Van Zile
Hawaiian Kealiinohomoku
Hebrew Abramowitz, Aron, Ginsburg, Gross, Narrowe, Slyomovics, Von Ins
Himalayas Bishop, Hart, Oppitz
Hindi Erdman, Grimshaw, Hart, Kirkpatrick, Östör
Hispanic Americans Brown, Burns, M. Collier, Cuéllar, Elder, Eyde, Farrer, E. Hall,
  Keefe, Lane, Perez-Tolon, Quintanales, Richardson, Rollwagen, Skylar, Trotter,
  C. Williams, J. Williams
Honduras Johnson-Dean
Hungarian Bán, Bosko, Östör, Rasson
Hungary Bán, Östör, Rasson, Winner
Ifugao Conklin
Igbo Jell-Bahlsen, Ottenberg, Wescott (*Ibo*)
India Bannister, Chin, Durrans, Erdman, Gardner, Grimshaw, Gropper, Hart, Hockings,
  Kirkpatrick, Lerner, McGilvray, Nanda, Östör, Pratt, Singer, Skylar, Wizelman, C. Young,
  Van Zile
Indians, American [see **North America (Native Americans), South America,
  Central America**]
Indochina Halpern, Holleman, Tapp
Indonesia Abrams, P. Asch, T. Asch, Belk, Bruner, Caldarola, Dewey, Geertz, Heider,
  Holaday, Hoskins, Lansing, Lewis, Lüem, Scheerer, Volkman, D. Wagner, Wood, Zeller
Indonesian (or *Indonesian-Malay; Bahasa Indonesia*) Abrams, T. Asch, Belk,
  Bruner, Caldarola, Conklin, Dewey, Geertz, Heider, Holaday, Hoskins, Lansing, Lewis,
  Luehrsen, Lüem, Scheerer, Simons, Volkman
Iran Martin, Safizadeh, Tapper
Ireland Gmelch, Hockings, C. Young
Isoko Peek
Israel Bruner, Narrowe, Remmers, Sever
Italian Adra, Allen, Behar, Birdwhistell, Cedrini, Chiozzi, Di Sparti, Farrer, Henley,
  Hoskins, A. Jablonko, M. Jablonko, Kellers, Lomax, Margolies, Nichols, Simic,
  Singer, Tapper, Weatherford, Weibel-Orlando, Wescott, Wizelman
Italy Bán, Cedrini, Chiozzi, Di Sparti, A. Jablonko, M. Jablonko, Lacy, Lomax,
  McConochie, Singer, K. Young
Jamaica Long
Jamaican Patois Long
Japan Beatty, Chin, De Brigard, Graburn, E. Hall, T. Johnson, Quiatt, Seaman
Japanese Beatty, de Brigard, T. Johnson, Seaman
Java Dewey, Heider, Holaday, Lüem
Javanese Dewey, Geertz, Lüem
Jewish Americans Aron, Ginsburg, Kugelmass, Mintz, Sherman, Spiegel
Julwasi Marshall
Kenya Bruner, Hart, D. MacDougall, J. MacDougall
Kíhêmbá P. Blakely, T. Blakely
Kodi Hoskins
Kordofanean Nuba (*Fungor*) Faris
Korea Cho, Eyde, T. Johnson, Van Zile

Korean Cho
Kumaoni Hart
Laotian Rynearson, Scheder
Latin Coggeshall, Edson, Erdman, Lacy, Oppitz, Östör, Sherman, Von Ins, Wescott
Latin America [see also **Caribbean**] Abrams, Albers, T. Asch, Ascher, Barrow, Behar, Belk,
    Benedict, Bick, Biella, Brown, Bugos, Burns, Campos, Cancian, Clements, J. Collier,
    M. Collier, Cone, Cuéllar, de Brigard, De Friedmann, Desmond, Doughty, El Guindi, Eyde,
    Fabian, Field, Flowers, Ford, Gonçalves, E. Hall, Heath, Henley, James, Johnson-Dean,
    Kaplan, Lane, Lee, Leeds, Malcolm, Margolies, McGee, O'Nell, Oliver-Smith, Pader,
    Perez-Tolon, Quintanales, Remmers, Richardson, Rollwagen, Scheder, Seubert, Simic,
    Skylar, Staples, Stearns, Trotter, D. Whitten, N. Whitten, C. Williams, J. Williams,
    Wright, Zantzinger
Lesotho Coplan, Zantzinger
Liberia d'Azevedo
Limba Ottenberg
Lithuanian Baskauskas
Malay [see also ***Indonesian***] Holaday
Malaysia Holaday, Rosenfeld
Mali T. Blakely, A. Roberts, C. Young
Manam Lutkehaus
Mandinka Weil
Marshallese Carucci
Marshall Islands Carucci
Maya Abrams, Burns, McGee, Stearns
Mediterranean [see **Africa (North)**, **Europe**, **Middle East**]
Melanesia Alpers, Barker, Belk, Eyde, Gardner, Geddes, Heider, A. Jablonko, M. Jablonko,
    Leininger, Lutkehaus, Mitchell, Olsson, Volkman, Weiner, J. Young
Mesoamerica [see **Central America** and **Mexico**]
Mexican Americans [see **Hispanic Americans**]
Mexico Abrams, Albers, Behar, Burns, Cancian, Clements, M. Collier, Cone, Cuéllar,
    Desmond, Doughty, El Guindi, Eyde, James, Kaplan, Lane, Lee, Malcolm, Margolies,
    McGee, O'Nell, Scheder, Stearns, Trotter, Wright
Miao Tapp
Micronesia Bishop, Burns, Carucci
Middle East Adra, Andrews, T. Asch, Ascher, Balikci, Bertocci, Bruner, Damon, El Guindi,
    Faris, E. Fernea, R. Fernea, Gilbert, E. Hall, Martin, O'Brien, Olsson, Oppitz, Remmers,
    Safizadeh, Slyomovics, Tapper, Tezcan, Trotter, Von Ins, D. Wagner, J.G. Wagner, Watson
Minangkabau (Austronesian) Heider
Moba Kreamer
Mohawk Beatty
Mooré Finnegan
Morocco Damon, E. Fernea, D. Wagner
Namibia T. Asch, Cabezas, Marshall, Volkman
Nepal Bishop, Kirkpatrick
Nepali Hart, Oppitz
New Guinea [and **Irian Jaya**] Alpers, Barker, Belk, Eyde, Gardner, Heider, A. Jablonko,
    M. Jablonko, Leininger, Lutkehaus, Mitchell, Olsson, Volkman, Weiner
Nicaragua Doughty, Field, Remmers, D. Whitten, N. Whitten
Nigeria Barrow, Drewal, Gardner, Jell-Bahlsen, Kaplan, Ottenberg, Peek, Rosenfeld, Wescott
North America [see also **Canada, Mexico, U.S.**, and the following 2 categories]
    Belk, Button, J. Collier, Crowdus, Dekin, Duncan, Gatewood, Gidley, Halpern,
    C. Heidenreich, V. Heidenreich, D. Johnson, Kolodny, Koons, Krouse, Lacy, Lomax,
    O'Brien, Orth, Quimby, Rasson, Rubel, J. Schmidt, Sherman, Tarabulski, J.G. Wagner,

Watson, C. Williams, D. Williams, K. Young

North America (Ethnic groups) [see also **African Americans, Asian Americans, Hispanic Americans, Jewish Americans, Native Americans**] Baskauskos, Beatty, Birdwhistell, P. Blakely, T. Blakely, Bogue, Brown, Burns, Buxbaum, Chalfen, Chin, Coggeshall, M. Collier, J. Collier, Cuéllar, De Friedmann, Dornfeld, Drewal, Elder, Erickson, Eyde, Fabian, Farrer, Field, Ginsburg, Gonçalves, Graves, Hammond, Homiak, Kealiinohomoku, Lane, Linklater, Lomax, Marks, Matthews, Mintz, O'Brien, Peek, Perez-Tolon, Quintanales, Rasson, Richardson, Rollwagen, Rynearson, Scheder, Simic, Simon, Slyomovics, Stull, Trend, Trotter, Winner, Zantzinger

North America (Native Americans) Abromowitz, Albers, Andrews, Arlen, Ascher, Balikci, Beatty, Birdwhistell, Bishop, Blackman, Blount, Bogue, Brandt, Brooks, Brown, Callaghan, Chalfen, J. Collier, M. Collier, Cone, Davidson, d'Azevedo, Dekin, De Peña, Diaz-Granados, DiMichele, Duncan, Faris, Farnell, Farrer, Feest, Field, Gearing, Gidley, Graburn, E. Hall, Hanisch, Hart, Hauck, C. Heidenreich, V. Heidenreich, Hymes, Jacknis, James, Kendall, Koolage, Krouse, Lane, Lobo, Luskey, Magdanz, Malcolm, Manley, McGee, Peters, Quimby, Pilling, Rachlin, Rasson, Sair, Saltman, Scheder, Scherer, J. Schmidt, N. Schmidt, Seubert, Sims, Skylar, Stearns, Stevens, Stull, Tarasoff, Trubowitz, Tefft, Topper, Trettevik, Walter, Weatherford, Weibel-Orlando, C. Williams, J. Williams, Wright

Oceania Alpers, P. Asch, Ascher, Barker, Belk, Bishop, Brooks, Burns, Carucci, Durrans, Eyde, Gardner, Geddes, Hammond, C. Heidenreich, Heider, Holaday, Holmes, A. Jablonko, M. Jablonko, Kealiinohomoku, Leininger, Lewis, Luskey, Lutkehaus, D. MacDougall, J. MacDougall, Manley, Mitchell, Olsson, Peterson, Pilling, Rubel, Scheder, See, Trigger, Weiner, D. Williams, J. Young

Pakistan Bannister, Iqbal, Kirkpatrick, Pratt, C. Young

Paraguay Bugos

Pashto Tapper

Persian Dallalfar, Martin, Olsson (*Farsi/Dari*), Safizadeh, Slyomovics, Tapper

Peru Clements, J. Collier, M. Collier, Doughty, Margolies, Oliver-Smith, Perez-Tolon, Stone, D. Whitten, N. Whitten

Philippines Bannister, Bishop, Blanc-Szanton, Conklin, Dumont, Singer

Plains Sign Language Farnell

Poland M. Jablonko, Winner

Polish M. Jablonko

Polynesia Brooks, Geddes, Hammond, Holmes, Kealiinohomoku, Scheder, J. Young

Portugal Leeds

Portuguese Barrow, Behar, Bick, Birdwhistell, de Brigard, Drewal, Field, Flowers, Gonçalves, Henley, Kaplan, Lane, Leeds, Lewis, Lobo, Margolies, Quintanales, N. Schmidt, Wizelman, Yoder, Zantzinger

Puerto Rico Alegria, Bishop, Elder, Quiatt, Rollwagen

Punjabi Iqbal

Quichua (dialect of *Quechua*) Irvine, D. Whitten, N. Whitten

Romanes Gropper

Romanian Edson, Hauck

Russian Bick, Hauck, M. Jablonko, Kellers, Lane, Lansing, Lass, Leeds, O'Brien, Simic, Singer, Stearns, Tapper, Tarasoff

Samoa Holmes, Scheder

Samoan Holmes, Scheder

Sanskrit Erdman

Sara Sikka Lewis

Senegal (and **Senegambia**) Von Ins, D. Wagner, Weil

Serbo-Croatian Halpern, Lockwood, Rasson, Simic, Winner

Sesotho Bosko, Coplan

Sierra Leone Hardin, Ottenberg
Slovak Lass
Slovene Winner
South Africa Coplan, Luskey, Zantzinger
South America T. Asch, Ascher, Belk, Bick, Bugos, Campos, J. Collier, M. Collier,
    Clements, De Friedmann, Diaz-Granados, Doughty, Drewal, Dumont, Flowers, Gonçalves,
    Heath, Henley, Irvine, Leininger, Lobo, Luskey, Margolies, McKee, Perez-Tolon, Seubert,
    Singer, Stone, Weatherford, D. Whitten, N. Whitten, C. Williams, Wizelman, C. Young
Spain Behar, Burns, Doughty, Leeds, Lomax, Mintz, Oliver-Smith, Perez-Tolon, Quintana,
    Staples
Spanish Abramowitz, Abrams, Alegria, Albers, Aschenbrennen, Baskauskas, Beatty,
    Bednarek, Belk, Bertocci, Biella, Birdwhistell, Blystone, Bogue, Brandt, Brooks, Bugos,
    Burns, Button, Campos, Cancian, Carucci, Clements, J. Collier, M. Collier, Cone,
    Conklin, Cuéllar, de Brigard, De Friedmann, de Peña, Desmond, Dewey, Diaz-Granados,
    Doughty, Drewal, Dry, Dumont, Duncan, El Guindi, Eyde, Fabian, Faris, Farrer, Feest,
    Field, Flowers, Gardner, Geertz, Gonçalves, Graves, Griffin, Grimshaw, Gropper, Heath,
    C. Heidenreich, V. Heidenreich, Henley, Hoskins, Husmann, Hymes, Irvine, James,
    Jell-Bahlsen, D. Johnson, Johnson-Dean, Kaplan, Kealiinohomoku, Kellers, Kendall,
    Kirkpatrick, Lacy, Lane, Lee, Leeds, Lobo, Lockwood, Lomax, Long, Lüem, Lutkehaus,
    Margolies, McGee, McGilvray, McKee, Mintz, Oliver-Smith, Olsson, Orth, Pader, Peek,
    Perez-Tolon, Peters, Quiatt, Quimby, Quintana, Quintanales, Richardson, Rynearson,
    Saltman, Scheder, J. Schmidt, Seremetakis, Sherman, Simic, Simon, Sims, Skylar,
    Slyomovics, Staples, Stearns, Tefft, Trend, Trotter, Weibel-Orlando, D.Whitten,
    N. Whitten, Wizelman, Wright, C. Young, Zantzinger
Sri Lanka McGilvray
Sudan Faris
Sulawesi Volkman
Sumatra Heider
Sumba Hoskins, Scheerer
Swahili (Kiswahili) P. Blakely, T. Blakely, Malcolm, Nichols, A. Roberts, Yoder
Sweden Baskauskas, Becker, Narrowe
Swedish Becker, Hoskins, Narrowe, Stearns, C. Young
Switzerland A. Jablonko, Lüem, Von Ins
Tagalog Conklin
Tahitian Hammond
Taiwan Bogue
Taiwanese Seaman
Tamil Hockings, McGilvray
Tanzania A. Roberts
Thai Moerman, Tapp
Thailand Blanc-Szanton, Geddes, Linklater, Moerman, Quiatt, Tapp
Tibet Gropper
Togo Kreamer
Tokpisn Alpers, Lutkehaus
Toraja Volkman
Trinadad Biella
Trobriand Islands Weiner
Twi Kreamer
Turkana D. MacDougall, J. MacDougall
Turkish Adra, Aron, Bass, Kellers, Safizadeh (*Azeri Turkish*), Tapper, Tezcan
Turkey Bass, Tapper, Tezcan
United Kingdom Beatty, Becker, Gmelch, Hockings, Leeds, Lomax, D. Williams,
    C. Young

U.S. Abramowitz, Abrams, Aibel, Albers, Andrews, Arlen, Aron, Aschenbrennen, Ascher, Barrow, Baskauskas, Beatty, Bednarek, Belk, Birdwhistell, Bishop, Blackman, P. Blakely, T. Blakely, Blaustein, Blount, Blystone, Bogue, Borchert, Boyer, Brandt, Brooks, Brown, Burns, Button, Cabezas, Callaghan, Chalfen, Chin, Cho, Coggeshall, J. Collier, M. Collier, Cone, Davidson, d'Azevedo, Dekin, Diaz-Granados, Dornfeld, Dry, Duncan, Edson, Elder, Erickson, Eyde, Fabian, Faris, Farnell, Farrer, Field, Fleischhauer, Gatewood, Gearing, Gidley, Gilbert, Ginsburg, Graves, Griffin, Grimshaw, Gross, E. Hall, S. Hall, Halpern, Hammond, Hanisch, Haratonik, Hardin, Harper, Hauck, C. Heidenreich, V. Heidenreich, Heider, Holleman, Homiak, Hymes, Jacknis, James, D. Johnson, T. Johnson, Jones, Kealiinohomoku, Keefe, Kendall, Krouse, Kugelmass, Lacy, Lane, Leeds, Leininger, Lerch, Lerner, Lobo, Lockwood, Lomax, Luehrsen, Luskey, Lutkehaus, Magdanz, Malcolm, Manley, Marks, Marshall, Matthews, Maynard, McGee, Mehan, Mintz, Moerman, O'Brien, Olsson, Orth, Pader, Perez-Tolon, Peters, Pierce, Potterfield, Quimby, Quintanales, Rachlin, Rasson, Richardson, J. Roberts, Rollwagen, Ruby, Rynearson, Sair, Sank, Scheder, Scherer, J. Schmidt, Schwartz, See, Seubert, Sherman, Simic, Simon, Sims, Skylar, Slyomovics, Spiegel, Staples, Stearns, Steele, Stull, Tarabulski, Tarasoff, Tefft, Topper, Trend, Trettevik, Trotter, Trubowitz, J.C. Wagner, Wallendorf, Walter, Wanner, Weatherford, C. Williams, J. Williams, Wilson, Winner, Wright, C. Young, J. Young, K. Young, Zantzinger

U.S. Appalachia Birdwhistell, Blaustein, Dornfeld, Fleischhauer, Jones, Keefe, Matthews, Potterfield, Zantzinger

U.S. East (New England, Mid-Atlantic, D.C.) Aibel, Bednarek, Bishop, Bogue, Borchert, Cabezas, Chalfen, Dry, Elder, Gatewood, Gearing, Graves, Griffin, Gross, Harper, Kugelmass, Leeds, Lerch, Marshall, Mintz, O'Brien, Potterfield, Rachlin, Rollwagen, Ruby, J. Schmidt, Seubert, Slyomovics, Spiegel, Trubowitz, Wescott

U.S. Midwest Aschenbrennen, T. Blakely, Bogue, Borchert, Brown, Coggeshall, Cone, Davidson, Diaz-Granados, Ginsburg, Griffin, Harper, Kendall, Lacy, J. Schmidt, Schwartz, Spiegel, Steele, Stull, Winner

U.S. South Bishop, Burns, Callaghan, Heider, Fabian, Fleischhauer, Gilbert, Lomax, Manley, Richardson, Simon, Tefft, Trend, Trubowitz, Wilson, C. Young

U.S. Southwest Albers, Blystone, Brandt, Brown, Burns, Chalfen, J. Collier, M. Collier, DiMichele, Faris, Farrer, E. Hall, Kealiinohomoku, Lane, Manley, McGee, Mehan, Rachlin, Sims, Skylar, Stearns, Topper, Trotter, C. Williams, J. Williams

U.S. West (Far West, Intermountain West) [see also **Alaska, Hawaii**] Abramowitz, P. Blakely, T. Blakely, Blount, Brooks, d'Azevedo, Duncan, Farnell, Fleischhauer, Hammond, C. Heidenreich, V. Heidenreich, T. Johnson, Peters, Sherman, Walter

    California Aron, Blount, J. Collier, M. Collier, Duncan, Lerner, Lobo, Luehrsen, Malcolm, Marks, Olsson, Pader, Peters, Sheerer, Simon, J.C. Wagner

U.S.S.R. Baskauskas, Edson, Tarasoff, Winner

Urdu Iqbal

Venezuela T. Asch, Bugos, Henley, Margolies, C. Young

Vietnamese Trend

West African Krio Hardin

West African Pidgin English Geary

Wolof Von Ins

Yemen Arab Republic Adra, D. Wagner

Yiddish Kugelmass, Slyomovics, Wizelman

Yoruba Drewal, Wescott

Yugoslavia Halpern, Luehrsen, Rasson, Simic,

Zaïre P. Blakely, T. Blakely, A. Roberts, Yoder

Zambia A. Roberts

Zimbabwe Zantzinger

Directory of Visual Anthropology

The Society for Visual Anthropology is compiling a Directory of Visual Anthropology which will be published as a reference volume. The Society seeks to include everyone working in fields bearing directly on visual anthropology,[1] not only members of the Society. Please complete the following biographical/professional data sheet and return it to Thomas D. Blakely, Department of Anthropology, 700 Kimball Tower, Brigham Young University, Provo, Utah 84602.

Name: _____

Primary mailing address: _____

Other addresses (home?, office?, summer?...) please specify: _____
_____
_____
_____

Phone: _____

Other phone numbers (please specify, as above): _____
_____

Profession(s): _____

Institutional affiliation(s), if any: _____

Professional specialization(s)/interests[1] (e.g. ethnographic filmmaking, teaching with ethnographic film, proxemics, choreometrics, and so forth.)
_____
_____
_____
_____
_____
_____
_____

[1] "Visual Anthropology" includes a variety of approaches to visual symbols, phenomena, and media (film, video, photography) in anthropological research, teaching, theory, methodology, and practice. The Society for Visual Anthropology aims to encourage and support those who are using visual means of description and analysis to study and interpret human (or humanly relevant) perception, behavior, interaction, or communication in context, and those who are interested in such topics as: the analysis of visual symbolic forms; visual theories; relationships among different channels and modes of communication; the visible expression of emotion; proxemic and other analyses of space and territory; kinesic and other systematic study of body motion communication, gesture, or dance; the structuring of reality as denoted by visual productions and artifacts; the study of art, artifacts, or performance from social, cultural, historical, folkloristic, semiotic, or aesthetic points of view; forms of social organization involved in planning, producing, and using visual signs and systems of signs; writing systems and other visible forms of language; visual contexts of speech or verbal art; visual approaches to the ethology of human and other life forms; film/video/photo archiving; anthropological teaching with visual media; visual analyses and methods in the professional practice of anthropology; using media in cultural feedback; the study, production, and use of ethnographic, archaeological, or other anthropological film, photography, or video.

Pertinent professional/academic training: _____
_____

Completed/"published" works related to visual anthropology (films, slide-tapes, photo essays, books, articles, study guides, ...); list up to **eight** works you wish listed in the directory:
_____
_____
_____
_____
_____
_____
_____

Work in progress: _____
_____
_____

Geographic/area focus (foci): _____
_____

Languages (note reading, writing, speaking levels): _____

Additional technical expertise: _____
_____

Other information not covered above: _____
_____
_____